G000115765

# South Africa reborn

To Susan!
Happy Reading!
Heather Deegan (1998)

# South Africa reborn

## Building a new democracy

Heather Deegan

UCL PRESS
UCL PRESS
Taylor & Francis Group

© Heather Deegan, 1999

This book is copyright under the Berne Convention.
No reproduction without permission.
All rights reserved.

First published in 1999 by UCL Press

UCL Press Limited
1 Gunpowder Square
London EC4A 3DE
UK

The name of University College London (UCL) is a registered
trade mark used by UCL Press with the consent of the owner.

**British Library Cataloguing-in-Publication Data**
A CIP catalogue record for this book is available from the British Library.

**Library of Congress Cataloging-in-Publication Data are available**

ISBN: 1–85728–709–6 HB
1–85728–710–X PB

Typeset by Graphicraft Limited, Hong Kong.
Printed by T. J. International, Padstow, UK.

# Contents

CONTENTS

# List of figures

# Chronology of events

1910  Union of South Africa formed as self-governing British dominion; Parliament limited to whites; General Louis Botha, leader of Afrikaner-English coalition and supported by General Jan Smuts, becomes first prime minister.

1912  South African Native National Congress, first national African political movement, founded to overcome ethnic divisions and oppose racial segregation; renamed African National Congress in 1923.

1913  Native Land Act limits land purchases by Africans, 70 per cent of the population to reserves, which equal 7 per cent of the land.

1924  General Hertzog, leader of the National Party, becomes prime minister in coalition with English-speaking Labor Party.

1930  White women enfranchised.

1948  National Party, led by Malan, wins narrow victory; introduces 'apartheid', which codifies and expands racial segregation.

1949  Prohibition of marriage between Africans and whites extended to coloureds and whites. ANC adopts Progamme of Action.

1950  Population Registration Act requires racial classification of all South Africans. Group Areas Act requires segregated residential and business areas for whites, coloureds and Asians. Prohibition of sexual relations between whites and Africans extended to whites and coloureds.

1951  Bantu Authorities Act abolishes Natives' Representative Council and establishes basis for ethnic government in African reserves or 'homelands'.

1953  Public Saftey Act empowers government to declare stringent states of emergency. Companion legislation authorizes severe penalties for protesters, virtually eliminating passive resistance as a tactic. In opposition to mission-run schools, Bantu Education Act imposes government control over African schools.

1956  Coloureds removed from common voter's roll and placed on separate roll to elect four whites to represent them in Parliament. Government issues passes to African women. Twenty thousand women of all races, organized by the Federation of South African Women, march in Pretoria to protest issuance of passes to African women. Legislation prohibits formation of racially mixed unions and requires existing unions to split into segregated unions. Enactment of Riotous Assemblies Act provides for control of public meetings of 12 or more persons.

1958    Dr Hendrik Verwoerd, theoretician of apartheid, becomes prime minister.

1959    Promotion of Bantu Self-Government Act provides for an end to African representation by whites in Parliament and envisages that all Africans will belong to one of eight ethnic 'national units' that will eventually become independent.

1960    In Sharpeville, police kill unarmed Africans during demonstration against pass laws.

1961    South Africa leaves Commonwealth. ANC abandons policy of non-violence.

1962    Sabotage Act provides for prolonged detention without trial.

1964    Nelson Mandela, Walter Sisulu and Govan Mbeki sentenced to life imprisonment after admitting sabotage and preparation for guerrilla warfare.

1966    Prime Minister Verwoerd assassination; succeeded by John Vorster.

1967    Terrorism Act broadens the definition of terrorism and provides for indefinite detention.

1968    Legislation outlaws multiracial political parties. South African Students' Organization formed under leadership of Steve Biko.

1972    Black People's Convention formed to advance black consciousness outside schools and colleges.

1976    Soweto students, protesting against inferior education and use of Afrikaans language as a medium of instruction, are fired on by policy; countrywide protest results in deaths of estimated 1000 protesters during following months. Internal Security Act broadens government's power to crush dissent. Transkei becomes first homeland given 'independence' (Boputhatswana follows in 1977, Venda in 1979 and Ciskei in 1981).

1977    Steve Biko dies after police beatings while in detention. Mandatory arms embargo imposed against South Africa by UN Security Council.

1980    Thousands of black high school and university students begin prolonged boycott of schools.

1983    The United Democratic Front (UDF), a coalition of anti-apartheid organizations sympathetic to the Freedom Charter, launched nationally.

1984    Desmond Tutu awarded Nobel Peace Prize for non-violent opposition to apartheid.

1986    Nationwide state of emergency imposed. Pass laws repealed; indirect control over movement remains.

1987    Oliver Tambo, head of exiled ANC, meets with US Secretary of State, George Shultz in Washington.

1989 Nelson Mandela and President Botha have an unprecedented meeting in Cape Town. Botha resigns as president. De Klerk is elected president for a five-year term. Walter Sisulu, former ANC secretary-general and 11 others released from long-term imprisonment.

1990 Nelson Mandela released from jail after 27 years of imprisonment. First formal talks between ANC and South African government produce progress on release of political prisoners and return of exiles. Fighting between Inkatha and UDF/ANC supporters spreads from Natal to townships around Johannesburg. SACP holds first public rally in 40 years.

1991 ANC holds first legal national conference in South Africa since banning in 1960; elects Nelson Mandela president, Oliver Tambo national chairman, Walter Sisulu deputy president and Cyril Ramaphosa secretary-general.

1994 Nelson Mandela elected President of South Africa.

(*Source*: Tom Lodge and Bill Nasson, *South Africa: time running out*, 1991)

# Preface

In 1994 momentous democratic changes took place in South Africa: universal enfranchisement, national elections, constitutional reform and an end to the old structures of apartheid. This study looks at the aftermath of those reforms. How has the democratic system taken shape? What do parties, youth movements, women, civil society and pressure groups think of the way in which democracy has developed? Has public participation and interest in the policy-making process been successful? How far have economic benefits extended to the wider population? Has South Africa managed to consolidate democratic practices over this transitional period?

This work is based on a series of interviews and meetings with the ANC general secretariat, elected representatives of the ANC, Inkatha Freedom Party, the Democratic Party and the National Party, officials of the ANC Youth Movement, research institutes, women's group leaders, legal experts, economists and organizations that conduct public opinion surveys. The book reflects the attitudes of South Africans, black, coloured and white, and assesses the degree to which empowerment and political rights have contributed to a greater collective sense of unity and responsibility. The future cannot be predicted but the events of the recent past can demonstrate the commitment a country can make to democratic change.

The research was conducted in South Africa between 1995 and 1997 and was funded by an award from the Nuffield Foundation. During that period the writer was a Visiting Fellow at the Africa Institute of South Africa, Pretoria and was invited to participate in a South African Democratization Commission headed by Professor Goran Hyden. The book considers a number of areas that are especially important in the nurturing and maturing of newly democratic states: the role played by the constitution, political parties, civil society, citizenship and identity, women, youth, local democracy and electoral processes, and relations between the political and economic spheres. The contemporary discourse concerning the nature of democracy provides a conceptual framework for the examination of these themes. The concluding chapters focus on the achievement of South Africa's transition to democracy and the potential challenges the future holds.

The writer would like to thank all those who participated in interviews and meetings: Dr Denis Venter, Kenneth Kotelo and Elizabeth Wessels of the Africa Institute of South Africa; Dr Caroline White of the Centre for Policy Studies, Johannesburg; Professor Tom Lodge and Professor Noam Pines of the University of Witwatersrand; members of the African Studies Association of South Africa, the Southern Africa Study Group of the Royal Institute of International Affairs and all those who assisted in the accessing and collection of research information. The writer, alone, however, is responsible for views and opinions expressed within the work.

# Introduction

South Africa faces a future filled with both challenge and hope. In the early years, our democracy brought celebration of our very freedom and common humanity; if those first three years of freedom meant the outpouring of national pride...then we are now coming to better appreciate the difficulties of change.

President Mandela's New Year message 1998

In April 1994 South Africa was viewed as a standard bearer for democracy within the wider African continent and as a beacon for democratic change globally. The move away from the politics of white supremacy and apartheid and the granting of majority voting created a great resonance in the developing world. An international audience gazed with awe as the country shifted from authoritarian to democratic rule. Some commentators spoke of the miracle they felt witnessing such a long-dreamed-of, but always remote and unlikely event; others simply took a deep breath and hoped that nothing would go wrong, no act of devastating violence would halt the proceedings and render all hopeful anticipation of democratic reform meaningless. In fact, even South African politicians themselves were not certain that the first elections would actually go ahead until a matter of weeks before they were due to take place (Carolus interview).

That time of political renewal was one of enormous expectation and deep sentiment, but although those heady days are long gone, South Africa still has the power to excite strong emotions and can equally disturb, delight and dismay, sometimes all at the same time. The country presents an array of contradictory images, some of which are profoundly depressing: cold, under-clad children huddled outside shacks juxtaposed with all the urbanity of high-rise, modern society; groups of unemployed young men idling on street corners or rummaging through rubbish bins; and the continuing poverty of under-resourced rural areas. Conversely, a whole range of sights are immensely positive, for example, confident, emancipated individuals, for the first time taking opportunities previously denied them; the belief of a range of political representatives in public service and commitment to the community; and the genuine feelings of many black, coloured and white South Africans that all people can work together in peace and harmony. These very different scenes run in parallel with each other and present the government with insistent problems: 'a skyscraper (white) economy surrounded by a (black) shanty-town' (Turok 1997). Equally, they have given rise to alternative impressions of the future: one envisages a hazardous picture of a declining democracy, in thrall to a dominant party with little effective political opposition, presiding over economic collapse, increasing lawlessness and corruption. The other, a rather more optimistic prognosis, points to a South Africa capable of building a prosperous and more equitable economy harnessed by racial harmony and the rule of law.

The first prediction is deeply pessimistic in its simplification of political conditions in the country, but more importantly it overlooks the fact that South Africa is in an early transitional phase, which at times can be problematic. Transitional democratic societies often display certain features: the introduction of multi-party politics and the inclusion of groups whose political culture has been influenced by liberatory struggle or authoritarian pressures; liberation movements and dominant parties; instances of charismatic leadership and social/economic disequilibrium. Institutional development, bureacratic management, executive responsibility, financial probity and representative government all form part of the transition. But there can be difficult phases, perhaps times when past authoritarian instincts prevail, or criminality and corruption emerge, or simply when plain incompetence and inefficiency threaten to engulf democratic trends. Certainly, patterns of political exchange shift and mutate during a transitional period which of itself is unsteadying and destabilizing, constantly demanding flexibility and adaptability from the wider community.

The question of institutional legitimacy is a recurring theme within transitional democratic societies. The government must continually demonstrate its ability to govern in order to gain the support of the population in the political process. At times, public expectations of government can be high, in fact, overexaggerated, especially with regard to the delivery of certain 'economic goods'. A newly enfranchised polity may hold unrealistic, almost utopian views of governmental capabilities which, if unfulfilled, render the electorate increasingly vulnerable to disappointment and disenchantment. Under these conditions, newly democratizing societies can have problems retaining the loyalty and trust of sections of the population whose anticipation of the benefits of a new government may be overly optimistic. Additionally, the threat of conflict and resistance to authority is inherent in transitional states, especially if elements within a political culture have formerly accepted confrontation as a means of resolving differences. A culture that sees a recourse to conflict as a preferable strategy is likely to be found in societies that have experienced a long liberation struggle. Clearly, a sense of political moderation and negotiation has to be inculcated at the mass level in order to encourage the development of more consensual attitudes.

But this task is not an easy one, particularly during a transitional process which itself may contribute to a climate of instability and violence as groups within society adapt to changing political and economic scenes. Criminal behaviour may ensue as groups reject the rule of law as socio/economic/ political disparities emerge. Although a democratic pluralist society represents competition between different groups and thrives on diversity and opposition, an overriding commitment by all groups to the rules of society must be present. Greatly polarized transitional societies are especially vulnerable to violence and criminality if sections of the population have yet to regard democracy as the best form of government. The polity may seek order but not necessarily a democratic order. Deeply held collective beliefs in strong government and paternalistic notions of political behaviour do not easily connect with democratic participation. Equally, if parties or liberation movements find the transition too difficult and fail to adapt to different circumstances, the new democracy can be undermined. Cultural and social changes create an ideal environment for the emergence of a 'charismatic' personality who provides a point of popular identification at a time of confusion. Nelson Mandela is repeatedly referred to as a 'charismatic' figure whose dignity and *gravitas* consolidated political changes, but too close an identification of democratic South Africa with a charismatic personality can inflict a damaging uncertainty about succession and stability after the transitional phase. Interestingly, no one refers to Thabo Mbeki as a charismatic figure.

There are both structural and cultural components of democratic transitions. Structural transformation is, of course, more obvious, for without such changes the actual institutional mechanics of representative democracy would not emerge. The cultural component is more complex. At times democratic credentials may be presented at an elite level whilst the political cultures of wider society may be traditional, fragmentary or inconsistent. In these circumstances, although democracy may be regarded as good in itself it may not be perceived as an actual material form of government. In other words, people may believe in democracy as an ideal, but may not act as democrats (Cuadra 1992). These attitudes, however, permeate society and it is equally possible to detect non-democratic behaviour in both political and business elites.

Although purely intellectualizing about democracy has limitations, theoretical assumptions do need to connect in some way with practical politics. Values, beliefs and behaviour all inform and, to a degree, delineate political practices. But there also has to be a theoretical framework against which to measure those practices and, perhaps, to improve on them. South Africa's recent political experiences, the policies of the new government and the changing emphasis of the economy have all contributed to much discussion within the country about the 'nature' of democracy. That is, is liberal democracy 'democratic' or too socially divisive and inequitable to warrant the term? Is it possible to have an egalitarian, redistributive democracy that will recognize and respond to the needs of the poor? Is 'socialist' democracy completely vilified? Do corporatist structures enhance or undermine democratic tendencies? Is the current preoccupation with the rights and responsibilities of the individual at the expense of the collective social experience? Definitions of democracy are evolving and questions of participation and process, accountability and inclusion preoccupy contemporary political practitioners and theorists. Post-authoritarian states are in a pivotal position to move their democratic experience forward, especially now that the whole issue of democracy and development is acquiring a new orthodoxy. Equally, the agency of citizenship and civil society in furthering popular democratic involvement continues to attract attention. These concepts are important as transitional states and societies graft on to their newly emerging democratic practices, progressive ideas of how to create greater public involvement in the political process. South Africa has already demonstrated its commitment to greater public participation in the drawing up of the Constitution, which is widely acclaimed internationally as one of the most democratic documents written. New ideas are constantly emerging that have relevance for South Africa, for example, Paul Hirst's views of 'associative' democracy and new forms of 'social and economic governance', and David Held's notions of 'democratic autonomy' with 'citizen juries' and 'voter feedback' (Hirst 1994; Held 1996). South Africa, both intellectually and politically, should contribute to this newly invigorated discourse.

Essentially, any process of democratization or theory of democracy contains assumptions about what people may be able to achieve, in a sense, their potentialities; their ability to move from one political sphere to another. In order to grasp an understanding of political practicalities and the propensity for change, certain determinate circumstances or conditions that influence political participation must be considered, that is, political parties, electoral procedures, local government and civil society. These are important elements within the democratic process as the plurality of society can be harnessed to a sense of neighbourhood or community commitment. Liberal democracy is concerned with the relationship between the citizenry and the political elite: the degree of trust between the leadership and the people, the level of independence afforded to the individual and the limits to the encroachment of power over the population. But what of the general social/economic environment? What of political culture and identity? What of women and the young? What of local representation and participation?

In examining the search for democracy in South Africa this study seeks to knit together several threads including: a theoretical debate about democracy; legal and formal structures of government (the constitution, local government); the political process (parties, electoral behaviour); political culture (civil society, the role of women and the young, citizenship and identity), political economy and public attitude surveys. Of course, these threads are subject to change and amendment at different paces: the political process is changing rapidly; political culture is changing but more slowly; whereas the constitutional legal framework is intended to stand indefinitely, although it will be reintepreted over time. Chapter 1 explores the discussion surrounding democracy, legitimacy and development and contrasts some early studies with newer contemporary works. To an extent, the nature of transitional democratic societies highlights some issues that were raised 30 years ago, at the time of the emergence of post-colonial, independent states, namely: societal integration, national identity, institution-building and participation. The linkage between development and democracy continues to be critical for it raises both socio/economic and political questions. Chapter 2 examines South Africa's unique undertaking of the drawing-up of the constitution, whilst Chapter 3 considers the main functions and purposes of political parties and their roles in articulating political preferences. Parties and politicians are immensely important in building democratic norms, but so too are the activities of groups and organizations. Civil society, then, is the focus of Chapter 4 together with a consideration of the notions of citizenship and identity. What does it mean to be a South African now? Are rights and responsibilities upheld in the new South Africa?

Women and youth provide the central concern of Chapter 5. Although both groups require a more nuanced assessment, they have much to contribute towards furthering democratic behaviour. The local government elections of 1995, their aftermath and the pointers they raise for community democracy are examined in Chapter 6. It is worth remembering that whilst electoral knowledge is often taken for granted, the newly enfranchised citizens of transitional societies have to be educated in the practical mechanisms of how to vote, which is a very difficult, arduous and costly task. Chapter 7 makes a close examination of the relationship between politics and the economy. The future direction of economic policy and its likely impact on democratic opportunities is one of the key preoccupations of South Africans. The concluding chapter draws these different themes together, whilst the afterword raises specific areas which currently challenge democracy: the economy, crime and corruption.

Perhaps at this point it is appropriate to return to Nelson Mandela's New Year address and his call for all spheres of government to 'fulfil the trust which citizens have placed in them'. This statement highlights the very core of representative democracy and reminds us of the constant need for government to remain accountable to the people. This study hopes to illuminate our understanding of the practical concerns confronting South Africa while also providing insights into the democratic process itself.

# ONE

# The democracy debate

Democracy must be taken to the people. It brings rights and responsibilities.
Cheryl Carolus, ANC Deputy Secretary-General, interview, 1996

## Conditions

From Ancient Greek notions of direct democracy within a city state and
utilitarian models of representative democracy, to Joseph Schumpeter's 'competitive theory of democracy' and the pluralism and polyarchy of Robert A.
Dahl, definitions of democracy have been many and varied. In fact, Dahl
maintains that it is precisely this evolution of democratic ideas that has
produced 'a jumble of theory and practices that are often inconsistent' (Dahl
1989). However, the term 'democracy' is used as a statement of commenda-
tion, even though in its classical mode it was vague, with the 'power of the
people' or 'will of the people' open to various interpretations. In the writings of the nineteenth-century theorist John Stuart Mill, democracy was
inextricably linked with representative government, which in order to exist
at all had to meet three fundamental conditions: 'People should be willing
to receive it; they should be willing and able to do what is necessary for its
preservation; and they should be willing and able to fulfil the duties and
discharge the functions which it imposes on them' (Mill no date: 68). For
Mill, the participation of a country's citizenry in communal activities, and
specifically political affairs, was crucial to the development of representative government. To be denied active participation and be consigned to a
life of passivity created a sadly impoverished people deprived of intellectual stimulus and lacking 'any potential voice in their own destiny' (*ibid.*).
Participation through the ballot box would reveal the general interest of the
community at large and render society more cohesive, in that powerful
groups would be absorbed into society, thus reducing the need for recourse
to violence and disorder. Voting would provide the key to participation,

but it was not simply to be a carefree act of indulgence: the voter was under an absolute 'moral obligation to consider the interests of the public, not his private advantage and to give his vote to the best of his judgement' (*ibid*.). Voting, or indeed any form of political activity, had to be informed, impartial, thoughtful and self-improving.

It has been the intention of Dahl 'to set out an interpretation of democratic theory and practice, including the limits and possibilities of democracy, that is relevant to the kind of world in which we live or are likely to live in the foreseeable future' (Dahl 1989: 2). The divide between 'normative' and 'empirical' accounts of democracy has further muddled the debate. Normative accounts stress the notion of a 'good' society which looks to human capabilities, potentialities and aspirations, whilst empirical approaches emphasize the applicability and efficacy of political practices in the real world. In a major work on democracy, Diamond, Linz and Lipset separated the political arena from other spheres in order 'to insist that issues of so-called economic and social democracy be separated from the question of governmental structure' (Diamond, Linz and Lipset 1988). The inescapable issue of how democracy is understood in the post-Cold War period is associated with the degree and depth of electoral enfranchisement afforded to all peoples, in other words, the democratic universality of electoral choice. However, according to Dahl, democracy, or 'polyarchy' requires certain essential conditions. First, extensive competition among individuals, organized groups, and political parties for government positions; second, political participation in the selection of candidates and potential leaders through regular and fair elections; third, a level of civil and political liberties that provides a framework for society and permits citizens to express themselves without fear of punishment (Dahl 1989: 221). These conditions are far wider than simple electoralism. People are granted rights and responsibilities, accorded freedoms and duties to exercise in a legitimate manner and within encoded parameters. A pluralist society represents competition between diverse groups, but although diversity and opposition are highlighted and groups are permitted to disagree on particular issues, there must exist an overriding commitment from all groups to the rules of society. In the phrase of Almond and Verba, 'a meaningfully structured cleavage in society' must exist to give adequate choice to the electorate (Almond and Verba 1963: 358). In essence, 'consensus and cleavage' politics are essential, but more crucially, there should not be too much of either: too much consensus leads to 'a community in which politics is of no real importance to the community' and choice means little; too much cleavage renders a democratic society 'in danger of its existence' (Berelson, Lazerfield and McPhee 1954). Competing interests should not, therefore, be extremist and potentially threatening to the structures of the state and the political system as a whole.

Joseph Schumpeter was a chief proponent of the notion of a 'competitive theory of democracy', which he defined as an 'institutional arrangement for arriving at political decisions in which individuals acquire the power to decide by means of a competitive struggle for the people's vote (Schumpeter in Kariel 1970: 40). Thus, 'free competition for a free vote' became a fundamental condition of a democratic system. Where no effective competition existed, the system ceased to be one in which the leaders were responsive to the independent wishes of non-leaders. The general model of the competitive theory is that of groups competing at the top for the votes of the majority during election periods. The electorate is enabled to join in a process of selection or rejection of candidates who openly compete for public office. This system of pluralism is identified with liberalism and the acceptance of certain values: for example, the rule of law, which separates the legislative function from the executive one; the preservation of the liberties of the people; freedom of speech, freedom of association, freedom of the press and freedom of assembly, which a government would be unable to violate; responsible government that is accountable to the people via elections; and the political equality of one person, one vote and equal-sized constituencies. Schumpeter defined democracy not as a utopian concept concerned with ideal societies, but rather as a descriptive, realistic and empirically accurate process.

When elections were held in South Africa in April 1994, 22 million people were eligible to vote, 17 million of whom had never voted before. For Cheryl Carolus, Deputy Secretary-General of the ANC, the elections were a 'precursor of democracy but not complete democracy, yet without them, nothing could have happened' (Carolus interview, 3 June 1996). Elections legitimize political decisions through the 'mechanisms of participation, representation and accountability' (Held 1996: 297). By gaining the consent of the electorate the government is granted the right to formulate policy. Since 1994 variants of liberal democracy have been practised in South Africa. A system of consociationalism lasted in a quasi formal sense until the National Party left the government of national unity (GNU) in 1996.

## Consociationalism

Consociational forms of democracy attempt to unite disparate groupings within society by permitting politicians representing differentiated interests to govern at national level in a coalition with the leaders of other parties and groups. By modifying the oppositionist tendencies inherent in liberal democracy, 'fragmented but stable democracies' can be achieved (Lijphart 1977: 145). Through a system of proportional representation it is possible for leaders of various groups to participate at the decision-making level. This procedure permits all sectors of society to have a stake in the political environment of the country. As such, it was deemed to be an appropriate form of democracy to adopt during South Africa's transitional phase. Consociationalism does, at first sight, appear to override the so-called 'mobilization of bias' in the community, that is, the dominant set of values, rituals and institutions that tend to favour the vested interest of one or more groups over others. Yet one major criticism has been levelled at the way in which an 'elite cartel' can often emerge, which then leads to the development of a system of 'patron-clientelism' (Poole 1991). Lijphart admits that the elitism of this type of democracy should not be compared with any ideal of equal power or citizen participation (Lijphart 1977: 50). Consociationalism is not chiefly concerned with citizen participation over and beyond enfranchisement, and elite structures exist. But there is not just one ruling political elite, as is the case in one-party or dominant party states.

The consociational model is inclusive of societal, ethnic, cultural and religious differences rather than exclusive. In a sense, it is this aspect that attracts greater criticism, that is, the virtual immobilization of the governmental body which, without consensus, can lead to a situation of policy stagnation and inefficiency. Often the larger the coalition, the more sluggish the policy-making procedures become. Certainly, commentators suggested that during the period of GNU the policy-making process appeared to be unwieldy. Although good ideas emerged, they were very difficult to put into practice (Hyslop 1996). Equally, critics complained of the 'government not doing enough' or not processing effective policies sufficiently quickly in order to meet people's expectations (Barnes 1996). National Party representatives claimed that the party's decision to withdraw from the GNU rested on the fact that the ANC refused to make concessions on power-sharing arrangements that would permit cabinet posts and the deputy presidential position to be awarded to the second strongest party. The National Party asserted that it wanted to move away from the constrictions of national unity and adopt the role of a strong opposition party (Radue interview, 1996). Lijphart concedes that the government-versus-opposition cycle has the advantage in that 'dissatisfied citizens can cast their vote against the government without voting against the regime', whilst in the consociational model the government and regime coincide, thereby turning dissatisfaction with the government performance into a far more damaging 'disaffection with the regime' (Lijphart 1977: 52).

Another difficulty identified with consociationalism is the potential lack of agreement. Donald Horowitz maintains that even if leaders committed themselves to a policy of consensus, 'centrifugal forces from among their own followers and from among their more extreme electoral competitors would easily undermine the durability of the government' by inhibiting agreement over policy-making (Horowitz 1991: 142). In a sense, it is the form of democracy a country adopts together with its exposure to the structure's demands that serve to create a future democratic trend. According to Seymour Lipset, whose seminal work continues to have relevance for new democracies, a democratic system, once established, 'gathers momentum' and creates its own institutions to ensure its continued existence. Lipset maintains that even young democracies will attempt to survive by facilitating the growth of other conditions necessary for its continuation, such as autonomous private organizations (Lipset 1960: 46–7).

## Participation, process and legitimacy

Jean Cohen and Andrew Arato view the elite competitive model of democracy with its emphasis on secret ballots, civil rights, electoral choice, regular elections and political parties, to be 'central to every modern conception of democracy' (Cohen and Arato 1995: 6). Yet they are also attracted by the 'normativist critique' of the model, especially against 'the elite model's tendency to extol apathy, civil privatism and the necessity to shield the political system from "excess" demands of the population' (*ibid.*). Elite and competitive theories, of course, were developed in the 1950s as political scientists and sociologists investigated voting behaviour in the United States and discovered that a significant proportion of the electorate were politically ignorant, indifferent, or both. In Berelson's opinion: 'If the democratic system depended solely on the qualifications of the individual voter it seems remarkable that democracies have survived through the centuries' (Berelson 1970: 69). The difficulty was that societies that called themselves democracies revealed a high degree of apathy among the electorate. Empirical studies of voting trends clashed with normative political theory. If enfranchised people actually failed to vote in stable democratic countries in the second half of the twentieth century, this actuality sharply confronted theoretical assumptions about the efficacy of participation in a democracy. Consequently, electoral apathy came to be seen as essential in maintaining stability whilst mass participation was associated with societal disorder and a tendency towards totalitarianism (Kornhauser 1957).

Yet the theoretical emphasis on political participation did not disappear from the debate as academics pointed to the potential sterility of the minimalist competitive model with its stress on a reductionist form of democracy that assumed society was 'little more than a series of market relations between individuals' (Macpherson 1973: 158). As Cohen and Arato assert:

> By restricting the concept of democracy to a method of leader selection and to procedures regulating the competition and policy making of elites, the (competitive) model sacrifices the very principles of democratic legitimacy on which it is nevertheless parasitic. It loses all criteria for distinguishing between formalistic ritual, systematic distortion, choreographed consent, manipulated public opinion, and the real thing. (Cohen and Arato 1995: 7)

If democratic exercises are confined to a periodic vote, David Held believes there will exist few opportunities for citizens to act as citizens, that is, to be participants in public life (Held 1996: 323). He elaborates a view of 'democratic autonomy' which he defines thus:

> Persons should enjoy equal rights and, accordingly, equal obligations in the specification of the political framework which generates and limits the opportunities available to them; that is, they should be free and equal in the determination of the conditions of their own lives, so long as they do not deploy this framework to negate the rights of others. (*ibid.*: 324)

The key features of 'democratic autonomy' are the state and civil society operating under a set of general conditions: open availability of information to ensure informed decisions in public affairs; the introduction of 'citizen juries' and 'voter feedback' in order to enhance the processes of enlightened participation; overall investment priorities set by government in discussion with public and private agencies, but with extensive market regulation of goods and labour and the minimization of unaccountable power centres in public and private life (*ibid.*: 324–5). Civil society would be diverse with social, cultural, economic and welfare groups being largely self-managed or co-operatively organized. Held makes clear, however, that whilst the principle of autonomy stipulates the right of all citizens to participate in public affairs, they are under no obligation to do so. So in practice, there could always be a non-participatory section of society, if not especially apathetic, then certainly disinclined to engage in political activity. Richard Kuper asserts that a popular view has emerged that believes 'participation is of itself good; representation, by definition, is alienating' (Kuper 1995). With the notion that participation is empowering, a great emphasis has been placed on 'widening the circle of those who can participate'. Accordingly a range of approaches designed to increase levels of participation have been developed. First, the use of quotas has been advanced as a suitable strategy to ensure that women and ethnic minorities are fully represented in organizations. Second, trigger mechanisms which decide that certain outcomes are not acceptable, for example, less than 40 per cent of women on any leading body of an organization would automatically trigger a remedial action. Third, opening up representative bodies to other groups that express an interest, for example, NGOs. Fourth, having more than one type of constituency electing representatives. Fifth, the allocation of leadership roles by lot, that is, a genuine randomization of those eligible to serve in order to enlarge the circle of participants (*ibid.*). Yet these options are not without problems as Kuper observes: 'Opening decision-making processes to those who believe they have an interest or stake in the decision can be a powerful means for broadening participation but, in the absence of a fair distribution of resources, may merely empower the already mobilised (*ibid.*).

The participatory model of democracy maintains that the exercise of power is good for citizens. In this sense, democracy would allow all citizens, and not only elites, to acquire a democratic political culture. There are, of course, echoes of J. S. Mill within participatory theory, in that an assumption is made that through the process of political experience citizens develop a conception of civic virtue, a tolerance of diversity, a rejection of extremism and egoism and a willingness to compromise (Cohen and Arato 1995: 7). In other words, the whole procedure is both self-improving and selfless. Without a 'decisive narrowing of the gap between rulers and ruled, to the point of its abolition, polities are democratic in name only' (ibid.). However, as Cohen and Arato point out, when it comes to conceptualizing alternatives, 'participation theorists offer institutional models that are meant to substitute for rather than complement allegedly undemocratic forms of representative government' (ibid.). Held concedes that participation within his 'democratic autonomy' model is not without difficulties. Whilst the principle of autonomy ensures the right of all citizens to participate in public affairs, 'What exact obligations would citizens have to accept? And under what circumstances could they legitimately refuse such obligations?' (Held 1996: 326). Certainly, there is considerable stress on public participation in South Africa and numerous media campaigns have been devoted to both educating and mobilizing the electorate. In part these attitudes have been conditioned by the need to legitimize the country's political institutions. Continuous statements reiterate the need for 'people to be involved' or for 'democracy to be taken to the people', and great consultation campaigns have been conducted, particularly over the formulation of the 1996 Constitution (Nhlapo, Carolus interviews, 1996). In a sense, extending participation is both practical and not without effect in enlarging the possibilities of democratic decision-making, but as Kuper reminds us there are dangers in 'assumptions that interests are pregiven and merely reflected democratically, and of a new elite emerging, this time of the activists' (Kuper 1995). Equally, the 'interests' of communities or citizens at grassroots level can differ from those identified and articulated at regional or national arenas.

The notion of democracy as 'process' offers a rather different perspective on democratic trends by focusing less on the rather congested participatory school of thought and more on 'what the purpose of democracy is'. Kuper delineates: 'The democratic task is surely not to aggregate the interests of persons seen as "bundles of preferences to be maximally satisfied" but to elaborate a process which can give expression to a notion of citizens as reasoning creatures' (ibid.). And Habermas muses:

> I can imagine the attempt to arrange a society democratically only as a self-controlled learning process. It is a question of finding arrangements which can ground the presumption that the basic institutions of the society and the basic political decisions would meet with the unforced agreement of all those involved, if they could participate, as free and equal. (Habermas 1979: 186)

Within this form of democracy, there is no onus on individuals to participate directly in the policy-making process so long as they can identify the process as legitimate. The question of legitimacy is crucial in any democratic process. According to Jean Blondel, legitimacy stems from individual support when members of the polity 'are favourably disposed towards the political system' (Blondel 1990: 54). Support may be diffuse and may vary in strength over time. Passive support is widespread, argues Blondel, as large segments of the population often have little contact with national authorities (*ibid.*: 55). Yet in industrial societies the majority of the populace is affected by the state through certain mechanisms, for example, social welfare, public works and taxation.

Seymour Lipset argued in a seminal work that the 'stability of any given democracy depends not only on economic development but also upon the effectiveness and the legitimacy of its political system' (Lipset 1960: 77). For Lipset legitimacy was defined as the capacity of a system to engender and maintain public confidence in its efficacy. However, he acknowledged that the extent to which a democratic political structure was perceived as legitimate depended largely on how 'key issues which have historically divided the society have been resolved' (*ibid.*). Sometimes there is a crisis of legitimacy at a time of change or transition to a new social structure. Crucially, if after the establishment of a new structure, it is unable to sustain the expectations of major groups within society for a sufficiently lengthy period of time in order to develop legitimacy, Lipset believed a crisis could develop (*ibid.*: 78). Tocqueville referred to a crisis of legitimacy occurring particularly when countries moved from one form of political system to a new democratic republic. He used the example of the shift from an old aristocratic monarchy to a democracy: 'epochs sometimes occur in the life of a nation when the old customs of a people are changed', citizens can then have 'neither the instinctive patriotism of a monarchy nor the reflecting patriotism of a republic, . . . they have stopped between the two in the midst of confusion and distress' (de Tocqueville quoted on Bradley 1945). Kornhauser adopted a similar theme: 'Where the pre-established political authority is highly autocratic a rapid displacement of that authority by a democractic regime is highly favourable to the emergence of extremist mass movements that tend to transform the new democracy in anti-democratic directions' (Kornhauser 1957: 125).

These views are, of course, dispiriting but Lipset considered the issue from a different angle. He raised the question of how different societies handle the 'entry into politics' of previously excluded social groups' and when that decision is made to admit them to the political process (Lipset 1960: 79). Whenever new groups become politically active, for example, in post-colonial or post-authoritarian states, easy access to legitimate political institutions can win their loyalty to the system. However, this loyalty rather depends on the extent of struggle or force that has to be exerted in order for them to join the body politic. Groups that have to push their way into the system by a measure of force often 'over-exaggerate' the possibilities of political participation and their hopes remain unfulfilled. Under those conditions, newly democratic states have problems winning the loyalties of the

8

masses. For Lipset a major test of legitimacy is the extent to which nations develop a 'secular political culture' through the adoption of national symbols. Yet the legitimization of political institutions requires a degree of knowledge and understanding within the electorate. A stable democracy requires relatively moderate tension among its contending political forces. But its best conditions are those of economic development: the growth of urbanization, education, communication and increasing wealth. These factors also establish legitimacy and tolerance (*ibid*.: 80–81).

Blondel believes that political integration plays a role in the process of legitimization. He regards it as a form of 'indirect' legitimacy, which is channelled and mediated by groups. Political integration has been defined as 'a pool of commonly accepted norms regarding political behaviour and a commitment to the political behaviour patterns legitimised by these norms' (Ake 1967: 3). Or put another way, integration refers to the 'process of bringing together culturally and socially discrete groups' (Weiner 1967: 150). 'Integrative behaviour' relates to 'the readiness of individuals to work together in an organized fashion for common purposes and to behave in a fashion conducive to the achievement of these common purposes' (*ibid*.: 163). Formally, these forms of organizations were seen as filling the so-called 'gap' between the government and the people, in other words, the engagement of the public in civic politics. More recently, the focus of the debate on democracy and democratization has shifted to the role of civil society.

## Civic politics

According to Clifford Geertz:

> The peoples of new states are simultaneously animated by two powerful, thoroughly interdependent, yet distinct and often actually opposed motives – the desire to be recognised as responsible agents whose wishes, acts, hopes and opinions 'matter', and the desire to build an efficient, dynamic modern state. The one aim is to be noticed: it is a search for an identity, and a demand that the identity be publicly acknowledged as having import, a social assertion of the self as 'being somebody in the world'. The other aim is practical: it is a demand for progress, for a rising standard of living, more effective political order, and greater social justice. (Geertz 1967: 167)

Primordial loyalties would beckon, that is those affinities of racial identity, language, religion, locality and so on, but the modern state demanded that those forces be subordinated to the aims of political and national integration. Whilst societies would be multiracial, multi-ethnic and multi-linguistic these separate identities and differences had to be negotiated. Transitional political systems often found that they were less integrated, on the one hand, sometimes displaying the features of a modern state, whilst on the other, still carrying aspects of traditionalism. In some polities, the state would play a dominant function in creating new organizations, as it alone had the capacity to expand and mobilize (Weiner 1967: 153). Clearly, as the functions of a political system expand, a new level of integration is required. In more modernizing societies, organizational capacities were likely to be evenly spread throughout the population and individuals could form various groups. Integration, then, involves the often newly enfranchised citizen's in a common political process and they are provided with the facility and legitimacy to organize themselves into autonomous groups. The integration of both political structures and governmental procedures with an active and organizationally appropriate civil society enables the nation to mediate diversity.

More recently a new discourse has centred upon the notion of 'associative' democracy (Hirst 1994: 15). According to Paul Hirst associationalism as a concept developed in the nineteenth century as an 'alternative to both liberal individualism and socialist collectivism, and as a criticism of state centralisation and the growth of bureaucracy' (ibid.). The idea contained two distinct arguments: it favoured a decentralized economy and a federalist structure. Associative democracy, as defined by Hirst, 'makes a central normative claim that individual liberty and human welfare are both best served when as many of the affairs of society as possible are managed by voluntary and democratically self-government associations' (ibid.: 22). Associationalism is concerned with changing the forms of organizations into accountable units, directly answerable to their members and to arbiters. As Hirst puts it: 'Associationalism does not strip down and diminish the public sphere as economic liberalism does, but actually revitalises it and extends it' (ibid.: 22).

The relationship between the state and civil society also concerns Dahl. In the kind of modern, dynamic, pluralist society identified by Dahl as being desirable, the governments of economic enterprises should in part be chosen by and legally responsible to the owners, that is private persons or collectivities (Dahl 1989: 324). Such an economic order should serve not only consumers, but also human beings more generally. Society is not made up of producers and consumers within a market mechanism in isolation from other factors. In fact, Dahl sees the liberties associated with democracy as being unlikely to emerge from market decisions. In his democratic vision, 'Political equality must be maintained by a definite set of legal and constitutional arrangements, supported by general opinion and enforced if need be by law, that effectively guarantee each citizen certain rights, opportunities and obligations necessary, and if fully achieved, perhaps even sufficient to ensure political equality among citizens' (ibid.: 326). Freedom within such a democratic order must centre on the self-determination of its citizenry to participate in the political process. Associations, for example business companies, consumer organizations, social and educational groups, would need to be democratically governed. In a sense, the economic order should strengthen the democratic process, but not in a dominant command economy manner. 'Inequalities in resources, strategic positions and bargaining strength' among the citizenry of a democratic state can threaten to undermine the democracy itself (*ibid*.: 333). Such is the nature of international and transitional forces and relations, that democratic nation states are constantly affected by shifting patterns of powers and constraints (Held 1996: 341). The inability of states to determine the precise trajectory of their economies creates a tension between the domestic political scene and economic imperatives. Group activity or civil society can then become internationalized with the effect that the policy-making process becomes increasingly complex (Dahl 1989: 336). Even Hirst admits that 'not all economic activities can be carried out by co-operative small and medium-sized firms, nor can all economic regulation be collaborative or regionally-based'. A central political authority would inevitably be required to ensure public 'rights of entitlement, standards of service and principles of equity' (Hirst 1994: 42). Civil society is both desirable and functional within a democracy, but Dahl does not imagine a society in which every citizen would be informed and active on every major issue. All that is basically required is a 'critical mass of well-informed citizens' that is large and active enough to "anchor the process" of democracy' (Dahl 1989: 339).

## Democracy and development

Forty years ago Seymour Lipset pointed out that 'Men may question whether any aspect of this interrelated cluster of economic development: . . . gradual political change, legitimacy and democracy is primary, but the fact remains that the cluster does hang together' (Lipset 1960: 71). Liberal democracy requires a supportive economic climate and as a prerequisite some degree of social cohesion and political consensus. 'The process by which democracy is liberalised is a key one', argues Richard Joseph, 'for it ties together notions of capitalist development, class formation and class conflict, as well as such essentials of liberal democracy as competitive parties and majority rule' (Joseph 1987: 20). In the 1950s political development was intimately connected with the process of modernization. This model assumed many guises but tended to coalesce around certain characteristics that had been factors in Western political development, namely: rationalization, national integration and nation building, democratization and participation. Whilst Dankwart Rustow defined political development as 'Increasing national political unity plus a broadening base of political participation' (Ward and Rustow 1964: 7), Karl Deutsch viewed modernization as a complex process of social change which was 'significantly correlated with major changes in politics' (Deutsch 1967: 153). Increasing urbanization, improved literacy rates, expanding economies and exposure to mass communications were all factors that would combine to mobilize the population and increase

11

demands for governmental services. Political participation was to be the key that opened the door to modern political development and thus distinguished the traditional society, which was non-participatory, separating people 'by kinship into communities isolated from each other and from a centre', from an advancing modernizing state (Lerner 1958: 48–50). A 'new world political culture', announced Almond and Verba (1963: 4), would be one of 'participation' and Frederick Frey (1963: 301) suggested that the 'most common notion of political development is that of a movement towards democracy'.

The debate at that time, although linking development with democracy, focused on a set of preconditions a country would have to undergo in order to achieve a 'good society'. As Lipset put it in a chapter titled 'The end of ideology?' in what might be regarded as a precursor to Francis Fukuyama's (1992) later deliberation on the inevitability of the global drift towards the highest stage of political expression, that is, liberal democracy: 'Democracy is not only or even primarily a means through which different groups can attain their ends or seek the good society; it is the good society itself in operation' (Lipset 1960: 403). Yet despite its desirability, not all countries could avail themselves of liberal democracy, for its development depended on a rigid set of conditions. Truly democratic countries were considered to be those with a high standard of living and a reasonable spread of income, which tended to diminish social unrest. Therefore, poverty, illiteracy, hunger and ignorance all served to render a country unlikely to sustain democracy, and with one sweep of analysis practically half the globe was condemned to undemocratic government (Lipset 1960: 71). Developing countries were seen to face enormous obstacles in achieving national unity. Divisive and destructive forces would savage any attempts at unity and in the absence of a general toleration of varied opinions, opposition could not be institutionalized. In fact, Samuel Huntington argued that if there was to be such a concept as political development, and it must be remembered that by 1971 he had rejected the term in favour of 'political change', it had to embrace the notion of 'political decay' and the circumstances that brought it about (Huntington 1967: 241).

Political decay was a depressing but empirically salient notion as newly developing countries became increasingly beset by coups and violence. Huntington argued that in its early stages, economic development – precisely that factor which had been hailed as the harbinger of political potential and advancement – created dislocation in new nations with fragile political institutions. If governments failed to govern, 'political degeneration' would occur and any attempts to democratize would vanish in a haze of tyranny. When rates of mobilization and participation were high and the rates of organization and institutionalization were low, democracy was in danger (*ibid.*: 207). Institutionalization was the process by which organizations and procedures acquired value and stability within society. In turn, the level of institutionalization of a political system could be defined by the adaptability,

12

complexity, autonomy and coherence of those organizations and procedures. But political institutions needed time to mature, they could not be 'created overnight' without running the risk of failing. If democracy were to survive it was necessary for political parties to become functionally adaptable within the system: 'A nationalist party whose function has been the promotion of independence from colonial rule faced a major crisis when it achieved its goal and has to adapt itself to the somewhat different function of governing a country' (*ibid*.: 218). If the party found the transition too difficult and failed to adapt to the changed circumstances, the new democracy would be under threat. Of course, when empirical evidence is considered, the new post-independent democracies of over a generation ago were clearly frail, vulnerable and, at that time, unsustainable.

However, more recently there has been an obvious shift in the development debate. As Adrian Leftwich points out: 'Now a new orthodoxy prevails in official Western circles which systematically connects democracy to the question of development in an entirely new way. It is now claimed that democratic good governance is not an outcome or consequence of development, as was the old orthodoxy, but a necessary condition of development' (Leftwich 1996: 4). Democracy is now seen to be within the grasp of every nation irrespective of economic or social factors. No longer is there an emphasis on the inability of a nation to cope with democratic norms, which so preoccupied the modernization theorists 30 years ago. Democracy is now part of the development process that will lead to its 'sustainability and accountability' (Chalker meeting, 1994). Yet it is important not to lose sight of the fact that former attempts at democracy by a range of newly independent states failed and that fact gave rise to the critique of the universality of democracy. A modern political system, James Coleman instructed us in the past, had to have 'a high degree of differentiation, explicitness and functional distinctiveness of political and governmental structures' (Coleman 1960: 532). Now the contemporary focus has shifted to the issue of good governance, that is, administrative competence, probity and accountability. This shift is partly conditioned by a combination of factors: the demands of international aid agencies, the changed global political scene and the increasing unacceptability of unelected authoritarian forms of government.

For some academics questions still remain unanswered. Certainly, Leftwich poses some important points: 'What does democratic governance mean? And is the question of governance, that is the form of government, really the right question to focus on when considering the appropriate political arrangements and institutions for the effective promotion of development?' (Leftwich 1996: 5). Equally, a fundamental question was posed in a study for the African Development Bank which went to the core of the issue when it asked to what extent democracy could be linked with economic success (van Hoek and Bossuyt 1993). The Overseas Development Institute, in a report on political liberalization and economic reform, found that national elections and the freedom to form different parties provided only a first, partial step towards political liberalization (Overseas Development Institute 1994a). For Leftwich the current emphasis on governance is misplaced because it is 'politics and the character of the state' that determine the form of governance and its effectiveness. In the case of South Africa, 'The enormous developmental tasks now to be achieved will depend critically on the politics of balancing the diverse and distinctive demands of very different interest groups. Everything will depend on politics and the capacity of the state to broker these demands and, where necessary, rise above them' (Leftwich 1996: 19).

So what can we make of the contemporary discourse on democracy and where does South Africa's recent political experiences fit into these elaborate democratic theories? Despite the obvious attraction of speculating on the normative and, perhaps, utopian ideas of a 'global democracy reflecting the will of the people through both processes and participation', a firm grasp of political reality is desirable (Held 1996: 337). This study pursues a number of themes and discusses a range of democratic trends because in the context of South Africa certain features are crucial to consider: How does multi-party politics actually work? What are the channels for effective opposition? How significant are local political structures? What is the significance of citizenship to the wider society? What is the nature of participation and political identity? How do people actually perceive their new government? And what is the relationship between politics and economics? The important aspect of any analysis of democracy is the readiness to steady theory with an understanding of political practice.

TWO

# Constitutionalism

We the people of South Africa,
Recognise the injustices of our past;
Honour those who suffered for justice and freedom in our land;
Respect those who have worked to build and develop our country;
and
Believe that South Africa belongs to all who live in it, united in our
diversity.
We therefore, through our freely elected representatives, adopt this
Constitution as the supreme law of the Republic so as to –
Heal the divisions of the past and establish a society based on demo-
cratic values, social justice and fundamental human rights;
Lay the foundations for a democratic and open society in which gov-
ernment is based on the will of the people and every citizen is equally
protected by law;
Improve the quality of life of all citizens and free the potential of each
person;
Build a united and democratic South Africa able to take its rightful
place as a sovereign state in the family of nations.
May God protect our people.

Nkosi Sikelel'iAfrika. Morena boloka setjhaba sa heso.
God Seen Suid-Afrika. God bless South Africa.
Mudzimu fhatutshedza Afurika. Hosi katekisa Afrika.
                Preamble to the Constitution of the Republic of South Africa
                                            Adopted 8 May 1996

### The 1993 constitution

In South Africa's short post-apartheid period, the country has had two constitutions. The first was a transitional document drafted in 1993 and intended
to provide a framework for democratic change. The second was a formal

15

document adopted by the Constitutional Assembly in May 1996. The objective in drafting the 1996 final constitution was to ensure that it is seen
as 'legitimate, credible and accepted by all South Africans' (Constitution
Explanatory Memorandum 1996). In order to assess the context in which
South Africa has changed into a constitutional democracy with a separation
of powers it is necessary to analyze the genesis and procedures of both
constitutions.

Every state requires a system by which a reasonably orderly process of
government may emerge. In modern states this process is generally defined
by a written constitution, which sets out the organs of government, their
mutual relationship and the relationship between government and the individual (Neumann 1960: 666). The concept of a fundamental order was known
in Greek and Roman times but the notion of a covenant between the people
and the law emerged in the sixteenth century. This gave rise to the idea that
'the state was based on a covenant into which all its citizens entered by an
act of consent'(ibid.: 667). As Neumann explains, the development of natural law and the belief that citizens had 'inalienable rights' that were not
received from the state or government but were 'inherent' contributed to
the modern concept of the constitution: 'a modern constitution would act as
a covenant agreed upon by the governed, having the characteristics of a
superior, fundamental law from which all other law is derived' (ibid.). Legal
authority, then, is both created and sustained by the will and consent of the
governed (Partridge 1975: 10).

In the period preceding the elections of April 1994, an emphasis was
placed on the approach, process and content of inclusive negotiations about
the form of political settlement to be reached. As the process developed it
became clear that a transitional period was needed during which the country would be governed under the aegis of a transitional constitution (Meyer
1995). This objective was realized with the adoption of a new constitution in
December 1993, which would serve for a transitional period of two years.
The 1993 constitution, then, was a product of negotiation and compromise.
At one stage the negotiations involved 26 parties, representing the whole
political spectrum. Gerhard Erasmus believes this procedure was a consequence of the nature of the political transition in a deeply polarized and
differentiated society (Erasmus 1994: 5–19). Certainly, one of the main challenges confronting South Africa is the question of how to normalize the
country's political life. This inevitably raises questions about the forms of
democracy to be adopted and how political institutions can be legitimized
in the eyes of the body politic. Equally, the constitutional process should
ensure that a just and viable democratic system of government can be sustained after the period of transition (Meyer 1995). Yet, intriguingly, 'constitutionalism is not identical with democracy' (Neumann 1960: 671). Supreme
laws may be observed and may direct procedures of government but they
may not be intrinsically democratic. For example, Iran observes constitutional
government according to Sharia law (Deegan 1993; Ehteshami 1995). What

matters is the extent to which the constitution imposes restrictions on the organs of government and prevents a concentration of power at the top.

The decision that the 1993 constitution would be reconsidered after two years was predicated on the fact that it was not the product of a democratic legislature. Yet the central achievement of the 1993 Interim Constitution is contained in Schedule 4 in which 34 clauses protect and enshrine democratic principles which can not be changed by a subsequent dominant party government (see Appendix 1 – Constitutional principles). In other words, a duly elected majority government could not simply rewrite the constitution to suit itself (Leon interview, 1996). Clause VI states: 'There shall be a separation of powers between the legislature, executive and judiciary, with appropriate checks and balances to ensure accountability, responsiveness and openness.' And Clause VIII pronounces: 'There shall be representative government embracing multi-party democracy, regular elections, universal adult suffrage, a common voters' roll and, in general, proportional representation' (Constitution of the Republic of South Africa 1993).

The basic values underpinning the essentially liberal democratic 1993 constitution include constitutionalism, the rule of law, freedom and equality, and the independence of the judiciary. Interestingly, R. W. Johnson and Lawrence Schlemmer point to the paradox that the three main parties involved in devising the constitution, the ANC, the IFP and the NP, had never been completely enamoured by liberal democratic principles:

> The NP had spent its whole period in power up until 1990 attempting to resist international pressure for such a constitution. The IFP, in its governance of Kwa-Zulu, had shown itself to be a party of conservative chiefly oligarchs. The ANC, for its part, had for a generation espoused the language of populist Marxism and had always taken as its goal a revolutionary, (and thus presumably single-party) seizure of power. (Johnson and Schlemmer 1996: 9–10)

The context for the 1993 constitution, both internationally and domestically, effectively excluded the possibility of parties drawing up any document that was not committed to a liberal democratic agenda. Essentially, if South Africa was to declare itself to be a democracy, there was no credible alternative to liberal democracy. Socialist democracy as defined by a dominant party had been undermined by the collapse of the Soviet Union; authoritarian, traditional rule was deemed intrinsically undemocratic and the iniquities of the former apartheid political structure were precisely the system from which South Africa was escaping. As Johnson and Schlemmer assert: 'The common ground between these somewhat unlikely partners in democracy turned out to be the classic discourse of liberal constitutionalism' (*ibid.*).

A constitutional state provides a framework of rules and institutions for deciding society's fundamental issues. Organs of state, powerful enough to protect and enhance public interests, are balanced by constitutional mechanisms to guarantee democracy and freedom (Erasmus 1994: 7). The 1993 constitution established the Constitutional Court, which is the highest in the country. According to Peter Leon this was a very important move as there existed so much widespread distrust of the courts because of their role in supporting apartheid. The ANC recognized the necessity to legitimize a Constitutional Court (Leon interview, 1996). The court has jurisdiction over 'any dispute of a constitutional nature between organs of state at any level of government' (Section 98(2)(e) 1993 Constitution). Nevertheless, as Gerhard Erasmus makes clear, the constitutional values of the new South Africa should always 'be viewed against the background of apartheid, exclusion and domination' (Erasmus 1994: 8). In a sense, of course, all constitutions are historical documents attempting to redress past injustices and grievances while simultaneously defining a politico-legal framework for the future. Yet South Africa was not emerging as an independent state following a process of decolonization and neither had it completely severed links with past political actors. This negotiated transition inevitably had implications for the manner in which the 1993 constitution was drafted: 'A large white population remains entrenched in a strong economic and bureaucratic position. Groups such as those represented through Inkatha Freedom Party enjoy considerable support. Their future participation is premised on the assumption that the constitutional deal will be honoured' (ibid.).

One of the interesting features of the transitional period was the emergence of a government of national unity (GNU) which was to last for a period of five years. The idea was originally conceived by Joe Slovo of the South African Communist Party (SACP) who introduced the famous and controversial 'Sunset Clause' which led to the birth of the GNU. Slovo's central view was that the sun was setting on apartheid and the ANC should accept a power-sharing formula for five years to enable those who supported the former government to make a dignified exit from power (Cronin interview, 1996; Adabunu 1995). However, the 1993 constitution did not explicitly establish or define an executive body to be a government of national unity, although R. P. Meyer refers to the exhortation to promote national unity in the Preamble to the Constitution and to Section 89(2): 'The Cabinet shall function in a manner which gives consideration to the consensus-seeking spirit underlying the concept of a government of national unity as well as the need for effective government' (Meyer 1995: 3). Whilst Section 82(2) of the constitution requires the President to consult the Executive Deputy Presidents both in the development and execution of policies and in all matters relating to the management and performance of the Cabinet, there is nothing in the constitution that obliges all the parties in the GNU to agree on all important issues (ibid.: 3–4).

Although the National Party left the GNU in 1996, primarily to focus attention on its role as an oppositionist force, it could, if it so desired, rejoin the government at any time until 1999 (Leon interview, 1996). Generally, the GNU has been regarded as a functional entity which operated adequately during a period of unease. Certainly, Cheryl Carolus, the ANC Deputy-

Secretary General, refers to the government as playing a crucial mediatory role and acting as a force between conflicting interests (Carolus interview, 1996). Meyer believes the GNU managed to achieve significant gains by initially creating an atmosphere of national reconciliation among the various political parties (Meyer 1995: 6). The GNU, then, is judged to have contributed to the creation of a culture of negotiation as the mechanism of co-operation and to have engendered 'a spirit of reconciliation' (Msimang interview, 1995). Previously, South Africa has had little experience of consensual decision-making and the GNU has been important in providing a framework for defusing potential problems within government. However, it has been necessary for parties to be aware that participation does not necessarily imply agreement on all policies. Equally it does not mean that differences between parties should be eliminated. What has been required is a process of operational consensus, that is agreements are reached whereby parties decide, regardless of their differences, to attempt to seek joint solutions in the best interest of the country (Meyer 1995: 8).

## Constitutional Assembly

The Constitutional Assembly (CA) was established as a forum to draw up the 1996 constitution. The public were invited to take a direct role in the constitution-writing process by submitting ideas or demands for inclusion through a range of access points; 1.9 million submissions were made to the Assembly (Nhlapo interview, 1996; Msimang interview, 1995). This approach was novel and exciting in that it potentially activated everyone and was 'a good way of involving people' (Nhlapo interview, 1996). The Community Agency for Social Enquiry (CASE) was commissioned by the Assembly to undertake an evaluation of the CA's media, public participation and education campaigns, in 1995. In 1996 CASE was requested to undertake the second, larger phase of the evaluation. This covered evaluating the plain language initiative as well as the internal structure of the CA in addition to the public and media campaigns. The full evaluation included:

- an inspection of the internal administration of the CA in order to understand the context in which the campaigns were undertaken;
- interviews with constitutional drafters in order to provide the background for assessing the plain language initiative;
- establishing nine focus groups among 'ordinary citizens' (although with some degree of higher education), one in each province, to test the plain language initiative;
- holding workshops with likely interpreters of the constitution, for example legal professionals, civil servants, and so on;
- participant observation and exit polls to evaluate the effectiveness of the local constitutional education meetings organized by the CA;

**Table 2.1**  The demographic profile of respondents

| | | | |
|---|---|---|---|
| Gender | Male | | 50% |
| | Female | | 50% |
| Highest level of education | No formal education | | 7% |
| | Primary | | 21% |
| | Jnr. secondary | | 31% |
| | Snr. secondary | | 30% |
| | Tertiary | | 10% |
| Age | 18–24 yrs | | 21% |
| | 25–34 yrs | | 28% |
| | 35–44 yrs | | 22% |
| | 45–54 yrs | | 13% |
| | 55–64 yrs | | 8% |
| | 65 + yrs | | 8% |
| Area & dwelling | Metropolitan | Formal | 35% |
| | | Backyards | 6% |
| | | Informal | 6% |
| | | Hostels | 1% |
| | | **Total** | **48%** |
| | Small urban | Formal | 19% |
| | | Informal | 2% |
| | | **Total** | **21%** |
| | Rural | Farmworkers | 4% |
| | | Farmsteads | 27% |
| | | **Total** | **31%** |
| Province | Gauteng | | 26% |
| | North-west | | 8% |
| | Northern Province | | 9% |
| | Mpumalanga | | 6% |
| | Free State | | 6% |
| | Northern Cape | | 2% |
| | Western Cape | | 10% |
| | Eastern Cape | | 14% |
| | KwaZulu/Natal | | 19% |

*Source*:  CASE 1996 (i)

- re-analyzing existing CA date dealing with the outreach of their public participation campaign; and
- conducting a national sample survey of 3,800 respondents aged 18 years and above. (A New Constitution for a New South Africa, Report by Community Agency for Social Enquiry, South Africa, April 1996)

The survey was nationally representative in that it covered all racial groups, all provinces and all areas – large metropolitan cities, smaller urban centres, rural areas including farm workers as well as homesteads and farms – and informal settlements in both metropolitan and urban areas. Table 2.1 sets out the demographic profile of the survey respondents.

The process of negotiating the final constitution for South Africa has been, not surprisingly, an arena of political contestation. The CA sought to forge an identity and a function in the minds of all South Africans and 60 per cent of all those interviewed by CASE had heard of the Assembly. Yet there were disparities. Those who had not heard of the CA were mainly drawn from disadvantaged communities and whilst 76 per cent of men knew of the Assembly only 55 per cent of women did (CASE 1996: 4). Rural dwellers and the elderly were the least likely to know of the CA, which in part reflects the country's unevenness in access to the media. Of those of who had heard of the CA, 39 per cent knew it was drawing up the constitution, while another 9 per cent pointed to it 'getting people's views' on key issues. For 22 per cent of those interviewed the CA was regarded as a law-making body (*ibid.*: 5).

Equally important is the fact that while 76 per cent of respondents first heard of the CA via mainstream media, 12 per cent were first informed of it by word-of-mouth, through a friend, at work, at school and so on. According to CASE this suggests that the CA campaign had been able to achieve one of the key goals of a social education media campaign, namely to 'generate interpersonal communication and enter political discourse' (*ibid.*: 6). A further 4 per cent heard about the CA from political rallies, civic or church meetings. The media campaign succeeded in reaching 73 per cent of all adult South Africans, equivalent to some 18.5 million people. The media campaign was wide-ranging, running from TV, radio and newspaper advertisements, to the *Constitutional Talk* tabloid, the Mandela Talk-line poster, as well as the CA logo. One of the major difficulties in rural areas is the widespread absence of electricity or other power sources in homes, which inevitably contributes to lower rates of media access. Clearly, then, people from different demographic backgrounds did not have an equal chance of being exposed to the TV advertisements. The CASE study found that generally, Africans, informal dwellers, that is squatters, and those living in rural areas, older people and lower-educated respondents were able to watch TV far less frequently than other groups. For example, 46 per cent of Africans seldom or never watch TV, compared with 22 per cent of coloureds, 15 per cent of Indians and 16 per cent of whites (*ibid.*: 8).

The Mandela poster was a successful item, reaching 34 per cent of all respondents. It depicted the President dressed formally outside a private home, holding a cellular phone and saying 'Hello, is that the Constitutional Talk-line? I would like to make my submission.' It was distributed via newspapers as an insert. More than half, 53 per cent, of newspaper readers had seen it. Yet, whites, women, rural dwellers, older people and those with low educational attainment were much less likely to have seen it than others. Of those, whites enjoy regular newspaper access, and the CASE study concluded that in some instances, a lack of recall may have reflected an absence of interest in the constitution-writing process (*ibid.*: 11). Interestingly, only 38 per cent of the respondents heard the radio advertisement

**Figure 2.1** Did the media teach you anything about the new constitution?*
(among respondents exposed to one or more component of the campaign)
(by race, gender and area)

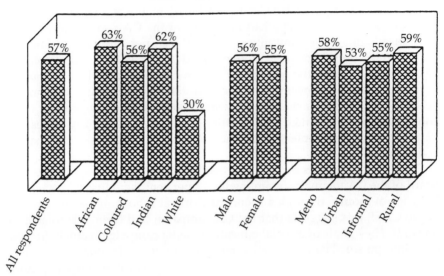

* Includes: TV and radio programmes and adverts; print adverts;
Mandela poster; CA logo; Const. Talk. Note, 73% of total sample were reached
by CA media campaign
CASE research for the Constitutional Assembly

*Source*: CASE 1996 (i)

compared with 48 per cent who had seen the TV version. More generally,
the newspaper advertisements did less well than the other forms of media,
largely because few South Africans read newspapers. Only 18 per cent of
the whole sample had seen the newspaper advertisement.

All respondents were shown a copy of the *Constitutional Talk* tabloid
newspaper, which included the draft constitution of 1993, and asked if they
had seen a copy before. Twenty per cent of the sample had seen it. More
Africans, 22 per cent, than other race groups had seen it as well as more
men, 24 per cent, than women, 17 per cent. Of those who had seen it, 63 per
cent reported they had learned something new. Respondents who had been
exposed to one or more of the components of the CA media campaign were
asked to assess whether their knowledge about the new constitution had
increased or not. Figure 2.1 shows the responses, categorized by race, gender and area. Over half, 57 per cent of those interviewed, said the campaign
had increased their knowledge and over a quarter, 28 per cent, felt their
knowledge had increased 'a lot' (*ibid*.: 14). The research project found that
the relatively low positive responses from whites reflected a general uncertainty and uneasiness about the political changes that were taking place.

**Figure 2.2** Did the media teach you anything about the new constitution?*
(among respondents exposed to one or more component of the campaign)
(by age and education)

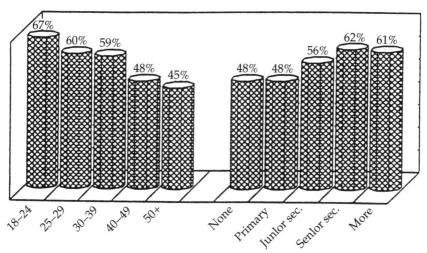

* Includes: TV and radio programmes and adverts; print adverts;
Mandela poster; CA logo; Const. Talk. Note: 73% of total sample were reached
by CA media campaign
CASE research for the Constitutional Assembly

*Source*: CASE 1996 (i)

Figure 2.2 charts the response to the same question: 'Did the media teach
you anything about the new Constitution?' Responses on this occasion were
categorized by age and education. Younger people were more likely to
have learned something from the campaign than their elders. Two-thirds,
67 per cent, of 18–24-year-olds said that the materials were educational
whilst only 45 per cent of people aged 50 and above responded positively.
Again those groups with higher levels of education tended to score more
highly. Clearly, any future political campaigns aimed at increasing knowledge and democratic awareness need to find a way of reaching older people
and those less well educated. As the study suggests, this is a serious concern and new ways and methods of accessing sections of the population
need to be explored creatively (CASE 1996: 13–14).

## The public participation campaign

The CA promotional campaign was concerned not only with advertising the
existence of the Assembly: its primary aim was to encourage public participation. The government felt that in order for people to become involved
and to understand better the democratic changes taking place within the

**Figure 2.3** Local meetings re Constitutional Assembly
(all respondents)

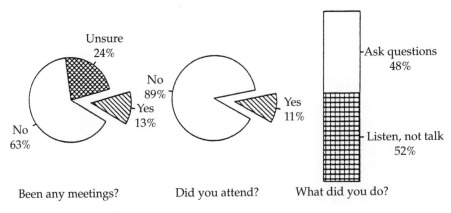

Unsure
24%

No
89%

No
63%

Yes
13%

Yes
11%

Ask questions
48%

Listen, not talk
52%

Been any meetings?        Did you attend?        What did you do?

*Source*: CASE 1996 (i)

country, public participation was both necessary and desirable. Equally, increased levels of participation could serve to legitimize the new constitution and serve to unite the nation. The CA organized a series of local meetings across the country with varying degrees of success. Figure 2.3 shows the responses to a series of questions: 'Have there been any meetings?; Did you attend?; and What did you do?'. The responses were not particularly encouraging, with a total of 87 per cent of responses to the first question being either negative or uncertain. Of the 13 per cent who were aware that public meetings were being held, only 11 per cent attended. The study acknowledges the low attendance rates but makes the point that when people did attend almost half, 48 per cent, reported they actively participated by asking questions. The meetings were deliberately designed to try to achieve broader than normal participation and the study felt that perhaps in this regard they could have succeeded. However, they concede that participation levels were very low and remark that with elections having taken place in 1994 and 1995, South Africans may well have suffered from 'meeting fatigue' (*ibid.*: 16).

It must be remembered, however, that open public meetings are notoriously poorly attended in most democratic countries unless they are supported or sponsored by elements within civil society. The CASE study looked at the role played by groups and organizations in informing their members of CA meetings. It found that few organizations had made a concerted attempt to draw their members into meetings or discussions about the constitution-writing process. As Table 2.2 indicates, of the respondents who belong to a range of societies, clubs or organizations, 79 per cent had not been informed about the CA process by their organization.

The same question was asked of those people who were members of trade unions and the response was more promising: 37 per cent had been informed about the constitution, 29 per cent had had the opportunity of

**Table 2.2**  Role of civil society in informing about CA
(Among those who belong to one or more organization:
43 per cent of sample)

| Question: 'Did your organization keep you informed about the CA process?' | | |
| --- | --- | --- |
| | Yes | No |
| Political organization | 9% | |
| Sports Club members | 2% | |
| Stokvel members | 2% | |
| Youth groups | 3% | |
| Civic members | 2% | |
| Church group | 2% | |
| Professional group | 1% | |
| Women's group | 2% | |
| Cultural organization | 1% | |
| Student organization | 2% | |
| Informed by none | | 79% |

*Source*: CASE 1996 (i)

attending meetings on the subject and almost three-quarters, 71 per cent, had done so. But it is important to remember that of the whole sample only 11 per cent were members of a trade union. The study felt that civil society partnerships which the CA needed to form for a successful public participation campaign were less effective than they could have been and had a limited follow-through (*ibid.*: 18). Where the CA was in charge of the process itself and less reliant on publicity about public meetings, the effectiveness of the campaign was more encouraging. Thus, almost a third, 29 per cent, of respondents knew that they were able to send in written demands to the Assembly. The study asked people, without any prompting, how they could take part in the process of drawing up a new constitution. The results set out in Table 2.3 show spontaneous responses to the question. Over half of all respondents, 56 per cent knew how to take part in the process.

It is important to note that while only limited numbers of people utilized the different participation channels mentioned in Table 2.3, the CA was successful in generating a level of discussion among South Africans. Earlier in the questionnaire, a spontaneous response revealed that 24 per cent of all respondents reported that they had discussed the CA and constitution-related issues with friends or family. Later in the questionnaire, the study found that 51 per cent of all those who had read parts of the draft constitution had discussed it with friends or family. The study points to these additional indicators as evidence that the CA campaign had reached a significant position whereby the issues it was promoting were entering public discourse (*ibid.*: 19).

**Table 2.3**  Participation channels

Question: 'How can people take part in the
constitution-writing process?'

| | |
|---|---|
| Contact your local organization | 18% |
| Write to the Assembly | 19% |
| Phone the Assembly | 11% |
| Use the Internet | 1% |
| Phone Talk-line | 10% |
| Raise it with my local organization | 8% |
| Contact a member of the Assembly | 8% |
| Contact my political representative | 9% |
| Attend a local meeting/workshop | 12% |
| Via local government | 9% |

*Source*: CASE 1996 (i)

## Attitudes towards the public participation campaign

Initially, the study wondered whether South Africans, in the post-liberation period, would suffer a stage of political saturation and want to be left alone rather than be called upon to engage in difficult notions of constitutionalism, human rights and the CA process. However, it found that just less than half, 48 per cent, of all adult South Africans felt part of the CA process, while just over a quarter, 28 per cent, did not. A further 24 per cent remained unsure. This is a considerable achievement, particularly in a country which had previously denied the majority of the population even the smallest degree of formal political participation. It is noteworthy that the positive feeling about the CA process is expressed nearly evenly across metropolitan areas, 48 per cent, and urban areas, 49 per cent, as well as the more disadvantaged areas, that is the informal dwellers from both metropolitan and urban areas, 43 per cent, and rural dwellers, 46 per cent. Less encouraging is the fact that men are more likely to feel positive, 52 per cent, than women 44 per cent. This gender differential stood out clearly in the study and has yet to be adequately understood, although the ANC is tackling the problem (see Chapter 4). In part it derives from the fact that politics has been seen as 'men's business' in many parts of South Africa, combined with the social, economic and political disadvantages faced by women, especially those living in rural communities. It must be recalled that this was reinforced by biases in media access, which at that time saw far fewer women than men able to access mainstream, and particularly prime time, media. This served to confirm existing forms of gender differentiation. Any campaign that relies in part on the media, as with the CA campaign, would obviously have to develop particular means and strategies to overcome bias in the future.

**Table 2.4**   Public faith in the public participation programme
(all respondents)

Exactly half of all adult South Africans believe that the CA wants 'ordinary people like us' to take part. Only a fifth do not believe this to be the case, while the remainder are uncertain.

Older people were less convinced that the CA wanted their involvement: only 38 per cent of those aged 50 and above answered positively, compared with 57 per cent of those aged between 18 and 24.

Belief that participation is genuinely sought by the CA rose with education levels: only 36 per cent of those with no formal education believed that the CA wanted their participation, compared with 42 per cent of those with primary school only, 50 per cent with junior secondary, and 58 per cent of those with senior secondary and with tertiary education.

*Source*: CASE 1996 (i)

The study revealed that 50 per cent of all adult South Africans believe that the CA genuinely wants them to participate in the constitution-writing process (Table 2.4). When respondents were asked whether they believed the Assembly would treat their submissions seriously, were they to send one in, a total of 41 per cent of respondents replied affirmatively. Forty-three per cent of rural dwellers believed their submissions would be treated seriously, compared with 42 per cent of urban dwellers, 40 per cent of metro-politan dwellers and only 39 per cent of those in informal areas. The highest level of scepticism came from whites, of whom only 16 per cent believed their submissions would be seriously treated, compared with 21 per cent of Indians, 29 per cent coloureds and 48 per cent of African respondents. The study considered the low response from whites to be partly associated with their antagonism towards the CA process.

While some degree of doubt seems to exist as to whether the Constitutional Assembly would treat individual submissions seriously, which contrasts with greater faith in the CA's call for public participation, the study felt the CA appeared to be doing what people wanted: namely consulting ordinary people about the new constitution. Eighty-three per cent of respondents stated that the assembly should be consulting the public about the constitution. There was little difference across race, gender or age cohorts in supporting the CA process. Irrespective of whether individuals felt their own submissions would be treated seriously if they sent them in, the overwhelming majority believed the Assembly to be right in consulting the public. The study saw the CA as setting a precedent, not merely in engaging in consultation with the public, but in the deliberate attempt to reach

**Figure 2.4** Will the new constitution reflect your views?
(all respondents: all quantities given are percentages)

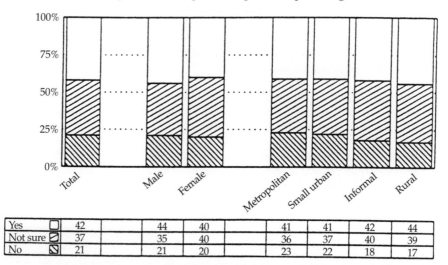

| | | Total | | Male | Female | | Metropolitan | Small urban | Informal | Rural |
|---|---|---|---|---|---|---|---|---|---|---|
| Yes | ☐ | 42 | | 44 | 40 | | 41 | 41 | 42 | 44 |
| Not sure | ▨ | 37 | | 35 | 40 | | 36 | 37 | 40 | 39 |
| No | ◩ | 21 | | 21 | 20 | | 23 | 22 | 18 | 17 |

*Source*: CASE 1996 (i)

marginalized communities. Other commentators have been more sceptical and see the process as essentially a public relations exercise. Although all submissions were collated, there is no evidence of the extent to which public, individual submissions have been included in the drafting of the 1996 constitution (*ibid.*: 23; Leon interview, 1996). Yet as the CASE study rightly recognized, the Constitutional Assembly could consider views submitted to it, but the constitution certainly could not reflect all shades of individual opinion. The constitution would be essentially a negotiated document which attempted to establish a broad consensus (*ibid.*: 26). There were few indications that the wider public believed the new constitution would reflect their views anyway, with consistently higher responses falling into the 'no/not sure' categories as Figure 2.4 demonstrates. Equally, Figure 2.5 outlines the responses to the question 'Did ordinary people help to write the constitution?' with very similar results: 65 per cent of all respondents replied negatively. In a sense, these responses indicate that the public were not being misled by the media campaign and retained what might be regarded as a healthy measure of political realism. An overwhelming belief in the efficacy of public involvement in the writing of the constitution might have suggested that the campaign had been one of political indoctrination rather than that of civil education.

Certainly, the CA media campaign succeeded in generating an interest among the public in reading the final constitution, which according to the study ran across race and gender lines. Support remained high across metropolitan and urban areas, 87 per cent and 86 per cent respectively, dipping slightly among rural dwellers and those from informal areas, representing

**Figure 2.5**   Did ordinary people help to write the constitution?
(all respondents: all quantities given are percentages)

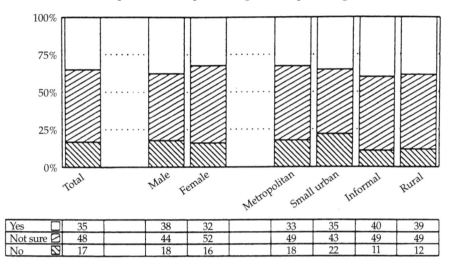

| | | Total | | Male | Female | | Metropolitan | Small urban | Informal | Rural |
|---|---|---|---|---|---|---|---|---|---|---|
| Yes | ☐ | 35 | | 38 | 32 | | 33 | 35 | 40 | 39 |
| Not sure | ◩ | 48 | | 44 | 52 | | 49 | 43 | 49 | 49 |
| No | ◩ | 17 | | 18 | 16 | | 18 | 22 | 11 | 12 |

*Source*: CASE 1996 (i)

80 per cent and 78 per cent respectively. Two-thirds of those with no formal education expressed an interest in the final document and the CASE study felt that the constitution might become a 'powerful adult education and distance learning tool'. The CA could also form partnerships with NGOs working in the field as an attempt at trying to reach groups with high illiteracy or semi-literacy rates.

The aspect which, perhaps, is of a potentially more serious and fundamental concern to the government is the range of issues that respondents wanted to see included in the constitution. As Figure 2.6 sets out, the most important issues for inclusion were: the provision of more jobs, more houses, better educational opportunities, crime prevention, water provision, return of the death penalty and equal opportunities for all. Of less concern, were issues that are generally associated with democratic constitutions, that is, free speech, religious freedom, national unity, rights for women, children and pensioners and so on. The CASE study found that these issues scarcely differed from those discovered in their questionnaires of 1995 when respondents also concentrated on jobs, houses, crime/violence prevention and better educational provision. The study conducted in 1996 maintained that there were possibly two interpretations. On the one hand, the results clearly strengthened those who wished to include socio-economic rights in the constitution. On the other hand, it might be that respondents were unclear as to the kind of issue that would be appropriate to include in a constitution. Consequently, they focused on their immediate needs. But in a sense, this is precisely the point that could be very worrying to a government that may not

**Figure 2.6**  Most important issue to be included in the constitution
(all respondents, first choice)
Open-ended question, no prompting

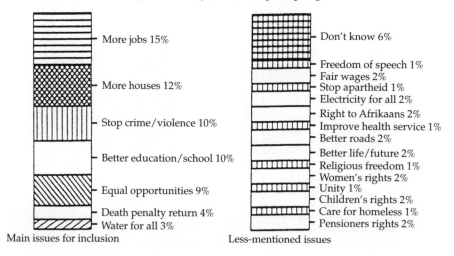

More jobs 15%

More houses 12%

Stop crime/violence 10%

Better education/school 10%

Equal opportunities 9%

Death penalty return 4%
Water for all 3%

Main issues for inclusion

Don't know 6%

Freedom of speech 1%
Fair wages 2%
Stop apartheid 1%
Electricity for all 2%

Right to Afrikaans 2%
Improve health service 1%
Better roads 2%

Better life/future 2%
Religious freedom 1%
Women's rights 2%
Unity 1%
Children's rights 2%
Care for homeless 1%
Pensioners rights 2%

Less-mentioned issues

*Source*: CASE 1996 (i)

be able to fulfil such socio-economic demands. In any case, many favour a slim constitution which outlines general principles but resists the temptation to define specific areas of policy (Neumann 1960: 673; Leon interview, 1996).

The CASE study suggests that there may be another element in the socio-economic dimension, in that South Africans are aware that previous constitutions and bodies of legislation were precisely the vehicles through which the government denied the wider population the right to vote and also the right to basic necessities such as jobs, houses, clean water, electricity and so on. The struggle against the tricameral parliamentary system during the 1980s and the ensuing heightened resistance which focused on bread-and-butter issues were still recent enough to have made a strong impression on people's notion of exactly what their rights should be. Only 6 per cent of respondents could not identify the kinds of issues they wanted to see included in a constitution.

A contradiction emerged in the responses of the study in that people were very clear about their demands but were less certain whether they would be included in the constitution. Having said that, however, the CA has recognized that it was working in a difficult area: trying to explain complex concepts to what were previously marginalized communities such as 'rural and informal dwellers, the elderly, women, and the under-educated, all groups suffering from extremely high illiteracy rates' (CASE 1996: 35). Looked at from this perspective, the campaign was a clear success in publicizing the constitution-writing process to the wider public. As the CASE study states: 'Many South Africans know of the CA and what it is doing;

know that they can take part in the process and feel part of that process, regardless of whether or not they have taken part' (*ibid.*: 34).

## The 1996 constitution

The Constitution of the Republic of South Africa as adopted by the Constitutional Assembly on 8 May 1996 contains 14 chapters and 7 schedules and is 'the collective wisdom of the South African people which has been arrived at by general agreement' (Constitution of the Republic of South Africa 1996). The process of drafting the text involved many South Africans in the largest public participation programme ever carried out in the country. After nearly two years of intensive consultations, the Constitutional Assembly negotiated the outcome, which is an integration of the ideas of ordinary citizens, civil society and political parties (*ibid.*: 1).

The chapters are concerned with a Bill of Rights, co-operative government, parliament, the president and the national executive, the provinces, local government, courts and the administration of justice, state institutions, security services, traditional leaders, finance, and general provisions. The schedules concentrate on elections procedures, oaths and solemn affirmations, the national flag, national and provincial legislative competence, transitional arrangements and the repeal of laws. Chapter 1 of the constitution delineates its founding provisions and declares that South Africa is one sovereign, democratic state based on certain values: human dignity, the achievement of equality and advancement of human rights and freedoms; non-racialism and non-sexism; supremacy of the constitution and the rule of law; universal adult suffrage, a national common voters' roll, regular elections and a multi-party system of democratic government, to ensure accountability, responsiveness and openness.

The constitution is the supreme law of the republic. Any law or conduct inconsistent with it is invalid and the duties imposed by it must be performed. There is a common South African citizenship and all citizens are equally entitled to the rights, privileges and benefits of citizenship whilst being equally subject to its duties and responsibilities. There are eleven official languages of the republic: Sepedi, Sesotho, Setswana, siSwati, Tshivenda, Xitsonga, Afrikaans, English, isiNdebele, isiXhosa and isiZulu and 'the state must take practical and positive measures to elevate the status and advance the use of these languages' (*ibid.*).

## Bill of Rights

The Bill of Rights contained in chapter 2 of the constitution proclaims that it is the 'cornerstone of democracy' in South Africa: 'It enshrines the rights of

**Table 2.5**  Human rights

Question: 'Could you please tell me what you understand by the term Human Rights?' (all respondents)

| Replies: | |
|---|---|
| Rights of the people | 25% |
| Don't know | 23% |
| Freedom of speech | 12% |
| Equality | 7% |
| Do anything if legal | 5% |
| Freedom for all | 4% |
| Women's rights | 4% |
| Needs of people | 2% |
| Our new laws | 1% |

*Source:* CASE 1996 (i)

all people in our country and affirms the democratic values of human dignity, equality and freedom' (Constitution of the Republic of South Africa 1996, see Appendix). Democracy has been seen as a 'complex interaction of forces, all of which must be enabled to operate with reasonable freedom from arbitrary restraint' (Sandifer and Scheman 1966: 44). In order to secure that freedom, the citizens of a state must be fully confident that the following rights will be operative: 'the right to life, liberty and security under which are included freedom of movement, the right to due process of law, freedom from arbitrary arrest and the right to privacy; equal protection of the laws; the right to free assembly and association; the right to peaceful petition; freedom of thought and expression; the right to the protection of impartial courts which includes the right to a fair trial and finally, the right to an education'. According to Sandifer and Scheman, some people may wish to add to this list, but it would be 'virtually impossible to subtract from it and leave any meaning to the word democracy' (*ibid.*). So in this sense, the Bill of Rights contained in the 1996 constitution can be regarded as truly democratic in that it safeguards and enshrines these various rights.

Interestingly, however, the CASE survey found that one of the key problems facing their evaluation was the difficulty of trying to develop an understanding of what people understood by the term 'human rights', which the surveyors felt 'underpinned the entire CA exercise' (CASE 1996: 30). They decided to adopt a procedure that they considered could be analyzed both qualitatively and quantitatively. Following an introduction to the survey which was read to all participants and which contained no reference to rights, all respondents were then asked two open-ended questions. Open-ended questions allowed respondents to give any answer they chose, which was later coded and grouped with other similar answers, to allow an approximate qualitative measure to be added to the quantitative exercise. The first question which respondents had to attempt with no prompting or explanations was: 'Could you please tell me what you understand by the term Human Rights?' It was hoped that by presenting questions in this format the survey could probe the extent to which respondents had any knowledge of human rights. Table 2.5 illustrates the responses.

The main answer to the question about human rights was the response 'the rights of the people', which could be regarded as a tautological reply, largely undefinable. If collated with the similar response, 'needs of the people', and the percentage replying 'don't know', a total of 50 per cent of respondents were uncertain about the meaning of the term 'human rights'. If one then groups the less ambiguous replies, namely: freedom of speech, equality, freedom for all, women's rights, a total of 27 per cent of those interviewed supplied some understanding of the question. An IDASA survey found that a 'strikingly high number of people' were unfamiliar with the political debate over specific rights. Twenty-eight per cent of their total sample could not list one thing they thought should be included in the constitution as a 'right'. These proportions increased drastically once people were pressed for a second or a third right: 43 per cent could not name a second right and a 'massive 61 per cent were unable to cite a third one' (IDASA 1996b). It is hardly surprising, then, that the CASE study felt that the CA campaign was ending at precisely the time of greatest need, that is, the moment at which the constitution was to be issued. They asked: 'Who will focus on illiterate and semi-literate South Africans, in order to explain their rights? Or to farm-workers and other similar groups? Who will mediate and explain it to ordinary people in the street?' (CASE 1996: 35).

Certain sections contained in the Bill of Rights are informed by the brutality of the apartheid period. Clauses on the protection of human dignity, the freedom and security of the person, the right to life and to privacy, the outlawing of slavery, servitude and forced labour are resonant with images of the past (see Appendix 2). The Bill of Rights also grants employees the right to strike without the often concomitant employers' right to 'lock out'. This clause has raised some criticism among lawyers, who feel labour relations should be excluded from constitutional matters (Leon interview, 1996). Peter Leon argues that although there is a 'good argument for requiring the Bill of Rights to recognise people's basic socio-economic needs, such as those to food, water, housing and health care, to include these needs in the Bill as directly enforceable rights could generate unrealisable expectations and lead the courts to usurp matters best left to the executive and the legislature' (Association of the Law Societies of the Republic of South Africa 1996: 2). On a legalistic point the Association of Law Societies believes socio-economic clauses may be included in the Bill under what is described as a 'standards of seriousness review'. This process empowers the courts to scrutinize the government's programmes but does not permit them to 'second-guess' governmental policy choices (*ibid.*).

Of more fundamental significance is the controversy about whether the Bill of Rights should have what is referred to as 'horizontal application'. The Association of Law Societies explains that there are two different explanations of horizontality. First, a benign interpretation assumes that fundamental rights govern all rules of law, whether the rules apply vertically, that is between the state and the person, or horizontally, that is between person and person. This process makes the constitution universal and ensures that particular classes or rules, such as common-law or private-law rules, are not exempt from the scope of the Bill of Rights. This kind of horizontality means that the constitution is the supreme law of the land and every rule of law should potentially be reviewable for conflict with a fundamental right. Second, a problematic interpretation of the horizontal application of a fundamental right means that it generates a right to sue a private person. This conception of horizontality dramatically widens the reach of the bill of rights and can lead potentially to high levels of litigation between individuals. The Association of Law Societies believes this form of horizontality can 'skew or disrupt government sponsored anti-discrimination programmes and affirmative action policies' (*ibid*.: 8). In the event, the final clause 39 of the Bill of Rights asserts: 'The bill of rights does not deny the existence of any other rights or freedoms that are recognised or conferred by common law, customary law or legislation, to the extent that they are consistent with the bill' (Constitution of the Republic of South Africa 1996, see Appendix 2).

## Amending the constitution/Constitutional Court

Under section 74 of chapter 4 of the 1996 constitution provision is made for bills of amendment. The constitution may be amended either by a bill passed by the National Assembly supported by a vote of at least two-thirds of its members or by the National Council of Provinces supported by a vote of at least six provinces. Peter Leon believes the constitution is too easy to amend and could be at risk of becoming a paper document that may be disregarded (Leon interview, 1996). The distinction between 'rigid' and 'flexible' constitutions is one of long standing. A flexible constitution is one that can be amended by the same agencies that enact laws and in the same manner. As Neumann points out: 'Most constitutions of the world are flexible because they may be amended by the legislature of their countries, but most of them are not completely flexible because there usually is provided a qualified vote' (Neumann 1960: 669). A rigid constitution, on the other hand, allows for amendments to be made through different agencies as in the case of the United States, which provides for four ways in which the constitution can be amended: through a proposal by two-thirds of both houses of Congress; or by a convention called by Congress on the application of two-thirds of the state legislatures; and ratification either by the legislatures of three-fourths of the states; or by conventions in three-fourths of the states (*ibid.*). This method is different from the legislative process and the president cannot veto any part of the process.

Neumann maintains that it is possible to have a constitution that is rigid in form but flexible in adaptability. This point rests on the extent to which the text may be interpreted. Whilst the constitution of the United States is both rigid in the classical sense and difficult to amend in the formal sense, Neumann argues that the terms such as 'due process of law' or 'freedom of speech' have changed radically in their interpretations since the constitution was written. In that sense formal amendments are not required very often. However, in countries with formally 'flexible' constitutions, as in the case of Germany, where their texts are so detailed and precise, amendments become a necessity (*ibid.*). It could be argued that the 1996 South African constitution runs the risk of being too detailed. As Neumann asserts, 'If a constitution is to be a superior document to which people are to look up as a symbol and guarantor of their way of life, very frequent changes are likely to defeat that aim' (*ibid.*: 670).

The Constitutional Court is the highest court in all constitutional matters and may decide only constitutional matters. It also makes the final decision whether a matter is a constitutional matter or whether an issue is connected with a decision on a constitutional issue. The Court is composed of eleven judges including the President and Deputy President of the Court and it is diverse in terms of representation, gender and race. Section 174 of chapter 8 of the constitution outlines the need for the judiciary to 'reflect broadly the racial and gender composition of South Africa' (Constitution of the Republic of South Africa 1996). The President of South Africa, as head of the national executive, consults with the Judicial Service Commission and the leaders of parties represented in the National Assembly and then appoints the President and Deputy President of the Constitutional Court. It is the composition of the Judicial Service Commission which has given rise to some criticism from the lawyers. The number of politicians on the Commission has increased from four to ten and it is feared it runs the risk of an increased chance of politicization. Andre Van Vuuren, Director General of the Association of Law Societies, maintains that a major party in parliament may choose or control the membership of the Judicial Service Commission and thus reduce the independence of the Constitutional Court (Van Vuuren interview, 1996). Another argument suggests that appointments to the Constitutional Court should be through 'a process of political party consultation led by the President on the recommendations of the Judicial Service Commission'. Such a process would 'recognise political realities but would also temper political bias by making the dominant party consult with ALL other parties' (Leon interview, 1996, Leon's stress on 'all'). However, in terms of an experiment in participatory democracy the process of drawing up the constitution provided a novel approach.

# THREE

# Parties and political cleavages

Political parties are essential features of the modern state and are critical forces in democratizing countries. The 400 members of South Africa's National Assembly represent seven parties (see Appendix 3). The ANC is by far the dominant party with 252 seats, followed by the National Party with 82 seats and the Inkatha Freedom Party with 43 seats. Parties in liberal democracies tend to play an integrative role, in that they bring people into the political process and provide channels of communication between society and political representatives. By building links with the public and articulating certain moral and social values, parties increase the legitimacy of political systems and thereby can reduce the likelihood of violent outbursts.

## Political parties: origins, nature and structure

Parties prevail in the large majority of countries in the contemporary world, both in liberal democratic and authoritarian states. The extension of the franchise boosted their emergence in nineteenth-century Europe, but as Epstein pointed out, parties could function with a limited electorate: 'Even when sizeable groups were excluded for racial or economic reasons, the franchise was sometimes wide enough for parties to function' (Epstein 1967: 20). This, of course, is precisely the situation which obtained in South Africa before 1994. Certain parties were permitted to function but others were banned and forced into exile. Once the franchise is extended, however, and other political organizations are no longer proscribed, existing parties must adapt through a process of reorganization and reorientation.

In less restrictive societies parties emerge when members of the polity begin to recognize the existence of conflicts of interest within society (Huntington 1967: 407). Historically, these conflicts have occurred over the diverse interests of capital and labour. Large social democratic parties were often forged in order to further the interests and opportunities of the working classes, whilst conservative parties often represented the interests of landowners, business, financiers and so on (Sartori 1976: 42–7). Industrialization and changing socio-economic patterns create differentiated class structures which, in turn, produce class-based parties. Consequently, the expansion of the working class was a pivotal factor in the historic development of the party system (Blondel 1995: 136). However, in countries where this feature is absent, class-based parties find it difficult to develop naturally: 'Socialist and communist parties thus emerge in a particular type of social structure' (*ibid.*). In those societies ideology plays a significant part both symbolically and practically in guiding parties and communities towards a common goal. Blondel sees communist and socialist parties as mobilizing organizations that attempt to educate the population to support the goals put forward by the regime (*ibid.*:137). Some third-world states have parties that closely resemble the traditional communist model. These parties use ideology as part of a national development strategy, or as Epstein asserts, they have functions to perform for the state that are 'incompatible with electoral competition' (Epstein 1967: 47). Yet Epstein concedes that communist party organization of the working class, using the cell instead of the branch as the basic unit, and orienting membership around the work-place rather than a geographically defined electoral district, can be effective (*ibid.*). Duverger saw the nature and size of the cell as being important in giving the party the ability to be constantly in touch with the membership at their place of work (Duverger 1967: 29).

The structure of a political party is also important. A poorly organized party is unlikely to achieve either representation or mobilization. According to some analysts three aspects of the structure of parties need to be considered: the internal arrangements, the relationship between parties and supporters, and patterns of leadership (Epstein 1967; Daalder and Mair 1983). The internal arrangements of a party include both the structure of the organization and the degree to which it exercises democratic principles. Hierarchical parties can be deeply centralized and less sensitive to the wishes of the rank and file membership. An executive body may decide policy with little reference to those outside its authority. Conversely, a democratically organized party may permit its membership to participate in the policy-making process.

Political parties are also the main mechanisms of political recruitment, in that candidates are selected and prepared for public office. To join a mass party the most usual procedure is to fill in a membership form, a printed document which generally includes a passage declaring that the signatory undertakes to observe the rules of the party. Subscriptions are then made to the party. Some parties are extensive and others are inextensive. As Blondel explains: 'An extensive party is one which is present all over the country; and inextensive party is one which does not aim at or does not succeed in being present at the periphery' (Blondel 1995: 141). Some parties operate on a clientalistic basis and therefore do not need to be extensive. Traditional parties also tend not to have 'branches' or 'sections' at the local level.

The classification of political leadership is an important aspect of parties in South Africa. Considering Max Weber's definition of three types of authority – traditional, bureaucratic-legalistic and charismatic – it is clear that traditional leaders of political parties owe part of their political power to the status of their family in a particular district, or to their ethnicity. This definition would appear to apply to the Inkatha Freedom Party and its base of support in KwaZulu Natal. Bureaucratic-legalistic leadership is often associated with professional politicians moving up the party hierarchy. In these cases the person holding the position of leader, chairman, president or secretary-general has usually made his/her career within the party. These forms of leadership appear in both multi-party liberal democratic countries and one-party states. Charismatic leadership has been typically associated with parties in the developing world but personalized forms of leadership have been apparent in both former communist countries and in fascist nations during the 1930s. Personalized leadership has become a feature of third-world countries largely because of the nature of former struggles for independence, but difficulties often emerge over the question of political succession. All countries, of course, have to confront the issue of succession at some stage. South Africa will be facing the issue in the 1999 elections and already commentators are beginning to speculate on how political affairs will develop after the next presidential and parliamentary elections, with obvious comparisons drawn between Nelson Mandela and Thabo Mbeki.

## The post-independence party

The political party has been regarded as the 'critical force for modernisation' which can assist in the construction of new political institutions (Apter 1967: 179; Huntington 1967: 212). By ensuring that social cleavages are represented in the political arena they provide the basis for institutional cohesion. However, some analysts have speculated that definitions of political parties have been 'too rigid' and determined by a Eurocentric understanding of what a political party should be (Randall 1988: 2). Looking at the example of the early post-colonial state, Clapham maintained that once independence had been achieved the role of the liberation/nationalist party often declined in importance as its leaders moved into the state bureaucracy (Clapham, 1985). As Foltz observed over 30 years ago, single, mass parties could be successful in leading the way to independence but they were equally adept at 'quickly consolidating control over the government and administrative apparatuses once independence was achieved' (Foltz 1967: 309). The strength of these parties was based on four central factors, some of which continue to have a resonance in the political environment of transitional democratic states. First, the notion of independence acted as a clarion call and became a unifying objective. Second, the single mass party generally included mostly all the modern elite, who had often been similarly educated, spent time overseas, and were committed to achieving the same goals. Those who were not in the party were often co-opted at a later stage, whereas those groups who had been too closely identified with the former regime were subsequently compromised by their previous political linkages. Third, often the single party dominated the political arena and left little room for the development of alternative forms of opposition. Finally, the party was usually well-organized, which generally resulted from the nature of the political struggle it had survived. The mass party, then, became 'the framework within which ethnic, caste, and regional differences among the population at large could be submerged in the search for a common goal. It both embodied and promoted a preliminary sense of national unity and identity' (*ibid.*: 310).

Once formal independence had been achieved, however, parties would be obliged to face the problems and demands of government. Sometimes newly independent governments chose new goals, for example economic development or national unity, which would attempt to serve the same symbolic purpose as the former battle for self-determination. It was often at this stage that difficulties arose when new administrative burdens and responsibilities were placed on government officials. The process of governing an independent country requires indigenous participation in a variety of new formally constituted units, for example a national army and a civil service (*ibid.*: 312). Although it would be both erroneous and misleading to categorize South Africa as an archetypal 'post-colonial' independent state or to regard the ANC as a stereotypical 'single, mass party', there are common features within transitional states, for example: the shift from exiled liberation movement to governing party; the emergence of a dominant party; declining popular euphoria once independence is achieved; and heightened public expectations of what government can deliver.

## The African National Congress and the liberation struggle

The African National Congress (ANC) regards itself as a democratic liberation movement whose policies are determined by the membership and whose leadership must be accountable to all members. Its primary aim and objective is to 'Unite all the people of South Africa, Africans in particular, for the complete liberation of the country from all forms of discrimination and national oppression' (African National Congress 1994a: 4). Its 1994 amended constitution declares that the ANC is recognized as the 'central organiser and inspirer of a vast popular upsurge against apartheid' (*ibid.*: 3). Included within the organization is a 'great array of social, cultural, religious, trade union, professional and political organisations' (*ibid.*).

The ANC, known as the South African Native National Congress (SANNC) until 1923, was formed in 1912. The declared intention of the SANNC was set out in its first constitution: '(The organization aims) to encourage mutual understanding and to bring together into common action as one political people all tribes and clans of various tribes or races and by means of combined effort and united political organisation to defend their freedom, rights and privileges' (cited in Worden 1995). However, as Tom Lodge points out, it was far from being a mass movement. It included some chiefs and rural leaders, but its members were still primarily middle-class men who feared 'being thrust back into the ranks of the urban and rural poor' (Lodge 1983: 2). The SANNC hoped to exert influence by petitions, delegations and journalism but the ineffectiveness of such approaches became clear by the end of the decade. However, the SAANC leadership was not wholly in favour of strike action and was fearful of the possible radicalization of labour protest (Worden 1995: 83).

The ANC was banned in 1960 and re-formed itself in South Africa's neighbouring states under the leadership of Oliver Tambo. At the Morogoro Conference in 1969 the organization confirmed a policy of violence against the South African government. During the 1970s it went through a period of political and military consolidation (see Beinart 1994 and Worden 1995 for accounts of the historical development of the ANC). In the organization's own literature, the 1940s are seen as the decade that gave the ANC new life and energy, in a sense preparing the movement for the organization it was to become (*Mzabalazo* 1994). It was changed from the 'careful organisation it was in the 1930s to the mass movement it was to become in the 1950s' (*ibid.*: 6). According to Nigel Worden, the ANC had been in decline during the 1930s: 'Its cautious and conservative orientation towards the reserve chiefs and the aspiring African commercial and middle classes provided little link with the majority of the population facing rural impoverishment and urban proletarianisation' (Worden 1995: 83). The ANC itself admits that it became inactive during the 1930s under its conservative leadership (*Mzabalazo* 1994: 5).

In 1944 the ANC Youth League was formed. The young leaders of the Youth League, including Nelson Madela, Walter Sisulu and Oliver Tambo, aimed to involve the masses of people in the struggle against repressive government policies. With more people moving to the cities in the 1940s to work in factories and industries, new community organizations formed such as the Squatters Movement and trade unions. In 1946, 75 000 African mineworkers came out on strike for higher wages. Many trade unionists were arrested and troops forced miners back to the mines with bayonets (*ibid.*). The Youth League drew up a Programme of Action calling for strikes, boycotts and defiance against the government. It was adopted by the ANC in 1949 and led to the Defiance Campaign of the 1950s. This action represented a break with the conciliatory policies of previous decades. It called for 'national freedom' and political independence from white domination, together with the rejection of all forms of segregation. Also it supported the use of boycotts, civil disobedience and strikes as a means of demonstrating against the government (*ibid.*: 8). The government, in turn, tried to stop the Defiance Campaign by banning its leaders and passing new laws to prevent public disobedience. But the campaign had made considerable strides and it forged closer co-operation between the ANC and the SA Indian Congress. It also led to the formation of new organizations, the SA Coloured People's Organization (SACPO) and the Congress of Democrats (COD), an organization of white democrats.

These organizations, together with the SA Congress of Trade Unions (SACTU), formed the Congress Alliance which canvassed people's opinions and presented what came to be known as the 'Freedom Charter'. The Freedom Charter stated: 'South Africa belongs to all who live in it, black and white, and no government can justly claim authority unless it is based on the will of the people . . . the rights of the people shall be the same regardless of race, colour or sex' (cited in Worden 1995: 106). It called for equal access to health, education and legal rights and demanded that all apartheid laws and practices should be set aside (*ibid.*). Worden maintains that the vision of a 'strongly democratic and multiracial' South Africa informed the ANC's thinking and provided an ideological benchmark of opposition to apartheid right into the 1990s (*ibid.*: 105–6). Certainly, the ANC sees the Freedom Charter as an expression of its policy of non-racialism. In fact, contained in the membership section of the 1994 constitution is the declaration that any new member must make a pledge to abide by the 'aims and objectives of the ANC as set out in the Constitution and the Freedom Charter' (African National Congress 1994a: 5). Also, the National Executive Committee of the ANC announced in 1996 the celebration of its adoption of the Freedom Charter in 1956 (African National Congress 1996a: 1). Nevertheless, during the 1950s it recognized that not everyone in the ANC agreed with the policy: 'A small minority of members who called themselves Africanist, opposed the Charter. They objected to the ANC's growing cooperation with whites and Indians, whom they described as foreigners' (*Mzabalazo* 1994: 14). The differences between the Africanists and those in the ANC who supported non-racialism could not be overcome and in 1959 the Africanists broke away from the ANC and formed the Pan Africanist Congress (PAC).

According to Tom Lodge, the ANC organizational structure until the late 1950s was largely federal in character, with 'each province constituting a fairly autonomous organisational unit, an arrangement which helped to sustain ideological diversity' (Lodge 1996: 191). Oliver Tambo drew up a constitution that gave more authority to senior bodies, although conference would elect leaders at all levels. Lodge maintains that until 1960 the ANC represented 'a broad church accommodating socially conservative and radical nationalists, democratic socialist, liberal constitutionalists and Marxists of various persuasions' (*ibid.*: 190).

The massacre of peaceful protesters at Sharpeville in March 1960 brought a decade of peaceful protests to an end. Sixty-nine people died, many shot in the back, and 180 were wounded. The government declared a state of emergency and arrested thousands of ANC and PAC supporters (*ibid.*). It is generally accepted that the Sharpeville shootings marked a dramatic turning-point in South Africa's history. Sharpeville revealed the weakness of non-violent resistance and forced a new approach from opponents of apartheid. Umkhonto we Sizwe (Spear of the Nation) (MK) was founded in 1961 as an underground guerrilla army to 'hit back by all the means within our power in defence of our people, our future and our freedom' (*ibid.*: 16). The ANC regards the formation of Umkhonto we Sizwe as one of its major 'pillars of struggle' against apartheid (African National Congress 1994b). In 18 months the organization carried out 200 acts of sabotage against government property and buildings. All cadres were under strict orders that no one be harmed during these actions. However, the government responded with even harsher methods of repression. Laws were passed to make death the penalty for sabotage and to allow police to detain people for 90 days without a trial. In 1963, police raided the secret headquarters of MK and arrested the leaders. This led to the Rivonia Trial where the leaders of MK were charged with attempting to cause a violent revolution. The Rivonia trialists included Nelson Mandela, Walter Sisulu, Govan Mbeki, Raymond Mhlaba, Elias Motsoaledi, Andrew Mlangeni, Ahmed Kathrada and Dennis Goldberg. They were all found guilty and sentenced to life imprisonment. The ANC admits that after the Rivonia Trial, the underground structures of the organization were all but destroyed (*Mzabalazo* 1994: 16). The ANC was banned after Sharpeville.

The ANC consultative conference held at Morogoro, Tanzania in 1969 committed the organization to an armed struggle against apartheid and to a campaign of mass political education and agitation. The non-racial character of the ANC was further consolidated by the opening up of its membership to non-Africans. The ANC mission abroad co-ordinated an international political campaign. The objective was to ensure political, military, economic and cultural isolation of the apartheid regime. It was also aimed at mobilizing political, material and human resources for the national liberation movement (African National Congress 1994b).

The 1970s and 1980s witnessed the emergence of 'black consciousness' movements, student uprisings in Soweto and elsewhere, strikes and demonstrations and the growth of community organizations such as civics, youth groups and women's organizations, all of which contributed to the formation of the United Democratic Front (UDF). One of the biggest organizations was the Congress of South African Students (COSAS) which had branches in towns and cities throughout South Africa. In many cases civic organizations developed out of parent–student committees which had been formed to support education struggles. Massive national school boycotts racked the townships in 1980 and in 1984/85. Labour organizations formed the Congress of South African Trade Unions (COSATU) in 1986. COSATU drew together independent unions that had begun to grow in the 1970s and committed itself to advancing the struggles of workers both in the workplace and in the community. 1987 witnessed the highest number of strikes ever, including a strike by over 300 000 mineworkers (*Mzabalazo* 1994: 22).

In 1985 the ANC called on township residents to make their localities ungovernable by destroying the Black Local Authorities which had been established by government. Under the 1982 Black Local Authorities Act community councils were given greater powers of administration. Elected by local residents, councillors were responsible for township administration on budgets raised by local rents and rates. The ANC admits that as administrative systems broke down an 'atmosphere of mass insurrection prevailed in many townships and rural areas across the country' (*ibid.*). As resistance to the government mounted, the regime became more draconian. A state of emergency was declared over many parts of the country in 1985, lasting for six months. By 1986 a national emergency was declared that lasted until 1990. The UDF was banned, COSATU was restricted from political activity and over 30 000 people were detained.

## Unbanning of the ANC

In his opening address to Parliament on 2 February 1990, F. W. de Klerk announced the lifting of the ban on the ANC and other organizations. For the ANC this development represented a 'strategic victory for the movement' (African National Congress 1994b: 4). It also led to the creation of political conditions that made it possible for the organization to pursue its aim of transferring political power to the people through a process of negotiation. Some commentators maintain that pressure from 'subordinate classes was the crucial agency in determining political transition in South Africa' (Lodge 1996: 189). Yet the ANC itself recognizes that political negotiations took place at a time 'when the end of the Cold War shifted the balance of forces internationally decisively in favour of the resolution of regional conflicts through negotiations' (African National Congress 1994b: 5).

Organizationally, Tom Lodge describes the ANC as 'an exiled insurgent body' which had acquired a 'disciplined and autocratic character' (Lodge 1996: 191). No leadership elections had been held for 26 years, between 1959 and 1985, and the South African Communist Party played a central role within the organization. The ANC exiles 'returned home with a well-developed set of authoritarian and bureaucratic reflexes'. Yet, as Lodge asserts, a very different form of political socialization had been taking place within South Africa itself (*ibid.*: 193). During the 1970s and 1980s 'two successive waves of organisation-building had endowed black communities with an unprecedented and dense network of voluntary organisations' (*ibid.*). Lodge sees the trade union movement as being the spearhead of community action, both politicizing and organizing the labour force. Equally, he points to the initiatives of the South African Communist Party (SACP) which established 'tight factory-based organisations, highly trained shop-steward leadership and a focus on workplace-related concerns' (*ibid.*). The success of this activity supports the views of both Epstein and Duverger, in that cell and work-based communist organizations can act as effective and efficient political agencies (Epstein 1967, Duverger 1967). In 1978 the Federation of South African Trade Unions (FOSATU) was established with the objective of gaining management recognition. FOSATU merged with a number of ANC-aligned unions in 1985 to form the Congress of South African Trade Unions (COSATU). The relationship between COSATU and the ANC has been viewed differently. Lodge argues that while COSATU acknowledged the 'moral authority' of the organization, loyalty to the ANC was not unconditional: 'When COSATU adopted the ANC's Freedom Charter in 1987 it did so with the understanding that the charter provided only a set of minimum democratic demands which did not in any way diminish COSATU's commitments to economic transformation based on working-class interests' (Lodge 1996: 192). Conversely, COSATU has been described as becoming the 'main organisational backbone' of the ANC (Johnson and Schlemmer 1996: 3). With the unbanning of the ANC and the release of political prisoners the ANC recognized that it had to begin to reconsider its own organizational structure and constitution. The ANC National Conference elected Nelson Mandela as President in 1991 and by 1994 the 49th National Conference amended and adopted a new constitution (African National Congress 1994a).

The amended constitution was intended 'to orient the structure of the organisation to conditions in the country since the 27 April (1994) election' (African National Congress 1994b: 15). The main amendments regarded the structures of the organization and their functioning. References to Umkhonto we Sizwe were removed from the existing constitution since the MK was integrated into the new South African National Defence Force. Similarly, references to overseas branches were removed as they too had ceased to exist. Apart from describing the ANC as a liberation movement, dedicated to the achievement of a united, non-racial, non-sexist, democratic South Africa, the constitution outlines a framework for democratic decision-making and accountability. The organizational structure is as follows:

- the National Conference which elects the National Executive Committee;
- the Provincial Conference which elects the Provincial Executive Committees;
- the Regional General Council which elects the Regional Executive Committee;
- the branch meeting which elect the Branch Committee.

(African National Congress 1994a)

The National Conference is the 'supreme ruling and controlling body of the ANC' and is composed of voting and non-voting delegates (see Table 3.1). Voting on key questions is by secret ballot or if at least one-third of the delegates demand it. Delegates at the 1997 National Conference voted to amend the ANC constitution and hold conferences every five years, instead of the previously agreed three-year period. The escalating costs involved in holding conferences was given as the reason for this decision, but clearly

---

**Table 3.1**   The composition of the National Conference

---

*Voting Delegates*

(i)    At least 90 per cent of the voting delegates shall be from branches which shall be represented by elected delegates. The number of delegates shall be in proportion to the paid-up membership.

(ii)   The number of delegates to be elected to National Conference by each province shall be fixed by the National Executive Committee in proportion to the paid-up membership of each province.

(iii)  The remaining 10 per cent of voting delegates at the Conference shall come from the Provincial Executive Committees, ANC Women's League, ANC Youth League and departments of the ANC.

(iv)   All members of the National Executive Committee shall attend ex-officio as full participants in the conference.

*Non-Voting Delegates*

The National Executive Committee may invite individuals who have made a special contribution to the struggle or who have special skills or experience to attend the conference.

---

(African National Congress 1994a: 8)

---

it extends the term of office for officials. The 1997 Conference also agreed to create a new forum, the National Council, which would be a scaled-down version of the full conference and would meet in the period between conferences.

The National Executive Committee (NEC) is the highest organ of the ANC between conferences and has the authority to lead the organization, but a new National Council could prevent the NEC from taking purely unilateral decisions (African National Congress 1994a: 9, Amendment 1997). Table 3.2 outlines the the powers of the NEC.

The 1994 constitution rationalized 14 ANC regions into the nine provinces of the new South Africa: Northern Transvaal, Eastern Transvaal, Gauteng, Orange Free State, North West Province, Northern Cape, Western Cape, Eastern Cape and KwaZulu Natal. The number of National Executive Committee members elected directly by Conference was increased (see Table 3.3).

Members of the NEC, except where otherwise stipulated, must be elected by secret ballot by the National Conference and may hold office, under the 1997 Amendment, for five years. Should a vacancy occur for any reason, the NEC shall have the power to appoint a replacement (*ibid.*: 10). It was agreed at the 1994 Conference that people who would have served on the NEC by

---

**Table 3.2** Powers of the National Executive Committee

---

(a) Carry out the decisions and instruction of the National Conference.
(b) Issue and send directives and instructions to and receive reports from the provinces.
(c) Supervise and direct the work of the ANC and all its organs generally.
(d) Ensure that the regional and branch structures of the ANC function democratically and effectively.
(e) Oversee the work of the Women's League and the Youth League.
(f) Establish departments and set up committees as it considers appropriate.
(g) Manage and control all the national and international property and assets of the ANC.
(h) Receive reports, supervise the work of, and delegate such functions to the National Working Committee as it considers necessary.
(i) Issue documents and other policy directives as and when it deems fit.
(j) Confer such honours as it may deem appropriate.

---

(African National Congress 1994a: 9)

---

**Table 3.3** The composition of the NEC

---

President, Deputy President, National Chairperson, Secretary-General, Deputy Secretary-General and Treasurer General – all elected at Conference;
60 people elected at Conference;
President and Secretary of the Women's League and Youth League ex officio;
Chairperson and Secretary of each province ex-officio;
5 people to be co-opted by the NEC.

---

(African National Congress 1994a: 9)

---

virtue of their positions in provinces or in the leagues and who have been directly elected to the NEC, could in special cases retain both positions. However, the affected province or league would not then gain an additional place on the NEC (African National Congress 1994b: 15).

The National Working Committee (NWC) is elected by the NEC and is constituted as follows: President General, Deputy President, National Chairperson, Secretary-General, Deputy Secretary-General and Treasurer General, plus no more than a quarter of the directly elected NEC members. NWC members need not necessarily be full-time, but the NEC has the authority to allocate specific people full-time posts. The Youth League and Women's League both appoint one representative to serve on the NWC. The duties of the NWC are included in Appendix 4.

The greatest structural changes to the ANC constitution is in the transformation of the 14 previous regions into nine provinces. This change required a redefinition of the nature of regional structures. Although the functions of the nine new provinces correspond to those of the 14 former regions, each province contains a number of regions, whose size and boundaries are determined by each province. Within each of these regions there are sub-regions, and at the local level there are branches (African National Congress 1994b: 15). The highest decision-making body of the province is the Provincial Conference, which meets every two years. A Special Provincial Conference can be called if requested by at least one-third of branches. The Provincial Conference elects the Provincial Executive Committee (PEC) (see Appendix 4). The NEC has determined a limit of 3000 delegates for the conference with 90 per cent of voting delegates coming from branches. Delegates are categorized into participating delegates and are then further categorized into voting and non-voting, observers and others.

## The aims and objectives of the ANC

The aims and objectives of the ANC are outlined in Table 3.4, whilst Table 3.5 lists the rights and duties of the ANC membership.

---

**Table 3.4**   Aims and objectives of the ANC

---

1. To unite all the people of South Africa, Africans in particular, for the complete liberation of the country from all forms of discrimination and national oppression.
2. To end apartheid in all its forms and transform South Africa as rapidly as possible into a united, non-racial, non-sexist and democratic country based on the principles of the Freedom Charter.
3. To defend the democratic gains of the people and to advance towards a society in which the government is freely chosen by the people according to the principles of universal suffrage on a common voters' role.
4. To fight for social justice and to eliminate the vast inequalities created by apartheid and the system of oppression.
5. To build a South African nation with a common patriotism and loyalty in which the cultural, linguistic and religious diversity of the people is recognised.
6. To promote economic development for the benefit of all.
7. To support and advance the cause of national liberation, women's emancipation, development, world peace, disarmament and respect of the environment.
8. To support and promote the struggle for the rights of children.

---

(African National Congress 1994a: 4)

---

**Table 3.5**   Rights and duties of ANC members

---

*Rights*
A member of the ANC shall have the right to:
(a) Take a full and active part in the discussion, formulation and implementation of the policy of the ANC.
(b) Receive and impart information on all aspects of ANC policy and activities.
(c) Offer constructive criticism of any member, official, policy programme or activity of the ANC within its structures.
(d) Take part in elections and be elected or appointed to any committee, structure, commission or delegation of the ANC.
(e) Submit proposals or statements to the branch, province, region or NEC, provided such proposals or statements are submitted through the appropriate structures.

*Duties*
A member of the ANC shall:
(a) Belong to and take an active part in the life of his or her branch.
(b) Take all necessary steps to understand and carry out the aims, policy and programme of the ANC.
(c) Explain the aims, policy and programme of the ANC to the people.
(d) Deepen his or her understanding of the social, cultural, political and economic problems of the country.
(e) Combat propaganda detrimental to the interests of the ANC and defend the policy, aims and programme of the ANC.
(f) Fight against racism, tribal chauvinism, sexism, religious and political intolerance or any other form of discrimination or chauvinism.
(g) Observe discipline, behave honestly and carry out loyally decisions of the majority and decisions of higher bodies.
(h) Inform his or her branch of movement to any other area and report to the branch committee secretary on arriving at any new area.
(i) Refrain from publishing and/or distributing any media without authorisation which purports to be the view of any organised grouping, faction or tendency within the ANC.

---

(African National Congress 1994a: 6)

---

Within these rights and duties provision is made for criticism to be exercised. However, in August 1996 the National Executive Committee castigated ANC members who 'publicly criticise and challenge the party' (*The Star*, 21 August 1996). The NEC believed that such criticism by the membership served only 'to aid and abet those forces who want to weaken the party and undermine democratic transformation', and the question of discipline was raised (*ibid.*). These statements raised comment in the media, particularly as the Health Minister Nkosazana Zuma had been embroiled in the *Sarafina 2* scandal, which involved the misspending of R10 million (*c.*£2 million) of taxpayers' money and occasioned considerable public outrage. (*Sarafina 2* was a play about AIDS which was an ill-considered project that was entrusted to a friend of Health Minister, Dr Nkosazana Zuma, without authorization. It ended sevenfold over budget. There was no account of the expenditure of money. Subsequently, an 'anonymous donor' attempted to give money to the government.) Allegations by the axed deputy minister General Bantu Holomisa of impropriety on the part of some ANC leaders was dismissed as 'anti-democratic' by the ANC, who maintained that all accusations resulted from the activities of a 'third force' determined to wreck all attempts at democracy (Nyatsumba 1996a). According to Kaizer Nyatsumba both the ANC and the government often refer to the fact that elements of the former 'dirty-tricks machinery' were fuelling opposition within the country. Although accepting that there would inevitably be disaffected groups within South Africa, he cautioned the party: 'It is time the ANC shrugged off its paranoia and began behaving like a governing party' (Nyatsumba 1996b). The *Sunday Times* also raised questions about the inability of the ANC to accept any constructive criticism and its tendency to always dismiss it as either 'a conspiracy or racism'. The ANC was undermining the principle of good government and threatening the basis of a young democracy (*Sunday Times*, South Africa, 15 September 1996).

Two important sections within the ANC are the Women's League and the Youth League. Although these issues are discussed in a separate chapter it is necessary to consider them briefly here. The ANC's Women's League is open to women who are members of the ANC. The League has the same basic national, provincial and branch structure as the ANC. Its objectives are to defend and advance the rights of women, both inside and outside the ANC, against all forms of national, social and gender oppression. It also aims to ensure that women play a full role in the life of the organizations, in both national life and what is referred to as the 'people's struggle' (African National Congress 1994a: 7). The Women's League functions as an autonomous body within the overall structure of the ANC and has its own constitution, rules and regulations. However, it remains an integral part of the ANC and must not act in conflict with either the constitution or policies of the ANC.

The ANC Youth League is open to all persons between the ages of 14 and 35. It also operates on a national, provincial and branch basis. The League's aims are to unite and lead young men and women in confronting and dealing with the 'problems of youth' (*ibid.*). It also hopes to encourage youth in the work of the ANC. As with the Women's League, the Youth wing is an autonomous organization but it remains an integral part of the ANC. Funding for the League comes from the ANC and it is guided by the policies of Congress (Majodina interview, 1996). The Youth League are aware of the role the young played in the fight against apartheid: 'The struggles waged by students and the young were always part and parcel of the national liberation struggle' (African National Congress 1996b). The Youth

League was originally formed in 1944 and by 1996 had 1077 branches nationally. The League is also regarded in some quarters within the ANC as a form of 'training ground for recruitment into the ANC' (Majodina interview, 1996). Nelson Mandela, Walter Sisulu and a host of other ANC leaders were all former members of the Youth League. Febe Polgieter, Secretary-General of the League, points to the need for the young to become involved in the new democratic South Africa (Polgieter interview, 1996).

## Inkatha Freedom Party

The constitution of Inkatha states:

> We declare ourselves a non-violent national cultural liberation movement . . . desiring to abolish all forms of discrimination and segregation based on tribe, clan, sex, colour or creed, and to ensure the acceptance of the principles of equal opportunity, justice, liberty, solidarity, peace, political, economic and social progress and determine that prosperity for people in all walks of life shall reign, free from poverty, disease and ignorance. (Inkatha Freedom Party 1987: 30)

The national Inkatha liberation movement claims to have grown from a cultural organization of the same name founded in the 1920s by King Solomon. The objective of that organization was 'to preserve the unity of the Zulu nation' at a time when people's rights were being undermined and their land removed (ibid.: 4). Hamilton and Mare maintain that ' "tradition", in the Inkatha sense, always meant loyalty to chiefs, to Mangosuthu Buthelezi and to King Goodwill Zwelithini' (Hamilton and Mare 1994: 77). Yet with the growing influence of Inkatha, power battles have emerged between the King and Buthelezi. The establishment of the National Cultural Liberation Movement in 1975 by Buthelezi has been seen as a demonstration of his political skill (ibid.: 76). Inkatha itself sees that period of rejuvenation as a time when it became an 'all-embracing national movement with its sights set on the liberation of all black South Africans' (Inkatha Freedom Party 1987: 4). But other analysts point to the fact that the movement still operated on an ethnically exclusive basis, with membership of Inkatha limited to Zulus (Hamilton and Mare 1994: 77). Yet Inkatha refers to a study conducted in 1977 by the Arnold Bergstrasse Institute of Freiburg University which shows that '40% of Inkatha's supporters in Soweto were not Zulus' (Inkatha Freedom Party 1987: 5). Inkatha asserts that its aim has been to 'work, in a multi-strategy approach, for the freedom of the people and for a united, non-racial, democratic country' (ibid.).

During the 1980s the KwaZulu/Natal Indaba attempted to set the mechanisms to establish within the existing apartheid nation of South Africa a

---

**Table 3.6**   Kwazulu/Natal Indaba Bill of Rights

---

*Guarantees*
To everyone the equal protection of the law, without regard to race, colour, ethnic origin, political opinion or economic status and, in particular:

*Enshrines*
The right to life and liberty.
The right to own and occupy property anywhere.
The principle of administrative justice.
The right of public education.
Ethnic, linguistic and cultural rights.

*Will be*
Part of the constitution of the new Province of Natal binding on provincial and local government in Natal enforced by the Supreme Court of South Africa.

---

*Source*: Inkatha Freedom Party 1987

'united non-racial democracy' in the region. Indaba, a Zulu word, means a 'decision-making body of leaders striving to come to an agreement' (*ibid*.). The Indaba contained a Bill of Rights (see Table 3.6).

In short the Indaba Bill of Rights accepted the democratic principles of freedom, equality, justice, and the rule of law. In terms of the constitutional proposals, a bicameral legislature was favoured based on the principle of universal suffrage, irrespective of race. Everyone would have two votes. The first vote would be for the first chamber of 100 members elected by proportional representation. For example, the party that gets 1 per cent of the vote gets 1 seat; the party that gets 30 per cent gets 30 seats, and so on. The second vote would be for the second chamber of 50 seats: 10 English, 10 Afrikaans, 10 African, 10 Asian and 10 South African – for people who choose not to identify with a specific historical background. Association with any group is voluntary. All laws would go through both chambers and, ordinarily, by a simple majority, although constitutional amendments may require a two-thirds majority. If one or more of the background groups in the second chamber object to legislation perceived to adversely affect their religious, language or cultural interests, if a simple majority (six out of ten) agree that this is the case, then a veto is cast. If a majority (26 out of 50) disagree, the law is not put through but is referred to the Supreme Court, which in turn is bound by the Bill of Rights in its decision-making.

Indaba recommended that the Executive consist of a Prime Minister and ten cabinet ministers. If, for example, the Prime Minister's party received 51 per cent of the vote in the election for the first chamber, he/she could appoint five cabinet members from his/her own party. The other five were to be filled in such a way that minority parties in both chambers are represented in relation to their relative strengths. The Indaba proposals represented a broad spectrum of nearly 40 black, white, Indian and coloured parties and interest groups. Inkatha argued that KwaZulu and Natal should be accepted as one region and should be given the opportunity to prove that a united non-racial system of government is both desirable and workable. It could also act as an example to the rest of the country. Chief Buthelezi is reported as stating at the time: 'The State President and the National Party must clearly understand that negotiation for me and the vast majority of the people of the KwaZulu/Natal region must be negotiations leading away from the politics of prescription. This is where the whole exercise of the KwaZulu/Natal Indaba has great significance' (Inkatha Freedom Party 1987).

According to Nigel Worden, Buthelezi trod an uneasy line: 'By moving away from the ANC's position of protest politics and international sanctions he won support from liberal whites, but was also regarded by Black Consciousness supporters as a government collaborator' (Worden 1995: 133). Conflicts arose between members of the United Democratic Front and Inkatha, with violence and killings exacerbated by covert actions of the government. Two moves further enhanced political tensions. First, in 1986 King Goodwill Zwelithini announced the formation the United Workers' Union of South Africa (UWUSA) as a counter to COSATU and called for 'Zulu' attendance. Second, he attended an Inkatha rally in Soweto and made an 'address to the Zulu nation'. Zwelithini asserted that Inkatha was the 'largest black liberation movement in the history of South Africa' and that unlike the exiled ANC it was in 'total contact with the oppressed masses on a day-to-day basis' (Inkatha Freedom Party 1987).

Events rather overtook Inkatha's Indaba constitutional proposals as attention focused on the national stage when F. W. de Klerk made his landmark speech in February 1990. However, the IFP believe that Indaba demonstrated the movement's commitment to democratic norms some years before political events hastened the pace of change (Mzizi interview, 1996). The lifting of the ban on the ANC and the release of Nelson Mandela clearly placed Inkatha in a much weaker position. Analysts argue that Buthelezi immediately recognized the need to place himself within the national political arena and by July 1990 the movement had transformed itself into a political party: the Inkatha Freedom Party (Worden 1995, Hamilton and Mare 1994). Inkatha representatives strongly refute the widely held view that its power base resides only in the KwaZulu Natal region. Support also exists within the Eastern and Western Cape and Gauteng (Razak interview, 1996). During the 1994 election the IFP gained over 10 per cent of the national vote although around 90 per cent of that support was based in KwaZulu Natal. However, in Gauteng support for the IFP was not as great as the party had hoped. This was partly because of the tension and conflict between the IFP and the ANC (ibid.). However, the party managed to gain over 170 000 votes which gave it 3.7 per cent of the vote in the country's most populous province. According to Andrew Reynolds that electoral support came from the 'Zulu migrant-hostel areas' (Reynolds 1994: 195). Nevertheless, the IFP felt cheated of its potential support in Gauteng and allegations of electoral fraud were made against the ANC at the time (Razak interview, 1996; Johnson 1996: 307). The party sees itself as suffering from intimidation exercised by the ANC. As Musa Myeni, MPP, states: 'In the townships the majority of the people are illiterate, therefore, it is easy for the ANC to manipulate or intimidate them' (Myeni interview, 1996). Fourteen ballot boxes were lost in the local elections of November 1995 (*ibid.*). There are three IFP members of the Gauteng provincial legislature but representatives, mindful of being marginalized, feel they do not receive an equitable share of administrative assistance (*ibid.*). Equally, the party sees itself as being treated unfairly by the media and complains of the seemingly constant supply of 'bad news about the IFP' stories (*ibid.*). Although this accusation may not be entirely true, with the Johannesburg *Star* regularly presenting a balanced picture of events in KwaZulu Natal, there is a distortion in some images of IFP supporters. As Johnson points out, some parts of the media tend to present 'the stereotypical IFP member as a young male warrior waving a shield and spear' (Johnson 1996: 15). A more accurate picture would be that of 'a middle-aged or older woman living in rural poverty' (*ibid.*).

Interestingly, the IFP has a significant amount of white support. Originally, Inkatha attracted a fringe of liberal whites, then later some 'notably right-wing figures'. However, in 1994, the IFP gained a very much wider band of white support, taking around 15 per cent of the vote for the national election and a 'staggering' 40 per cent of the provincial assembly vote in many KZN white suburbs (*ibid.*). Johnson maintains that this support cut across the usual class, language and political barriers: 'The IFP pulled the same 40% vote in the lower middle class, National Party voting and Afrikaans-speaking area of Kirkie Uys, Durban Bluff as it did in the affluent English-speaking and Democratic Party voting areas of Musgrave, Durban' (*ibid.*). Andrew Reynolds asserts that the 5 to 6 per cent of the white vote which the IFP gained in April 1994 was both a higher share than the ANC received and 'the highest white vote among any of the historically black political organisations contesting the election' (Reynolds 1994: 194–5). Yet, Alexander Johnston maintains that essentially both the ANC and the IFP are 'African parties' in terms of their core support (Johnston 1996: 2).

The Institute for Multi-Party Democracy (MPD) conducted a series of interviews under the leadership of R. W. Johnson, Lawrence Schlemmer, Mervyn Frost and Paulus Zulu which were designed to record and document the attitudes of voters and the level of support the parties enjoyed before the election in April 1994. Bearing in mind that the IFP did not agree to participate in the election until the last week of the campaign, the actual votes cast in the 1994 were considerably contested (Johnson and Schlemmer 1996: 13) (see Tables 3.7 and 3.8).

**Table 3.7**   Proposed party choice by group in KwaZulu Natal (%)
before April 1994 Election

| Party | Total | Whites | Indians | Coloureds | Africans |
|-------|-------|--------|---------|-----------|----------|
| ANC-SACP | 36.7 | 4.4 | 14.2 | 23.2 | 44.1 |
| IFP | 18.1 | 14.8 | – | 0.9 | 21.3 |
| NP | 13.9 | 40.5 | 71.9 | 37.1 | 2.1 |
| DP | 2.3 | 19.6 | 1.9 | 4.9 | 0.2 |
| FF | 0.8 | 7.0 | 0.2 | – | 0.1 |
| PAC | 0.8 | – | 0.1 | – | 1.0 |
| Don't Know | 10.5 | 6.1 | 7.1 | 12.2 | 11.5 |
| Won't Say | 8.4 | 4.8 | 2.9 | 8.5 | 9.6 |
| Won't Vote | 8.2 | 1.9 | 1.2 | 13.1 | 9.9 |

*Source*: Public Opinion in KwaZulu Natal in Johnson and Schlemmer 1996: 201

**Table 3.8**   KwaZulu Natal April 1994 Election results

| Party | Vote (%) |
|-------|----------|
| ANC-SACP | 31.61 |
| IFP | 48.59 |
| NP | 15.76 |
| FF | 0.45 |
| PAC | 0.61 |

*Source*: Adapted from Johnson and Schlemmer 1996: 379

Considering the 1994 election in hindsight, Johnson accepts that some of the opinion polls MRD conducted in KwaZulu Natal suffered from 'a large lie factor, with IFP voters by far the most likely to disguise their preferences' (*ibid*.: 14). Johnson believes that one of the most significant indicators of IFP versus ANC preferences rests on what he describes as the 'entitlement culture'. Questions posed to test the extent to which an 'entitlement culture' existed were set in September 1994 as part of a post-election survey: 'two-thirds of ANC voters believed that people should keep their houses and services even if they did not pay their mortgages or rates. While 59% of IFP voters believed the opposite' (*ibid*.). Johnson explains that given the ANC's dominance around the country, it was not surprising to find the pro-entitlement view favoured by a national majority. However, in KwaZulu Natal alone, 60 per cent of voters took an anti-entitlement view. Certainly, the IFP regards itself to be ideologically at variance with the ANC, in that it is openly capitalistic, in favour of the free market and a multi-party system, of strict law and order enforcement, of improved economic and trade relations, of greater ministerial accountability and against quasi-socialist, state-led policies (Mzizi and Ndlovu interviews, 1996). IFP representatives dismissively refer to 'ANC top leaders' as having 'no real policy, just words' (Myeni interview, 1996). In terms of economic policy, Gertrude Mzizi asserts that the ANC-dominated government must decide 'whether it is the government of COSATU or of the wider economy' (Mzizi interview, 1996). There is no doubt that economic factors confront the government, and as Denis Venter states there exists an ideological divide between those who support a socialist, state-centred approach to policy and those who favour a liberal free-market model. Within the ANC there are 'great divisions as to the direction the economy should follow', and consequently this contradiction is felt by the government (Venter interview, 1996).

The deputy provincial secretary of the party in the Gauteng province when asked what the IFP had to offer a wider ethnic population, replied that the party's emphasis on KwaZulu Natal was 'strategic rather than ideological'. The IFP was not only an ethnic movement and although its largest support came from KwaZulu Natal it had always attracted 'Sotho and other groups' from its inception (Razak interview, 1996). However, the distribution of electoral support in 1994 did not reflect this partisanship, in part because of the rivalry between the IFP and the ANC. The IFP regards itself as upholding democratic principles and does not want a centralized state. It feels this is a position on which it will not compromise (ibid.). But the party acknowledges the constitution as the 'supreme law of the country' and firmly believes in the concept of constitutional review. Sam Razak maintains that areas such as 'education, housing, infrastructure, policing and welfare should be in the realm of the province, whilst foreign policy, defence and macroeconomics should be in the sphere of central government' (ibid.). The IFP would like a devolved system of government so that 'corruption could be avoided at the centre' (ibid.). Yet when both Razak and Gertrude Mzizi, a member of the Gauteng legislature, were questioned about the party's decision to withdraw from the Constitutional Committee at the time it was devising the new constitution, they maintained that their decision resulted from a point of principle. The reason the party left the negotiations was because 'Nelson Mandela had made an agreement that International Observers would be present and then he reneged on his agreement' (Mzizi interview, 1996). It was widely believed that the IFP had made a tactical error and would have gained ground on the new constitution's proposals had it chosen to stay. Razak agreed that different currents of thought existed within the IFP as to whether it had been tactically correct to withdraw (Razak interview, 1996).

Gertrude Mzizi was also asked what the IFP felt about the policy of affirmative action. Affirmative action, she explained, should be concerned with abolishing glass ceilings: 'There should be a meritocracy not a quota system because standards will be lowered. There should be open and equal opportunities but affirmative action can lead to a culture of entitlement and privilege. This must not happen to black people' (Mzizi interview, 1996). The party wishes to be the main oppositional force to the ANC but cautions that the last thing the ANC wants is a 'strong black opposition' (ibid.). Sam Razak asserts: 'We are seeing a repetition of the apartheid days under the ANC in that the treatment of opposition is just as oppressive. Now, however, it is not just white against black, but black against black.' One hundred and twenty-five IFP political leaders have been killed between 1994 and 1996 (Razak interview, 1996). Humphrey Ndlovu, also a member of the Gauteng legislature, maintains that South Africa, for all its level of economic development, is not a modern state but 'a dual system of the first and third worlds which should not be viewed only in terms of urban society. Policies which are right for the cities might not be automatically appropriate for the rural areas' (Ndlovu interview, 1996). It was important that the ANC recognized this division and did not completely 'override the culture of large sections of the society' (ibid.).

Whilst the IFP looks to the future 'we have a country and a responsiblity' other commentators suggest that its days as a political force are numbered. Richard Cornwall of the Africa Institute asserts that 'The IFP is unlikely to succeed after Chief Buthelezi' (Cornwall interview, 1996). Other analysts believe that the IFP, under a rather different leadership, could exert greater political influence (Hyden interview, 1996). For Alexander Johnston, the IFP has three choices as to its future role:

> First, it can join the NP in a centre-right coalition which emphasises opposition to the ANC's alliance with COSATU and the South African Communist Party and stakes a claim to be the bearer of Christian Democrat values, like the centre-right in European politics. Second, it can settle its differences with the ANC and explore ways of giving expression to a re-worked African nationalism in association with its former antagonist. Third, it can carry on its adversarial relationship with the ANC and continue to articulate a regional identity and claim to autonomy. (Johnston 1996: 5)

Johnston also points to the fact that around 35 per cent of the electorate does not vote for the ANC. However, that vote is divided between the National Party's stronghold in the Western Cape and the IFP's support base in KwaZulu Natal. He argues that if the opposition to the ANC is not to be 'hopelessly balkanised' then these different constituencies need to be realigned (ibid.: 2). Yet, if the IFP moves closer to the ANC it may reduce its effect as an oppositional force and if it aligns with the National Party it may become tainted with that party's uncomfortable past. Talks have taken place between the ANC and IFP and their first meeting in May 1996 resulted in the recognition of Inkatha as part of the liberation movement. As Jacob Zuma, provincial leader in KwaZulu Natal and newly elected Deputy-President of the ANC, asserts: 'The political orientation of the two parties is very different: one traditional, the other progressive, but it is possible to pursue divergent political agendas without violence' (Zuma 1997). Certainly, relations between the ANC and IFP are easing as negotiations take place about KwaZulu Natal. In fact, IFP representatives were invited to attend the ANC National Conference in December 1997 and there was some talk, instigated by President Mandela and later denied, that the two parties should form an alliance. Meanwhile, however, the IFP's central concern is that South Africa moves into the next century with a strong government (interviews with Razak, Mzizi and Ndlovu, 1996).

## The National Party

At the Congress of the National Party in September 1996, the premier of the Western Cape, Hernus Kriel, announced that the party's policy had to be 'fair and based on what was right and not what was popular' (*Cape Times*, 25 September 1996). The party leader, F. W. de Klerk, attending the congress of 700 people, stated that it was clear the country was beginning to 'reap the bitter fruits' of the abuse of affirmative action and insufficient financial control. The National Party, he urged, had to prove it could govern better than the ANC (*ibid.*). In any other country, this could be the usual, run-of-the-mill, party politicking banter of an opposition party. But in post-apartheid South Africa the story is different. As one newspaper leader put it on the occasion of Pik Botha's resignation from parliament in June 1996: 'Here is a man who served in the National Party during the years in which it visited horror upon horror on the majority of the country's citizens' (*Sunday Independent*, 2 June 1996).

The National Party has an uneasy past as the architect of the apartheid system. The questions which must be posed in the context of the development and sustainability of South Africa's new democracy are whether the National Party will continue to have a role to play in the future and, perhaps more interestingly, whether it actually matters if it does not. When Cheryl Carolus, Deputy-Secretary General of the ANC, was asked for her comments on the success of the National Party in the May 1996 local elections in the Western Cape, largely because of the support of the coloured vote, she replied that the event could only be explained as something akin to the 'battered-wife syndrome'. Opposition parties, including the IFP and the NP represented the 'interests of the past' (Carolus interview, 1996). There is some debate in the IFP as to whether the NP will continue or not, with some representatives feeling it may not and others seeing the party's future only in terms of continuing racial segregation (Razak and Mzizi interviews, 1996). In respect of support nationally, the NP attracts around 49 per cent from the white community, 31 per cent from the coloured, 7 per cent from the Indian and 13 per cent from the African communities (James 1996). Whether the party could appeal to a greater number of black voters, as F. W. de Klerk has suggested, is open to debate. As Wilmot James states: 'Who among the African community, in significant numbers, would support the NP in opposition to the ANC?' (*ibid.*). Dr Theo Alant, a National Party MP, claimed that the party hoped to expand and attract black voters and that 'eventually the NP might have a black leader'. Another Nationalist MP thought it might be as long as ten years before the party had a black leader (van Heerden interview, 1996). The NP intended to adopt an 'across-the-board campaign to the emerging black middle class, property owners and union members' (Radue interview, 1996). Senator Radue also emphasized the possibilities of recruiting blacks based on Christianity (*ibid.*). However, the party did not have high expectations of attracting black votes in 1999 but was looking towards the 2004 elections (Alant interview, 1996).

Wilmot James believes it would take 'a leap of faith and a radical reorganization of politics to expect the NP to make major inroads in established constituencies belonging to other parties' (James 1996). However, the issue of a non-white leader was raised again at the National Party Congress in September 1996 as concerns were expressed about accusations of white supremacy in the party hierarchy. The congress decided to oppose any such move at that time which might be regarded as tokenism and emphasized that what was needed in 1996 was 'expertise and strength'. Nevertheless, the newly elected Peter Marais, MEC for local government and deputy leader of the NP in the Western Cape, warned that the NP would lose voter support if it was seen to be 'wilfully preventing people of colour from moving into leadership positions.'(van Heerden interview, 1996; *Cape Times*, 23 September 1996; *Cape Argus*, 24 September 1996). Hernus Kriel, the provincial premier was elected unopposed at congress. This result shifted power firmly to provincial level politicians and there was a decline in influence of national-level Nationalists, who are seen to be directly under the control of F. W. de Klerk.

The National Party leadership under de Klerk has, of course, made great strides towards reform but at the same time has attempted to defend itself from charges that it did not act in accordance with its mandate (Giliomee 1994: 46). Critics from other parties maintain that the NP has let down its main constituency, the white Afrikaaner, and that inevitably the party will have little or no support. Consequently, the onus of responsibility for opposition within the country will fall to the IFP, not the second largest party, the NP (Razak interview, 1996). Other commentators have suggested that it is the political culture in the NP supporting Western Cape province which needs to be examined (Mattes, Giliomee and James 1996: 1). Robert Mattes states that since the 1994 election, 'the province has come to be widely seen as politically atypical of South Africa as a whole both in terms of partisan preference as well as political culture' (*ibid.*). IDASA's Public Opinion Service held a wide and differentiated survey in the Western Cape in order to discern whether or not there existed views that were particular to the region. As Tables 3.9 and 3.10 reveal, citizens had 'a very negative view of the

**Table 3.9**   Trust in different levels of government (%)

|  | Western Cape | White | African | Coloured | National |
|---|---|---|---|---|---|
| National Government | 34 | 35 | 59 | 19 | 45 |
| Provincial Government | 32 | 37 | 29 | 28 | 32 |
| New Town Councils | 27 | 25 | 58 | 13 | 33 |

*Source*: Adapted from IDASA Public Opinion Survey No. 8, May 1996: 14 (IDASA 1996d)

**Table 3.10**   Negative views of government by racial/ethnic category

| Question | Coloured | White | African |
|---|---|---|---|
| No contact with MPs | 67 | 87 | 76 |
| Govt too complex | 59 | 39 | 44 |
| MPs not helpful | 46 | 33 | 16 |
| National govt does not represent people like me | 36 | 57 | 7 |

*Source*: Adapted from IDASA Public Opinion Survey No. 8, May 1996: 15 (IDASA 1996d)

**Table 3.11**   Satisfaction with democracy (%)

|  | Western Cape | White | African | Coloured | National |
|---|---|---|---|---|---|
| Satisfied | 13 | 6 | 27 | 12 | 12 |
| Fairly satisfied | 26 | 27 | 34 | 19 | 29 |
| Not very satisfied | 29 | 36 | 23 | 24 | 39 |
| Not at all satisfied | 29 | 29 | 12 | 40 | 18 |
| Don't know | 3 | 2 | 4 | 5 | 2 |

*Source*: Adapted from IDASA Public Opinion Survey No. 8, May 1996: 17 (IDASA 1996d)

representativeness and responsiveness of their elected officials and institutions and a much more negative view than the rest of the country' (IDASA 1996a: i). These views tended to run along racial lines, with black residents far more optimistic about the democratic changes than the white or coloured respondents. In fact, although whites held pessimistic views about their elected officials and institutions and were dissatisfied with democracy, the coloured citizens held the most 'cynical view of MPs'. They felt they had little influence over government and exhibited the least trust in government (*ibid.*).

As Table 3.11 demonstrates, a total of 39 per cent of respondents in the Western Cape report they are satisfied or fairly satisfied with the way democracy works in South Africa, and 58 per cent say they are dissatisfied.

**Table 3.12**  What if democracy does not work? (%)

|  | Western Cape | White | African | Coloured | National |
|---|---|---|---|---|---|
| Democracy always best | 45 | 53 | 60 | 27 | 47 |
| Strong, non-elected leader | 42 | 42 | 33 | 45 | 43 |
| Don't know | 14 | 5 | 7 | 28 | 10 |

*Source*: IDASA Public Opinion Survey No. 8, May 1996: 17 (IDASA 1996d)

However, these results were only slightly more pessimistic than the national public responses, in which 41 per cent were satisfied and 57 per cent dissatisfied. As Wilmot James asserts, the Western Cape appears to be broadly similar to the country as a whole regarding satisfaction/dissatisfaction with democracy (*ibid.*: iv). However, distinct differences appear within the province. Of the white and coloured population interviewed, 65 per cent and 64 per cent respectively were dissatisfied with democracy as opposed to a black response of 35 per cent. Nevertheless, in terms of a commitment to democracy the findings of the Western Cape survey were similar to those of national surveys. Yet the coloured response of 27 per cent was much lower than the national average together, with over a quarter of respondents registering a 'don't know' (see Table 3.12).

Wilmot James sees the coloured community in the Western Cape as displaying the 'least commitment to democracy over the long haul' either because of political apathy or alienation (*ibid.*: iv). There seems to be a disenchantment with political reform expressed in the view that the coloured community was undermined by apartheid and now feels itself to be ignored by the new government regardless of the fact that racial segregation is abolished. As one coloured respondent put it: 'We used to be squeezed by the whites now we are squeezed by the blacks' (non-survey interviews conducted with stall holders, shop workers and taxi drivers, Cape Town, 22–24 September 1996). Yet in a particular study of the election in the Western Cape, the coloured community was found to have a 'cultural affinity' with whites in terms of support for the Dutch Reformed Mission Church, the 90 000 coloured readership of the NP-supporting Afrikaans-language daily newspaper, *Die Burger*, and in general attitudes to 'family life' (Mattes, Giliomee and James 1996: 114). In May 1991, the then Cape NP leader, Dawie de Villiers predicted that 'coloured people would support his party because of their deeper affinity with whites' (*ibid.*).

As Mattes, Giliomee and James (1996) make clear, the relationship between coloured voters and the National Party is more complex. Partly, it is a result of the government's reforms in the 1980s, during which the National Party attempted to 'modernize apartheid' by introducing a limited form of power-sharing among white, coloured and Indian racial groups, the Tricameral system. The National Party split in 1982 as a result of this policy,

**Table 3.13**  Demographic figures

| Year | Total population | White % | Coloured % | Asian % | African % |
|------|------------------|---------|------------|---------|-----------|
| 1991 | 38 268 720 | 13.2 | 8.6 | 2.6 | 75.6 |
| 2000* | 47 591 000 | 11.4 | 7.9 | 2.4 | 78.3 |

\* Projected figures
*Source*: Democratic Trends Urban Foundation, Cape Town South Africa 1994

with its conservative flank breaking away, but the new system brought benefits to the coloured community: 'Locally elected coloured authorities were able to obtain real, albeit limited powers because they now had an important access point through their members of parliament and, at times, cabinet members, who took up their plight at national level' (*ibid.*: 115). As a result, development programmes were instituted and housing was increased and improved as more resources became available. In effect, what happened during that decade was the gradual 'embourgeoisement of coloured South Africans' (*ibid.*). If this process is taken in conjunction with the fact that the unbanned ANC seemed to be dominated by a black African agenda, or as Mandela stated, 'preoccupied with Africans and neglecting coloured people', then some explanations accounting for coloured support of the National Party become apparent. (See Mattes, Giliomee and James 1996 for further details and an excellent analysis of the election campaign in the Western Cape.) However, whatever the motivating forces behind the electorate's support of the National Party, what really matters is whether it can change sufficiently to attract black voters. As Table 3.13 makes clear, by the year 2000 black South Africans are expected to represent nearly 80 per cent of the total population. So in order to avoid increasing marginalization resulting from support coming from diminishing sections of the population, the party will be obliged to change. However, this may be quite difficult for some representatives of the NP. Responding to a question about whether the NP would encourage its members to apply for amnesty under Truth and Reconciliation Commission, MP Frik van Heerden asserted that the party did 'nothing wrong' and had 'nothing to hide' (van Heerden interview, 1996). Sectors of the media suggest the party has yet to provide evidence of the new 'vision and mission' which it alleges will make it a credible opposition (*Sunday Independent*, 2 June 1996; *Cape Times*, 4 June 1996). The newly elected NP leader, Marthinus Van Schalkwyk may steer the party in a more progressive direction although the decision of former NP officionado, Roelf Meyer, to form a new political organization, the United Democratic Movement, with Bantu Holomisa, may further split the party. In what is clearly a volatile period for the National Party, the Western Cape election results raise more questions than answers.

## South African Communist Party

The ban against the South African Communist Party (SACP) was lifted at the same time it was lifted for the ANC. Jeremy Cronin, Deputy General-Secretary of the SACP, which was founded in 1921 and banned in 1950, claims that 'the party came through exile more unifed and with greater prestige' (Cronin interview, 1996). In 1996 the party had 70 000 members. Its relationship with the ANC is close, or as Cronin puts it, 'the SACP is dedicated to the ANC' (*ibid.*). Cronin sits on the Executive Committee of the ANC; there are four SACP members of the Cabinet and 53 SACP/ANC MPs under the ANC whip in parliament. The SACP has considerable support among the ANC constituency, but the party does not operate as a caucus, or an entryist organization. It regards the ANC as a broad spectrum liberation movement (*ibid.*). Certainly, the SACP is regarded as having helped to maintain the 'organisational continuity' of the ANC and also provided a channel for funding and training in the Soviet Union (Beinart 1994: 215). Equally, it provided the ANC prisoners on Robben Island with a framework for political planning (*ibid.*).

Yet international events have rather eclipsed the political viability of communism. The collapse of the Soviet Union and the Eastern Bloc provided the backdrop to the political changes in South Africa. In fact, some analysts actually view the end of the bi-polar world as having the most 'important and dramatic' effect in forging reform in South Africa (Johnson and Schlemmer 1996: 130). So, in a sense, what are the political ideas of the SACP now? Discussions are taking place regarding the relationship between the ANC, SACP and COSATU about the future of the alliance. It could break up into its constituent parts. The SACP does not wish to leave the alliance, but it is not happy with the government's economic policies: 'An awkward stitching together of worthy social goals and liberal economic policy' (Cronin interview, 1996). Jeremy Cronin still speaks of imperialism and the revolutionary potential of South Africa's neighbouring states. He believes that 'competitive, multi-party politics is unlikely to sustain itself into the next millennium' and that the most appropriate form of government for South Africa would be 'a broad, popular-front' political movement: 'politics should not be sharpened into factions, it should be about people' (*ibid.*). How these views fit into the new democratic South Africa is open to question. The SACP may be regarded in some quarters as ideologically bereft, but it is important to remember that neo-Marxism is not regarded as a completely defunct project in South Africa. Marxist debates, so prominent in the West during the 1970s, are still presented in intellectual circles, journals and newspapers and to an extent they affect the public debate about government policies such as employment law, the role of trade unions, economic policy and so on. Although Marxism may be yesterday's dialectic in Western academe, it is not necessarily true of the intellectual climate of South Africa.

What has become clear since 1994 is the fact that the ANC is very much the dominant political organization. In fact, according to Johnston and Spence the ANC 'has no serious rival in popular political consciousness' (Johnston and Spence 1995). As a broad-based popular front liberation movement it has gained considerable support among the electorate. The pressing question now is how the ANC will comport itself in the future.

# FOUR

# Civil society, citizenship and identity

## Civil society

One of the most important issues discussed recently is the role played by civil society in promoting and sustaining liberal democracy. One central feature of a functioning democracy presented in the classic study by Almond and Verba in 1963 was the establishment of a supportive 'civic culture' (Almond and Verba 1963). The intention of Almond and Verba's study was to examine the extent to which 'a pattern of political attitudes and an underlying set of social attitudes' was supportive of a 'stable democratic process' (*ibid.*: 35). Cleavages within society could be managed and balanced by a civic culture that combined levels of citizen activity with passivity, tradition with modernity, political parties, interest groups, voluntary associations and a neutral media, which would contribute to a 'pluralistic culture based on communication and persuasion, a culture of consensus and diversity, a culture that permitted change but moderated it' (*ibid.*: 6). Central to Almond and Verba's theme was an understanding that the 'democratic model of the participatory state required more than universal suffrage, the political party and the elective legislature'. It needed a compatible cultural base: 'The working principles of the democratic polity and its civic culture – the ways in which political elites make decisions, their norms and attitudes, as well as the norms and attitudes of the ordinary citizen, his relation to government and to his fellow citizens – are subtler cultural components' (*ibid.*: 3). State and institutional structures cannot enforce or ensure democracy. Democracy is concerned with the relationship between the citizenry and the political elite: the degree of trust and identity between the leadership and the people, the level of independence afforded to the individual, the limits to the encroachment of power over the population. Civil society is both necessary and important. It can provide a ballast against the power of the state and permit_ the existence of channels of public expression in order that society's wishes can be articulated. A civic culture can thus emerge in this enlarged polity which is supportive of democratic practices. Without a civil society there is no motive for state actors to recognize the demands of society and all the temptations of arbitrary rule can become a reality.

Civil society is also seen as a way of 'securing substantive political rights and freedoms, essential for a functioning democracy, in an arena outside of state control' (Williams and Young 1993). The activities of groups and organizations such as trade unions, business associations, pressure groups, educational establishments, various voluntary societies, women's groups and religious groups operating with a free press are critical factors in sustaining democratic accountability. In other words, civil society operates in the space between the state and the people. In the 1990s interest focused on the role and importance of civil society in fostering democratic practices and in creating a demarcation line between what Habermas calls 'a public and a private sphere' (Habermas 1979). The distinction between these two arenas is decisive: the 'private' arena is that of economic and familial relations while the 'public' is that of the development of a 'public opinion' which increasingly demands that its voice be heard by the state. With the broadening and deepening of the space between state activity and that of the individual, increasing roles would be available for groups, especially economic groups, who could forge greater productive and economic benefits for the nation as a whole. Yet precise definitions of civil society have been discussed and Michael Bratton identifies five

> essential definitional notions about the nature of civil society and its relationships with the state: 1) civil society is a public realm between the state and the family; 2) civil society is distinguishable from political society; 3) civil society is a theoretical rather than an empirical construct; 4) state and civil society, although conceptually distinct, are best considered together; and 5) civil society is the source of the legitimation of state power. (Bratton 1994: 55–6)

In drawing a distinction between civil society and political society, groups would necessarily have to be separated into those which do not seek to govern or are not involved in any form of electoral activity and those organizations which seek office, such as political parties (*ibid.*). Yet clearly, there is often an overlap between personal and collective interests and political representation. For example, there are often close financial and institutional ties between trade unions and political parties and it would be practically impossible to separate the two components into political or civil activity.

Goran Hyden, in analyzing changing perceptions of the state, maintains that analysts differ in their perspectives depending on whether they see the state as 'an instrument of control and power or as a tool to solve societal problems' (Hyden 1996). If the state is viewed negatively, that is, as an instrument of oppression and exploitation, then according to one school of thought it must have a diminished role. Alternatively, if the state is seen in a positive light, as a force for the reconciliation of society's conflicting interests, it may be seen as being instrumental to the emergence of civil society (*ibid.*). A centralizing state, however, would be inimical to the development of legitimate government for, as Bratton asserts, 'the legitimacy of a political leader's claim to excercise state power derives from civil society' (Bratton 1994: 60). Mehl and Ashley point out that 'statism', the situation where central government exercises a high degree of control and takes extensive responsibility for the provision of services, is not only in decline but has actually disintegrated (Mehl and Ashby 1994). These developments have given rise to studies of civil society and political transition. O'Donnell and Schmitter have traced the nature of political transition from authoritarian structures to more democratic rule in Latin America and southern Europe (O'Donnell and Schmitter 1986). They argue that contours of civil society are shaped by social groups and classes that come out openly in favour of political liberalization. Social dissent can take varied forms: mass activity, workerist opposition, intellectual criticism or non-governmental organizations stressing human rights. Business and commercial elites abandon the regime if they perceive it as limiting their economic opportunities (*ibid*.: 56). Incumbent elites make the major political concession of the transition when they agree to convene competitive elections. O'Donnell and Schmitter believe that the impetus for this capitulation comes from activities of a wide-ranging civil society. However, some authoritarian states collapse under the weight of their dysfunctional and over-extended regimes. Nevertheless, when elections are called, it is the political arena which is important rather than civil society (*ibid*.: 57). Those who desire power, in other words, political parties, become the central players and they seek sanction and legitimacy from the wider society. Civic organizations can then reassess their roles and functions. Their position in transitional polities is as an agency for opposition to the former regime. Once democratic elections have taken place and there are legitimate political conduits for oppositionist opinion, civic groups can redefine their identities.

## Civil society in South Africa

Under the United Democratic Front (UDF), created in 1983 to organize and lead popular opposition to the tricameral parliament, a number of groups operated. The UDF was a multiracial confederation of affiliated labour, church, student and civic organizations which supported the then-banned ANC (Mattes, Giliomee and James 1996: 121). According to Mattes, Giliomee and James most UDF-affiliated organizations tended to move towards a national civic federation, which became the South African National Civic Organisation (SANCO) (*ibid*.). SANCO has its roots in the radical civics formed as part of the township resistance movement of the 1980s. These civic groups organized themselves around local basic issues such as rent and township services. However, more recently SANCO has found itself to be at a crossroads. W.-M. Gumede argues: 'The accelerating pace of political change since South Africa's first democratic elections in April 1994 has forced the whole spectrum of civil society organisations to redefine their roles' (Gumede 1996). Khehla Shubane believes that civics must make a shift from their 'apartheid-derived origins' and address 'a new set of issues and problems' (*ibid.*). Non-governmental organizations are one element of civil society. They are non-profit-making groups organized by communities or individuals to respond to basic needs that are not being met by either government or the market (Bernstein, A. 1994). The Development Resource Centre estimates that South Africa has around 54 000 NGOs operating in areas ranging from non-formal education, to community development projects, to feeding schemes, to medical and scientific research institutes. This figure excludes private schools but does include 22 000 church and religious organizations that engage in some kind of community activity. A total of 20 000 of the 54 000 NGOs are 'development' in character, which includes some 2000 civic organizations, 7000 educational agencies, 1000 organizations which provide finances and service to grassroots groups and 10 000 other community-based associations of various types.

The Development Resource Centre states that in 1992 the NGO sector as a whole raised over R6 billion of donated funds: R1 billion from foreign agencies, R1 billion from 'corporate social investment' and at least R4 billion from 'individual giving' (*ibid.*). This financial support during the apartheid era was seen as crucial to the development of community activities, solidarity and opposition to government policies and actions. As Bernstein asserts, 'often the funding was not motivated by an intrinsic and positive belief in the benefits of NGO activity as such, but rather in order to fill a gap or help defend community and individual interests in the face of an antagonistic state' (*ibid.*). Funding for NGOs from overseas has come from the United States, the European Union, Britain and Denmark, yet it was clear in 1994, after the elections, that foreign assistance would be reconsidered. A European Union policy document stated that future funding would be based on strict criteria: projects should take into account regional and national policy; they should seek to address poverty and the marginalization of sections of the population through discrimination; and they should make efficient use of financial, human and other available resources (*The Star*, 28 September 1994). It was clear that foreign donors had changed their priorities now that South Africa had a democratic government. In fact, as the newspaper the *Business Day* put it: 'One of the notable achievements of the extra-parliamentary opposition to apartheid was the mushrooming of NGOs' (*Business Day*, 1 September 1994). Clearly, the post-election period would bring a process of change. Some NGO leaders entered politics, standing in national, provincial and local elections on an ANC platform. Ann Bernstein believes that because the nature of NGOs is so wide they seem amorphous, to 'continually assume that the similarities between organisations outweigh the differences is misleading' (Bernstein, A. 1994). Different types of NGO need to be distinguished in categories:

voluntary associations driven by a cause, whether religious or charit-
able; membership-based community organisations; organisations that
support membership-based organisations and are sometimes accountable to them; organisations that provide a service, sometimes on a
contract basis for the public sector and hybrid governmental/non-
governmental organisations. (*ibid.*)

It is inevitable that NGOs need to reconsider their roles. South Africa's new
government, as Bernstein asserts, is accountable to its citizens for the first
time in the country's history and of necessity needs to play a more active
role in delivering services to the population. International funding will no
longer be interested in the opposition movements in the country, but will
support the new government in its difficult tasks (*ibid.*).

Albie Sachs believes that for NGOs to operate as a vibrant sector and
to contribute to solving national problems, attention must be paid to five
objectives:

- the right of these bodies to exist and function actively with the requisite
  degree of autonomy;
- their right to co-operate with each other and with the government to
  achieve the objectives of the constitution;
- the right to receive backing or benefits when undertaking certain activities that promote the national interest;
- the right not to be co-opted or muzzled when co-operating (or not co-
  operating) with the government; and
- the right to be consulted and to be involved in the process of elaborat-
  ing new legislation which touches their areas of interest, and to monitor the laws and ensure that they are applied in a just and effective
  manner. (*Sowetan*, 19 April 1994)

Bossuyt and Develtere point out that NGOs often find themselves dependent upon official funds in order to realize their civic agenda, but the changing nature of government support compounds their difficulties (Bossuyt
and Develtere 1995). This dependency presents a paradoxical situation for
civil society. Organizations that are fiercely independent and determined to
maintain autonomy feel potentially compromised in what often develops
into a tense relationship with government:

> At best NGOs fear a loss of freedom and flexibility. At worst, they
> see themselves being co-opted by governments as cheap executing
> agencies. Yet, in essence, both NGOs and government have to work
> together. Of course, there can be positive benefits if NGOs seek and
> accept official sponsorship but this requires a rejection of autonomy in
> favour of 'identity'. (*ibid.*)

However, a close funding relationship between the government and NGOs
rather undermines civil society supposedly operating in the 'space between
government and society'. Table 4.1 indicates the funding options open to

**Table 4.1** Four approaches to NGO financing

| Approach | Who takes the initiative | What is the task of the NGO | Who pays? |
|---|---|---|---|
| Programme Approach | the NGO | to execute its own programme | co-financing (NGO and government) |
| Project Approach | the NGO | to execute its own projects after approval | co-financing (NGO and government) |
| Window Approach | the NGO and the government | to execute its projects within a governmental framework | co-financing or 100% government financing |
| Quango Approach | the government | to execute projects identified by government (and to act as subcontractor | 100% government financing |

Quango = Quasi-Autonomous Government Organization
*Source*: Bossuyt and Develtere 1995

**Table 4.2** Employment figures

| Employment | African | Coloured | Indian | White |
|---|---|---|---|---|
| Non-profit institutions | 0.6% | 0.3% | 0.3% | 1.6% |

*Source*: Race Relations Survey 1994/1995

NGOs. The ideal option would be the Programme Approach with the NGO taking the initiative and running its own programmes, partly funded by the government, but in a sense this model is unrealistic. It is generally acknowledged that only those organizations that can deliver skills and services, efficiently and creatively, will survive (*Weekly Mail and Guardian*, 26 August–1 September 1994). Interestingly, in 1994 the Institute of Race Relations looked at employment ratios in non-profit institutions on the basis of racial group. Table 4.2 outlines the distinction between employment figures. The percentage of people employed in non-profit institutions represents 0.8 per cent of the total workforce (Race Relations Survey 1994/1995).

In 1996 SANCO organized a mass action campaign to counter evictions by banks on bond defaulters. It also campaigned against local authorities who were considering evicting residents for non-payment of rates and taxes. This action followed warnings made by Johannesburg Southern MSS executive chairman, Prema Naidoo, that strict control measures would be introduced because R300 million was outstanding in rates in the region. These measures included demand notices to debtors, followed by the disconnection of services, legal action and, as a last resort, the possible eviction from property. Only 4 per cent of certain communities had paid their rates and taxes and local authorities were determined to change the culture of non-payment that was entrenched in some areas (*The Star*, 5 June 1996). The action by SANCO further distanced it from the government, who were trying to encourage people to pay for services. But this is central to the difficulty between the two sides because SANCO complains that it was not consulted when the government introduced the Masakhane Campaign, which is aimed at encouraging the population to pay rates and taxes. However, despite the lack of consultation, the ANC urged civic associations to play a role in persuading residents to pay. The civic associations, on the other hand, wanted to see evidence of efficient service delivery before attempting to persuade people to pay (Gumede 1996).

It is not hard to see that the strictures of governmental responsibility forge a somewhat different perspective than that of organizations operating at grassroots level. Yet whichever way the situation is considered, national and local government must be able to collect rates and taxes from its citizenry. SANCO general secretary Penrose Ntlonti states: 'We are serious about these matters and will do everything possible to convince government about the importance of our role in shaping the future of this country' (*ibid.*). But SANCO's role and function is obscure. Partially co-opted into the government's National Economic Development and Labour Council (NEDLAC), it hardly commands an independent status in what is a semi-corporatist state. In fact, its relationship with the ANC, although strained at times, is on occasion too close to be comfortable. Caroline White's study of the Mzimhlope Civic Association demonstrates that there is an overlap between the leadership of the civic association and the ANC (White 1995a). Mzimhlope is an area located in the northern part of Soweto and forms part of a development of houses for Africans which was constructed in the 1940s. Relations within the community deteriorated in the 1980s, with clashes between Inkatha supporting hostel dwellers and the United Democratic Front supporters in the township. The Meadowlands Hostel had been constructed as single men's accommodation close to the mine shaft. According to White, during the late 1980s, Mzimhlope 'bore all the marks of a war zone: streets were patrolled at night, fire was exchanged with fire, nobody could enter or leave the hostel, money was collected from house to house to finance the purchase of food and ammunition, women cooked collectively and fed the "troops" and young men walked about openly parading arms' (*ibid.*: 11). Local associations, those which could withstand the conditions, were highly politicized. Mzimhlope Civic Association claims to be politically independent and therefore open to residents of all persuasions. But, as White points out, the association is affiliated to the Soweto Civil Association, which is allied to SANCO, and therefore the ANC. The chairperson of the local ANC is also an executive member of the Mzimhlope Civic Association. There

71

is no formal membership; anyone living within the area is deemed to be a member and the same executive members tend to be re-elected continuously. After the elections in April 1994, the civic association called for less tension in the area and held meetings with hostel dwellers and township residents, but such is the unrepresentativeness of the association that it was unable to resolve fundamental issues of crime, child abuse and mutual uncertainty. In a sense, perhaps these profound problems are simply too much for a single civic association to contemplate, particularly one that is seen to be politically compromised and distanced from its diverse community. As White asserts, there exists a 'degree of distrust in the civic's ability to represent residents adequately on issues which might challenge the informal political establishment of which the civic leaders are part' (*ibid.*: 25).

The divide is largely political, with the ANC the predominant political organization in Mzimhlope and the IFP dominant in the Meadowlands Hostel. White argues that associations that are 'spontaneous and politically unaffiliated' should be encouraged rather than viewed as a threat. Areas must not be 'colonised' by a political party to the exclusion of any other political players:

> Democratic culture and the civic-mindedness which is one of its crucial elements would be greatly strengthened if politicians accepted the likelihood that those people living in the areas where they are hegemonic, who do pursue their interests independently, are unlikely to change their political allegiances and that 'colonising' them by insisting that they direct their activities through the 'proper' political channels may do more to weaken democracy than to ensure active and committed party support. (*ibid.*: 49)

Attention is now focusing on local initiatives, such as the Utyani (Grassroots) Fund which raised R2 million for new houses then lent $1.3 million to borrowers who had no collateral. The unsecured loans are being repaid at an interest rate of 105 per cent. Utyani grew out of the Federation for the Homeless, which is supported by the Catholic Church. As Harvey Tyson reported, while projects are not easily achieved without aid and advice from government, the 'private citizens' involved in the projects did not want any 'fuss' but just wished to 'get on with it regardless of government and politics' (Tyson 1996).

## Citizenship

Two decades ago the Dutch academic, Herman van Gunsteren, lamented the demise of the concept of citizenship, which he claimed had 'gone out of fashion among political thinkers' (van Gunsteren 1978). Today the concept is very much in intellectual fashion. Indeed, in liberal democratic theory with its emphasis on the place of the individual's rights and responsibilities set within a legal framework, the citizen assumes a primary position. Under

Chapter 1 of the Founding Provisions of the Constitution there appears a declaration on citizenship:

1. There is a common South African citizenship
2. All citizens are:
    (a) equally entitled to the rights, privileges and benefits of citizenship, and
    (b) equally subject to the duties and responsibilities of citizenship.
3. National legislation must provide for the acquisition, loss and restoration of citizenship. (Constitution of the Republic of South Africa 1996)

Citizenship clearly constitutes the most basic conduit for integration into the state and defines a person's relationship with the political environment. Marshall defines citizenship as an individual's 'full membership of the community' (Marshall 1950: 34) whilst van Gunsteren sees the 'notions and practices of citizenship' to be 'variable and conflicting' containing ambiguities which truly reveal the 'conflicts and problems between a plurality of people whom history has brought together in relations of interdependence and dominance (van Gunsteren 1978). Yet citizenship implies the bestowal of certain rights and duties upon the individual and, as such, the good citizen will acknowledge and abide by the conventions and expectations of his or her society. Accordingly, there must be a procedure whereby 'citizens exert control over government and make it aware of their demands, but correspondingly, there must also be a readiness to allow the government to enforce policies' (Parry 1978: 40). In other words, citizens are enfranchised and may participate in the political process but equally are under a duty to accept being ruled; otherwise there might be a drift to mass politics, characterized by unruly large-scale activities of the citizenry outside the structure and rules instituted by society to govern political action. Mass politics is to be avoided at all costs for it involves violence against opposition, a lack of respect for minorities, the rejection of peaceful solutions to conflicts and the pursuit of short-term objectives (*ibid.*). The only way to counter this development is through the establishment of a pluralistic social structure, which will enable the citizenry to form independent and limited pressure groups and to facilitate the 'free and open competition for leadership, widespread participation in the selection of leaders and restraint in the application of pressures on leaders' (Kornhauser 1957: 55). Citizenship refers to a successive and increasing catalogue of rights, entitlements and obligations towards the full membership of the organized political community. According to Tunch Aybak, citizenship has the capacity to 'enhance the life chances of individuals and increase political participatory channels in civil society and public life (Aybak 1997). The role of citizenry, then, can be both stable and responsible. In J. S. Mill's opinion, the permanence of representative institutions depended upon 'the readiness of the people to fight for them in case of their being endangered' (Mill undated: 69). If the citizenry of a country are not committed to the nation they may very well undermine democratic development and retard any reforming process.

**Table 4.3**  Attitudes to perceived economic benefits of democracy (%)

| Question | Western Cape | White | African | Coloured | National |
|---|---|---|---|---|---|
| *Equal access to houses, jobs and a decent income:* | | | | | |
| Important | 93 | 92 | 93 | 93 | 91 |
| Not important | 4 | 5 | 5 | 1 | 6 |
| *Small gap between rich and poor:* | | | | | |
| Important | 48 | 36 | 47 | 61 | 60 |
| Not important | 46 | 62 | 46 | 26 | 36 |

*Source*: IDASA (1996d)

**Table 4.4**  Procedural vs. substantive views of democracy (%)

| | Western Cape | White | African | Coloured | National |
|---|---|---|---|---|---|
| Rule to elect representatives | 33 | 36 | 40 | 25 | 45 |
| In-between | 16 | 16 | 7 | 21 | 17 |
| A way to improve one's life | 41 | 40 | 52 | 36 | 29 |
| Don't know | 10 | 8 | 1 | 18 | 9 |

*Source*: IDASA (1996d)

## Public attitudes towards democracy

An IDASA study of political attitudes in the Western Cape looked at citizens' basic conceptions of democracy. It was important to know whether 'people see democracy as a set of procedures by which citizens can govern themselves, or whether their very definition of democracy includes expectations of improvement of their life circumstances' (IDASA 1996d: 6). If citizens regarded the 'substantive' aspects of democracy to be important then their belief in democratic government could potentially lessen if they failed to gain material advantages. Table 4.3 outlines their responses.

As Table 4.4 demonstrates, the balance of national opinion ran in the opposite direction with 45 per cent taking the procedural and 29 per cent choosing the substantive position. An interesting question about the extent to which violent protest was justified tested citizenship responses in order to gauge whether 'the repertoire of political protest developed during the struggle against apartheid would continue even with the existence of legitimately elected representative institutions' (*ibid.*: 5) (Table 4.5).

As the IDASA study demonstrates, a total of 23 per cent in the province believe that violent protest may be justified, against 21 per cent in the nation as a whole, whilst in the African and coloured responses the figures are 37

**Table 4.5** Is violent protest justified? (%)

|  | Western Cape | White | African | Coloured | National |
|---|---|---|---|---|---|
| 'Often justified' | 7 | 5 | 10 | 8 | 8 |
| 'Sometimes justified' | 16 | 5 | 27 | 24 | 13 |
| 'Almost never justified' | 10 | 4 | 29 | 8 | 11 |
| 'Never justified' | 56 | 86 | 23 | 40 | 61 |
| Don't know | 11 | 0 | 11 | 20 | 7 |

*Source*: IDASA (1996d)

**Table 4.6** Political deaths in KwaZulu Natal during 1994

| January | 172 | July | 91 |
|---|---|---|---|
| February | 180 | August | 74 |
| March | 311 | September | 66 |
| April | 338 | October | 52 |
| May | 104 | November | 60 |
| June | 79 | December | 75 |

*Source*: Human Rights Watch Africa 1994

per cent and 32 per cent respectively. It is perhaps inevitable that former patterns of political behaviour may encroach upon a full understanding of the demands made of citizens in a democratic South Africa, but these changes will have to be understood if a sense of lawlessness is not to prevail in some provinces. The Human Rights Watch Africa monitored outbreaks of violence particularly in KwaZulu Natal before and after the 1994 elections. Table 4.6 indicates the findings.

Following the decision of the IFP to participate in the 1994 elections, violence decreased in KwaZulu Natal and continued to do so after the elections. One aspect the Human Rights Watch team feared was the continuance, albeit at a lower level, of 'endemic feuding' in the province (*Human Rights Watch Africa* 1995). The ANC acknowledges that in order to end the era in which political problems and differences were resolved through violence, the government should support a comprehensive strategy to stop politically motivated violence (African National Congress 1994b: 26). Conflict and arbitrary killings violate the basis for democratic decision-making and undermine the duties and responsibilities of a nation's citizenry. Democracy is a process of self-definition through which people come to identify with political entities that best represent their interests and ideals. This process demands careful assessment of the visions and policy alternatives proffered by competing parties. If citizens are denied full and equal access to political groups because of violent outbursts or intimidation then their

**Table 4.7**  Observation of civic duties – payment of rates and taxes (%)

Question: To what extent should people have to pay for their rents, rates and services?

|  | Western Cape | White | African | Coloured | National |
|---|---|---|---|---|---|
| 'Always' | 60 | 84 | 52 | 39 | 54 |
| 'Only when they can afford it' | 21 | 4 | 24 | 39 | 10 |
| 'Only when they are satisfied with their houses and the delivery of their services' | 14 | 12 | 14 | 16 | 28 |
| 'Only when they approve of the local town council' | 2 | – | 5 | 3 | 4 |
| 'Never, these things are basic rights and should be provided free' | – | – | – | – | 3 |
| 'Don't know' | 3 | – | 5 | 3 | 1 |

*Source*: IDASA (1996d)

rights have been infringed. As G. A. Gotz states: 'It is the legitimate expectation of any citizen living in a democracy that he or she be able to pursue everyday activities free of the constant threat of violence' (Gotz 1995).

Chantal Mouffe interprets a radical democratic citizenship to be one in which the citizen is not simply the 'passive recipient of specific rights' under the protection of the law and sharing a common political identity, but one in which the citizen can assume a number of political identities. Citizens, then, become activated to participate in a range of social movements. She argues that the ideal of citizenship could 'greatly contribute to an extension of the principles of liberty and equality' (Mouffe 1995). The liberal conception of citizenship is viewed in terms of a set of principles that everyone must accept. As David Miller explains, in order to avoid open conflict between groups, the only option is to adopt liberal institutions that provide citizens with 'a set of rights and liberties' (Miller 1995). Yet whichever form of citizenship is undertaken in a plural society, there must be an agreement and consensus among the population to observe duties and responsibilities, for example abstention from violence and coercion, and a willingness to argue and listen to others' views and opinions (*ibid.*). In other words, these must be an observation of civic responsibilities together with a notion of political tolerance. Returning to IDASA's study in the Western Cape and the respondents' answers to questions dealing with both civic duties and political tolerance, Tables 4.7, 4.8 and 4.9 display interesting findings.

As Table 4.7 indicates, only 54 per cent of a national survey felt they would always pay their rates and taxes, which is a very low response. If attitudes do not change, government policy will be affected. Regarding levels

**Table 4.8**   Pre-election political intolerance

Question: Think of the party in your area to which you are the most strongly opposed and indicate whether it or a member of this party should be allowed or not allowed to take the following actions:

(% saying they would not allow the action to take place)

|  | Western Cape | White | Africa | Coloured |
|---|---|---|---|---|
| 'Hold a public protest in your town/city' | 45 | 51 | 51 | 41 |
| 'Make a speech in your area that criticises the party you support' | 46 | 31 | 61 | 44 |
| 'Teach at a school in your area' | 46 | 56 | 42 | 44 |
| 'Be associated with your friends' | 35 | 34 | 38 | 34 |
| 'Live in your neighbourhood' | 30 | 26 | 34 | 30 |
| 'Operate a business in your neighbourhood' | 31 | 28 | 39 | 32 |
| 'Visit people to enrol support for the party' | 36 | 23 | 51 | 35 |

*Source*: Launching Democracy, Institute for Multi-Party Democracy, in Johnson and Schlemmer 1996

**Table 4.9**   Post-election political intolerance

Question: You also mentioned that you were opposed to the XXX during the campaign before the elections. Please indicate whether it or a member of this party should have been allowed or not allowed to take the following actions:

(% saying they would not allow the action to take place)

|  | Western Cape | White | African | Coloured | National |
|---|---|---|---|---|---|
| 'Hold a public protest in your town/city' | 37 | 50 | 30 | 33 | 37 |
| 'Make a speech in your area that criticises the party you support' | 42 | 35 | 48 | 43 | 42 |
| 'Teach history at a school in your area' | 49 | 57 | 53 | 42 | 49 |
| 'Live in your neighbourhood' | 25 | 26 | 28 | 23 | 25 |
| 'Visit people to enrol support for the party' | 40 | 25 | 39 | 29 | 30 |
| 'Hold a mass rally/meeting in your area' | 41 | 52 | 32 | 38 | 41 |

*Source*: IDASA (1996d)

of political tolerance, Table 4.8 demonstrates that they were rather high before the 1994 elections, but Table 4.9 shows that there were some variabilities in attitudes after the elections. The understanding of the rights and responsibilities of citizenship is a crucial issue in the new South Africa and needs to be constantly reaffirmed in order that the population can nurture a democratic culture.

## Identity

After the 1994 elections Stanley Uys stated that the 'new pattern of political relations will still be race-based, but it is an immense improvement on long years of white domination' (Uys 1994). The question of identity has usually centred on racial, ethnic, religious, linguistic, national and gender categories. More recently, writers have suggested there may be theatrical and imaginary dimensions to identity and states can politically create their 'own world of meanings' through various procedures of ceremonial and symbolic significance (Wagner 1991, Mbembe 1991: 166). Myths and imaginings can be appropriated for political purposes and can be employed to justify conflict, war and repression. Michel Foucault maintains that history reflects 'relations of power'. However, power is not necessarily linked to the state but to a range of power associations: family, kinship, knowledge, technology and so on. According to Foucault each society has a 'regime of truth', that is a body of ideas or 'types of discourse which it accepts and makes function as true' (Foucault 1995: 75).

Religion, mysticism and story-telling, especially in regions where literacy levels are low and oral traditions exist, are all processes that contribute to perceptions and intepretations of truth and falsehood. But what of identities in the new South Africa? What does it mean to be a South African? Clearly such a polarized society will have many identities, memories and histories and, in a sense, images must be reclaimed and re-examined. Pieter Duvenage states that since South Africa moved into a democratic phase it is time for 'issues of memory, forgetfulness and history to enter the public sphere' (Duvenage 1995). He asks how should the people of South Africa deal with apartheid and to what extent is it possible to forget? The process of ensuring that the collective memory is engaged in recognizing the tragedy of the past is of contemporary importance for South Africans living in a multicultural democracy (ibid.).

The Truth and Reconciliation Commission is attempting to deal with the violence of the past in an appropriate manner and must complete its work in a maximum of two years. Operating in plenary sessions and through three committees, one dealing with human rights violations, another dealing with amnesty and a third dealing with reconciliation and reparation, the Commission has an initial budget of R50 million (£8.5 million). The work of the Commission involves hearing the stories of victims of gross human rights violations, considering application for amnesty from perpetrators of such violations, and making recommendations on both reparations to the victims and measures for ensuring that human rights abuses are not committed again. Human Rights monitors estimate that over 200 political assassinations took place during the apartheid era, while over 15 000 people died in factional violence and dozens of prisoners died in custody (*Human Rights Watch Africa* 1995).

For James, Caliguire and Cullinan, one way of understanding the rise of coloured political groupings and movements is to view them as a collective search for identity, which is undergoing a process of rigorous self-examination (James, Caliguire and Cullinan 1996: 10). This process, however, is not without difficulties as there is a tendency for people to define themselves under the old apartheid criteria, that is, coloureds regard themselves as non-black and non-white. The coloured community is an ethnic minority which tends to distinguish it from the dominant national category. Aybak argues that the term ethnic minority suggests a degree of marginalization and exclusion. This tendency can lead to a situation of actual or potential conflict, especially if there is a feeling among the community that they are of secondary status within the organized society (Aybak 1997). It is widely acknowledged that there is a 'palpable sense of marginalisation' from the new political system among the coloured communities in the Cape (James, Caliguire and Cullinan 1996: 14–15). In a sense, the distance is inherited from the divisive legacy of apartheid, which placed coloureds 'above' blacks and 'below' whites, with the effect that 'The resulting middle ground became home for the various coloured communities and has now become a place where uncertainty and ambiguity dwells' (*ibid.*). A crisis of identity has emerged within the democratic order, as people feel they are losing their past relative advantages or as James and colleagues put it: 'What limited benefits were provided in the past are gone and there is a sense of being excluded from the new resources to be distributed' (*ibid.*).

## Language

In considering identity it is necessary to appreciate the extent to which society still divides along linguistic/ethnic/racial lines. South Africa has 11 formal languages and numerous informal ones. Under the 1996 constitution a special clause is devoted to languages. The official languages of the Republic are Sepedi, Sesotho, Setswana, siSwati, Tshivenda, Itsonga, Afrikaans, Englis, isiNdebele, isiXhosa and isiZulu. The 1996 constitution states:

- Recognising the historically diminished use and status of the indigenous languages of our people, the state must take practical and positive measures to elevate the status and advance the use of these languages.
- National and provincial governments may use particular official languages for the purposes of government, taking into account usage,

practicality, expense, regional circumstances and the balance of the needs and preferences of the population as a whole or in respective provinces; provided that no national or provincial government may use only one official language. Municipalities must take into consideration the language usage and preferences of their residents.

• National and provincial governments, by legislative and other measures, must regulate and monitor the use of those governments of official languages. All official languages must enjoy parity of esteem and must be treated equitably.

• The Pan South African Language Board must:
    (a) promote and create conditions for the development and use of:
        i. all official languages;
        ii. the Khoi, Nama and San languages; and
        iii. sign language.
    (b) promote and ensure respect for languages, including German, Greek, Gujarati, Hindi, Portuguese, Tamil, Telugu, Urdu and others commonly used by communities in South Africa, and Arabic, Hebrew, Sanskit and others used for religious purposes. (Constitution of the Republic of South Africa 1996)

However, in a recent study it was clear that although South African parents defended their own language and culture, there was strong support for teaching to be conducted in English (IDASA 1995). An IDASA national survey asked people what language they generally spoke at home and found that none of the 1736 black respondents spoke English or Afrikaans as their primary language at home. The largest language groups nationally were Zulu (23 per cent), Afrikaans (17 per cent), Zhosa (15 per cent) and English (11 per cent). Sesotho, Setswana and Sepedi were spoken by between 8 per cent and 9 per cent respectively. Seswati, Venda and Shangaan were the three smallest language groups, each with 3 per cent. The study found that English and Afrikaans were spoken at home by white, coloured and Asian respondents only. Yet when asked in which languages the respondents would wish their children to be instructed, the survey showed that 81 per cent of black South Africans wished their children to be educated in English. Afrikaans speakers were the only major linguistic group who did not express a majority wish to have their children learn in English. However, at the same time, indigenous African language speakers also expressed a strong desire to retain their own languages as at least one medium of instruction. Yet among both English and Afrikaans speakers, only very small minorities wanted their children to be instructed in an African language. The survey also revealed 'strong majority support among all racial groups and all the major linguistic groups for guarantees to ensure that schools are taught in their language and culture' (ibid.). Tables 4.10 and 4.11 reveal the survey's findings.

IDASA dispute the argument that the 1994 elections divided along racial lines. Whilst accepting that most ANC, PAC and IFP support came from

**Table 4.10**   Language preferences

Question: What language would you like your children to be educated in?

| Zulu | Afrikaans | Xhosa | English | Sesotho | Setswana |
|------|-----------|-------|---------|---------|----------|
| English | Afrikaans | English | English | English | English |
| 83% | 88% | 92% | 96% | 79% | 58% |
| Zulu | English | Xhosa | Afrikaans | Sesotho | Setswana |
| 53% | 33% | 78% | 19% | 52% | 55% |
| Afrikaan | Xhosa | Afrikaan | Xhosa | Afrikaans | Afrikaans |
| 11% | 2% | 6% | 2% | 18% | 6% |

*Source*: IDASA 1995

blacks and most NP, DP and FF support came from whites, they maintain that this does not explain why people voted for these parties. When they conducted a survey and asked why people felt close to a particular party, '15% mentioned reasons connected to race or ethnicity' although they admit that certain parties, for example, the IFP, did attract supporters because of ethnic factors.

If South African society is to become truly multiracial all political parties will have to attract cross-ethnic support. Diversity can thrive when there is growth and development for all communities, but if one group benefits at the expense of another, identity politics can emerge. Apartheid defined everyone on the basis of racial classification and this formed part of the political socialization of the wider population. It perhaps is not surprising that political support may, on occasions, be demarcated on the basis of ethnicity and race. However, if democracy is to strengthen in a plural society a multicultural polity must be able to define and express cultural differences at the same time as moving forward in harmony and unity as a nation.

**Table 4.11** Language preferences by province

Question: What language would you like your children to be educated in, or to be used in your local school?

| W. Cape | N. Cape | E. Cape | Gauteng | N. West | Mpumalanga | Northern | Free State | KwaZulu/Natal |
|---|---|---|---|---|---|---|---|---|
| English 58% | English 64% | English 92% | English 56% | English 51% | English 67% | English 82% | English 77% | English 92% |
| Afrikaans 51% | Afrikaans 44% | Xhosa 68% | Afrikaans 25% | Seswati 41% | Seswati 25% | Sepedi 39% | Afrikaans 35% | Zulu 35% |
| Xhosa 7% | Seswati 9% | Afrikaans 24% | Zulu 21% | Afrikaans 18% | Zulu 22% | Venda 16% | Sesotho 32% | Afrikaans 12% |
| | | | Sesotho 8% | Sesotho 12% | Afrikaans 15% | Shangaan 16% | Xhosa 13% | |

*Source:* IDASA 1995

# FIVE

# Women and youth

One of the central planks of the new South African government has been to upgrade the role of women in society and to attempt to deal with the plight of young blacks. Women of all ages want their voices to be heard and regard equal rights between women and men and the equitable sharing of responsibilities to be vital to the well-being of humanity (*RDP News*, October 1995). As Thenjiwe Mtintso puts it 'the eradication of patriarchy depends on changing attitudes' (Mtintso 1996). In terms of the legal status of women, the Common Law rule, whereby a husband obtained marital power over his wife and her property, was repealed by the General Law Fourth Amendment Act in December 1993. The amendment meant that a married woman would now have the same management powers as her husband. The Guardianship Act of 1993 giving a married couple equal guardianship rights over minors came into effect in January 1994. Previously, only the father had been the natural guardian of a minor child born within marriage.

With the opening of Parliament on 24 May 1994, President Nelson Mandela raised the issue of women's rights. He stated that the objectives of the Reconstruction and Development Programme (RDP) could not be realized 'unless we see in visible and practical terms that the condition of the women of our country has radically changed for the better and that they have been empowered to intervene in all aspects of life as equals with any other member of society (*RDP News*, June 1995). The first White Paper on Reconstruction and Development refers to economic gender discrimination such as employment discrimination in public works projects, unpaid labour, credit constraints for women with limited collateral and insufficient resource allocation to childcare and education. The government intended to redress these inequalities by improving opportunities to benefit women.

## Women and violence

The debate on gender issues had been given an impetus in 1994 with the release of a report on the status of South African women in preparation for the United Nations World Conference on Women held in Beijing in September 1995. The document suggested that the government should develop a specific component of its work and resources for a broader national empowerment programme for women (*RDP News*, October 1995). Within its remit certain key issues would be included: the alleviation of women's poverty, improvements in health, education and job opportunities, and measures to combat violence against women. A Commonwealth Observer Mission to South Africa (COMSA) had visited South Africa before the elections of 1994 to consider violence within society. Their findings were sobering. They found that South African women, who constitute 53 per cent of the population, were among the worst victims of apartheid and violence. According to 1991 figures, almost half the female population is likely to be raped within her lifetime, and it is estimated that one in six women is battered by her male partner (COMSA 1993).

Empowering women was seen by COMSA to be essential in combating the particular effects of violence directed against females. Apart from socio-economic improvements, COMSA recommended the recruitment of women into law enforcement agencies. Policing approaches would have to reflect the new democratic political order of South Africa and reflect the diversity of the communities they served with appropriate levels of accountability and consultation (*ibid.*). The term 'violence against women' is described in the Draft Declaration for the Platform of Action of the Beijing conference as 'any act based on gender that results in physical, sexual, and psychological harm to women' (Human Rights Watch 1994). Violence against women embraces a wide variety of acts:

- Physical, sexual and psychological violence in the family, including battering, sexual abuse of female children in the family, marital rape, female genital mutilation and violence related to exploitation.
- Physical, sexual and psychological violence occurring within the general community. This includes rape, sexual harassment and intimidation at work, in educational institutions and elsewhere, trafficking in women and forced prostitution.
- Physical, sexual and psychological violence condoned by the State, wherever it occurs. (*ibid.*)

Cultural patterns and the historical manifestation that men are superior to women have led to the domination of women by men. Indeed, as Sophie Masite, Mayor of Soweto, stated: 'Culturally, women used to be placed in an inferior role to men' (Masite interview, 1996). Mmatshilo Motsei, who was initially the co-ordinator of gender equality within the RDP, asserted that women often lacked access to legal information, aid or protection. Yet the Global Report of Women's Human Rights reported that domestic violence was a leading cause of violence. The South African organization People Opposing Women Abuse (POWA) found that what they call 'intimate femicide' was the main cause of violent deaths among women. These deaths were brought about by their partners (White interview, 1996). The study, based in part on an examination of inquest records which included the magistrate's findings, statements from witnesses and the relatives of the victims as well as post-mortem reports, concluded that family murders were not only a 'white people's pattern but a South African pattern'.

The oppression of black women under the apartheid system is well documented, but it should be pointed out here that there was 'virtually a complete absence of child-care provisions for working mothers, or gynaecological services in a country with the highest cervical cancer rate in the world: 35 per 100 000 women, and an estimated 20 000 deaths per year from back-street abortions' (Unterhalter 1989: 162, Bernstein, H. 1983).

As Thenjiwe Mtintso maintains: 'The strategic objective of gender and women's struggle is the complete eradication of all forms of oppressive gender relations and equal roles in all spheres of life, including family roles' (Mtintso 1996). Yet the traditional aspects of black society have intruded into the political debate about the rights of women. Women who are subject to customary law have traditionally not had full legal capacity and were treated as 'minors'. According to customary law, the father or husband is the legal guardian of the woman. In KwaZulu, under terms of the KwaZulu Act on the Code of Zulu Law Act 1985, all persons became majors on marriage or on attaining the age of 21 years. A female who is a major is, therefore, no longer under the guardianship of any person in KwaZulu (Race Relations Survey 1994/1995: 3–4).

The position of customary law within the constitution was one of the more controversial issues surrounding the debate about women. Traditional leaders, at the time, insisted that customary law be included in and protected by the Bill of Rights, while women delegates argued that this would mean that women from communities that observed such customs, especially rural women, would not be protected by the constitution's equality clause. According to the established leaders, the institution of traditional leadership was hereditary and passed down through the male line. Women had not been traditional leaders and chiefs in the past. The traditional leaders were concerned that the equality clause would give women this right. They felt that by undermining the role of customary law the government was eroding the foundation of African culture. A female ANC delegate at the multi-party talks, Mavivi Manzini, now an ANC MP, together with representatives of other parties, the Women's National Coalition and the Rural Women's Movement, insisted that the institution of traditional leadership and the role of indigenous and customary law be subject to fundamental human rights, including equality of the sexes and the abolition of racial and gender discrimination. However, Manzini added that women recognized the fact that the institution of traditional leadership should continue and could play a positive role in society.

Mmatshilo Motsei, the co-ordinator of gender equality within the RDP, felt there had to be greater clarity about women's rights within the highly diverse South African society: 'The one thing that we are facing as women

is that we do not even know what our rights are' (Motsei 1995). The importance of a strong women's movement could not be overemphasized, but so
much had to be done: 'We can have the best policies, the best gender structure in government, but as long as women are not organised they will get
nowhere' (ibid.). Under the Bill of Rights, within the clause on equality, it is
clearly stated that the State 'may not unfairly discriminate directly or indirectly against anyone on one or more grounds, including . . . gender, sex,
pregnancy, marital status, culture' (see Appendix 2). However, although the
Bill of Rights is enforceable against the State, women employed in private
institutions and suffering discrimination would have to seek alternative
action. One policy which has had a direct influence on women since 1994 is
affirmative action.

## Affirmative action

The policy of affirmative action has had rather a mixed response since it
was introduced into South Africa. According to one view it has probably
been one of the 'most misunderstood and even feared features of the new
democratic order' (Infospec 1995). Whites have feared replacement or non-
promotion, coloured and Indian communities are apprehensive about increasing marginalization, some sections of the black community regret that
the policy might suggest they have been employed or promoted solely
because they are black and not on the basis of merit (ibid.). Because affirmative action embraces the issue of race and gender, it has heightened the
issues of racism and sexism. South African women across party lines have
begun to realize the importance of fighting sexism as vigorously as racism
or any other form of discrimination (Ramphele 1995). However, it is recognized that affirmative action would be a 'difficult and sometimes painful
process' (Infospec 1995).

Ramphele argues that gender must be seen as something 'distinct from
sex – a biological variable – which makes us male or female' (Ramphele
1995: 25). She argues that the construction of 'manhood' or 'womanhood' is
a social process, starting from birth, which encourages boys and girls to
develop self-identities according to their social locale, 'assigning different
roles to them as men and women' (ibid.). Gender issues, then, are not simply
women's issues. Affirmative action is concerned with providing employment and opportunities to black people, men and women, who have been
disadvantaged in the past. As Ramphele asserts, 'South Africa has many
psychological and social wounds to heal after decades of apartheid' (ibid.).
The pursuit of equality is enshrined within the constitution but 'equal treatment in all cases, in a society scarred by discrimination, also has the potential of reinforcing inequity' (ibid.: 26). Equitable treatment often demands
preferential policies in order to ensure that previous injustices are redressed.
Such was the racial division with South Africa under apartheid that when

we refer to women now we are not referring to a homogeneous group. White women regard their futures with uncertainty mainly because they fear that black women will stand a better chance of getting a job than they will (*Infospec* 1995). So the situation becomes more complicated. There are also very important distinctions between different groups of black women: coloured and African, African and Asian, middle-class and lower-class, older and younger, rural and urban, and so on (Ramphele 1995: 28). Middle-class women tend to benefit from affirmative action more than poor, ill-educated, rural women. The government recognizes this difficulty and is promoting the purchase of land by rural women. Grants and loans are offered as a means of promoting the project (*Mayibuye*, June 1996). Equally, free health care programmes for women and children have been instituted in rural areas. In the Northern province over 80 per cent of children under five years of age were immunized against polio and 25 new clinics were being constructed. Whilst the crucial role of environmental factors, such as clean water, sanitation, housing and education, are the fundamental aspects of improving the health of men and women, mother and baby clinics, ante-natal care and gynaecological services are exceptionally important for women, particularly rural women (*ibid.*). Equally, many women have stood for office in the local, provincial and national elections, which provides a visible sign that opportunities are available to women.

The local elections in 1995 resulted in a number of women becoming councillors and mayors. These new political representatives are in a position to make real differences to the lives of ordinary people and to provide role models for younger women. One woman, Maria Barnabas the daughter of a Xhosa shepherd, cleans the toilets at the local school but she is also mayor of Lamberts Bay (Hooper-Box 1996). Barnabas and other women like her were elected in 1995. Women now occupy just under 20 per cent of the seats in local government. Many of these new local leaders were vigorous opponents of the old apartheid councils. In fact, Sophie Masite was a key organizer of the Soweto rent boycott. She and other councillors with similar backgrounds now face the challenge of getting residents to pay for services. But these challenges are faced head-on and Masite has already instigated a scheme to allow people to pay by instalments (Masite interview, 1996). Judy Sibisi comes from a family of prominent IFP members but she represents the ANC as a councillor in Cape Town. She moved away from the IFP and sees her role now as encouraging people to participate in the 'broader political decision-making process' (Sibisi 1996). She is interested in setting up gender structures at the local level. Women must feel they can approach councillors through advisory committees and community groups. Her personal aim is to set up a gender advisory council at grassroots level. Julia Melato is the new black mayor of Petrus Steyn. She holds two degrees, is unmarried and was previously an ANC activist who helped form a squatter camp outside Petrus Steyn. Now she is attempting to provide the camp with water and sewerage. She believes the influx of women into councils has brought a more compassionate approach to issues (*ibid.*). Another mayor, a former community worker who founded two successful creches in Mpumalanga, Thuli Sitholi, believes women have a big role to play in politics because of the focus of their lives: 'The hard jobs are done by women. They must keep their kids safe and protected. Men look after their own needs first, not looking to the children, the community. Single-parent families are many and are headed by women. Some can't afford services. A woman councillor would understand their problems' (*ibid.*). Female political representatives are also tackling issues that have not been considered before: help and protection for battered women, homelessness and squatter camps. They agree that their success will depend on their ability to listen to their communities.

Yet life can be very difficult for rural women. Seventy per cent of rural women scratch a subsistence living from agriculture. Historically, because men worked away in the mines in the cities, these women had to take over agricultural production together with bringing up children, carrying water and struggling to find fuel. Rural areas had no electricity or infrastructure. As Anthea Billy explains: 'Rural women were at the bottom of the heap because of discrimination on grounds of race, class and gender' (Billy 1996). The Transvaal Rural Action Committee, a non-governmental organization that works with rural communities, states that rural women's voices should be heard: 'Rural women in particular have the least access to processes of political decision making' (*ibid.*). The legacy of the system of migrant labour, which allowed for men to be employed in urban areas, but not women, and the constraints of influx control, which admitted men under regulated circumstances but prohibited the movement of women into the cities, is that an asymmetrical demographic structure has emerged. Men of working age outnumber similar women in the urban areas, where there are some possibilities of employment, by 1.1 million, whereas women outnumber men by one million in the rural areas (White 1995b).

Many commentators suggest that customary law is still a potent force in the lives of rural women despite the Bill of Rights and the government commitment to gender equality (Billy 1996, White 1995a: 7). The main resource for rural women is land, to which their households have access under traditional customary arrangements. White points out that under customary law, women obtain access to land only through a male relative or their husband. So although they may be sole cultivators of the land 'they may not own the land nor make any important decisions about its use or disposal' (White 1995b). Equally, under the African communal system, grazing rights and rights to live and grow crops on portions of land are allocated by the chief to male heads of household (White 1995b). Because alternative forms of paid work are rare, women are dependent on the remittances sent to them by their spouses. With the unreliability of remittance payments, women sometimes raise animals for sale or run a shebeen. Billy argues that the only way to guarantee a gender-sensitive land policy that includes the needs of rural women 'is to construct suitable channels for reaching out to women and providing opportunities for them to make their voices heard' (Billy 1996). Certainly, the government is making moves to reform land owner-ship and has introduced the Communal Properties Association Act of 1996 which attempts to formalize the communal tenure system into associations with registered constitutions which must provide for the adequate repre-sentation of women.

## Women and employment

According to the census of 1991, the economically active population of the country is nearly 12 million, of whom about 4.5 million are women (White 1995b: 11). A further 4 million women are of working age but do not appear in the figures. In 1996 it was estimated that unemployment among young women was around 70 per cent (Polgieter interview, 1996). Young women become invisible, unlike men who are all too visible on street corners and in the crime figures (ibid.). Yet it would be both wrong and misleading to presume that women were disinclined to work. In fact, historically it is well documented that women in black South African society 'perform all the hard work, planting and tilling the earth, digging, thrashing besides cook-ing and collecting water' (White 1995b: 25). Recent studies have collated the time rural women spend collecting wood for fuel and it ranged between 90 minutes to three hours (ibid.). Women also travel long distances on foot to fetch clean water in areas such as the Eastern Cape (Haines interview, 1995). The distinction between men and women regarding domestic work is that men do very little within the home environment, or as White puts it: 'Men and boys are excused from almost any task associated with the home' (White 1995b: 9). Men see household management as the responsibility of their part-ners, states Thenjiwe Mtintso, and that attitude must change (Mtintso 1996). Despite the difficulties faced by women in the formal labour market, women find themselves under increasing pressure to obtain employment (Mini 1994).

Rural women have been imaginative in establishing savings and loan clubs or what have been called rotating credit associations, umbalelo (Buijs 1995). Gina Buijs has studied the saving and lending habits of women in the community of Rhini, in the Eastern Cape. Large-scale unemployment in Rhini and Grahamstown has led to women trading as hawkers. In 1993 these women started a money-lending club, which makes available loans of between R10 to R50 (£1.50 to £8) at a standard rate of interest of 40 per cent. Loans are recalled in September, all outstanding debts are collected in October, the money is banked and by December it is divided equally among members. Members introduce potential borrowers, although the member is liable for the debt if the borrower defaults (ibid.). Buijs found that the majority of credit association members in Rhini used their funds not only for personal or domestic purchases, but also 'to support business ventures' (ibid.).

A World Bank study of the characteristics and constraints facing black businesses in South Africa reported that women operate 62 per cent of all informal sector businesses. Enterprises owned by women, however, tended to be concentrated in the sectors with the lowest levels of profitability: food, beverage, tobacco, textiles and garments – dressmaking, knitting, crocheting – and retail. The study found that employment growth tends to be lower in sectors dominated by women than in sectors dominated by men. It also discovered that access to credit had not been immediately translated into increased employment opportunities for female-owned enterprises. Most female enterprises operate from home and these tend to have lower growth rates and lower profits than market-based firms because they reduce the firm's access to customers. The World Bank found that the obvious reason for the stagnation is that:

Women have dual domestic and productive responsibilities and lack time to invest in the growth of their business. Nonetheless, their businesses play an important role in providing for family welfare and are an important source of investment in the education and health of children and family members. They also contribute to the survival of families who are living on the margins of absolute poverty. These female-run enterprises do not have to be dynamic and large in order to play a critical role in contributing to overall household income. (World Bank 1993)

The sectoral breakdown in Table 5.1 reveals the concentration of low levels of turnover in the traditional, easy-entry activities in which female enterprises are concentrated. Yet it is clear that women are prepared to engage in a range of enterprises in their search for income-generating activities. In fact, as Buijs observes, a number of female-headed households, as many as 40 per cent in Rhini, participate in income-generating activities (Buijs 1995). These activities, for example hawking, the street-selling of food or running a shebeen, are within the informal sector. One sector where the participants are almost exclusively women is that of domestic service. Recently, the government has introduced legislation designed to bring domestic workers' pay and conditions into the reach of the law. Previously, domestic service had no minimum wage and conditions were poor, with long hours, very little time off, no working clothes, and so on (White 1995b). Buijs states that during the 1970s domestic service was not particularly favoured by African women, who only entered it out of necessity (Buijs 1995). Mtintso asserts that domestic labour has always been and still is exploited in white South African households in general, but she is concerned about the trend for upwardly mobile black women to be employing domestic labour (Mtintso 1996). In the midst of 'sisterhood', she argues, there is rarely any mention of the issue of black labour: 'The trend among black women, including those in parliament, has been to rake up some "relative" from

**Table 5.1**   Growth rates and gender of the proprietor of firms, by sector, in Mamelodi and Kwazakhele Townships, 1990

| Business sector | % of firms run by women | Sectoral growth rate |
|---|---|---|
| *Manufacturing:* | | |
| Food, beverage and tobacco | 72.2 | 19.4 |
| Textile, clothing, leather production | 63.1 | 13.0 |
| Wood and wood processing | 13.4 | 43.3 |
| Paper, printing and publishing | 100.0 | 27.3 |
| Chemicals and plastics | 16.7 | 129.0 |
| Nonmetallic mineral processing | 0.0 | 23.8 |
| Fabricated metal production | 6.3 | 38.1 |
| Other manufacturing | 43.2 | 21.1 |
| Construction | 0.0 | 33.1 |
| | | |
| *Trade:* | | |
| Wholesale | 69.2 | 11.2 |
| Retail | 69.9 | 25.1 |
| Restaurants, bars, shebeens | 62.2 | 28.6 |
| All trade | 68.7 | 25.6 |
| | | |
| *Services:* | | |
| Transport | 11.3 | 21.8 |
| Financial, real estate, business services | 60.8 | 2.0 |
| All services | 66.8 | 21.9 |
| | | |
| *All Enterprises* | 62.1 | 23.9 |

*Source*: World Bank, *Characteristics of and Constraints Facing Black Businesses in South Africa*, Washington, 1993

the rural areas to come and stay.' Some she admits are relatives, but this muddles the real relationship, that between employer and employee (*ibid.*).

Caroline White asserts that if jobs were distributed evenly, 35 per cent of professionals would be African women and about 9 per cent would be white women (White 1995b: 13) (see Table 5.2). The reality, however, is vastly different. Only 0.3 per cent of African women hold managerial positions. In the professions, engineers, doctors, lawyers, architects and so on, white women are the majority of the 25.7 per cent of the total. Although in jobs such as nursing, teaching and journalism, African women represent 23.6 per cent, this is still unrepresentative in terms of their demographic percentage. In secretarial, shop and office work, the percentage of African women is 14.2 per cent. Skilled and semi-skilled work is the prerogative of men, 68 per cent, whilst women work as cleaners and tea-makers. With the preponderance of mining work these figures might not be surprising,

**Table 5.2**  Racial breakdown of population

| Population aged 2 to 64 | Number | % of total population of working age |
|---|---|---|
| African women | 6 169 658 | 34.9 |
| African men | 6 243 918 | 35.2 |
| Coloured women | 834 463 | 4.7 |
| Coloured men | 794 199 | 4.4 |
| Indian women | 272 501 | 1.5 |
| Indian men | 265 716 | 1.5 |
| White women | 1 563 408 | 8.9 |
| White men | 1 585 382 | 8.9 |
| Total | 17 729 245 | 100.00 |

*Source*: Caroline White, *Gender on the Agenda*, 1995b: 13

although women of all races were excluded from apprenticeships during the apartheid years (*ibid.*: 14). White believes that women experience difficulty in finding jobs in the formal sector even at lower levels. She does not attribute this recruitment to educational attainment, although in 1991 of the 160 000 African girls who took examinations on leaving school only 14 675 passed, whereas of 120 000 African boys, 15 614 passed (*ibid.*: 15–16). At every level of the public tertiary educational sector, black women are under-represented, with the exception of the correspondence university, the University of South African (UNISA), and then their predominance is only in relation to black men. UNISA still had a largely white intake in 1995 (*ibid.*).

Black women are interested in being trained in business and commercial skills. Helene Rubin, the Principal of the private commercial college, Anchor College, started advertising for black students in 1984 and by 1996, 75 per cent of its intake was female and 25 per cent was male. Of the total, 60 per cent are black and 40 per cent are white. The college has two black partners and runs a selection of courses apart from business and commercial programmes, including agriculture, glazing, trucking and general empowerment and entrepreneurial courses. Students are placed with companies and although Rubin is fully aware that racism still exists in some businesses, Anchor College is prepared to confront those attitudes. Rubin believes that lack of confidence is the major drawback for young women entering either higher education or the labour market and she sees private colleges playing an important role along with the public educational sector in promoting positive attitudes (Rubin interview, 1996).

Another important factor that can lead to discrimination against women in the labour market is child-bearing and child-rearing. As White (1995b) points out, although sex equality is written into the constitution, no cases of sex discrimination have yet been brought before the constitutional court. Industrial courts can rule that dismissal on account of pregnancy is an unfair labour practice. However, the high fertility rate among African women, an average of 4.6 births per lifetime with 49 per cent of pregnancies occurring before a women is 20 years old, limits women's educational and training opportunities and employment chances. In 1996 legislation was passed that permitted abortion for the young, which did not necessarily rely on parental permission. It was seen at the time as a radical attempt by the government to lend some control to the increasing birth rate and to offer a choice to pregnant women.

Although some analysts believe that the women's movement in South Africa is currently in a state of flux because it has lost so many of it members to parliament, female ANC MPs are still calling for women's complete emancipation from patriarchy (Gouws 1996, Mtintso 1996). Patriarchy appears as a feudal relic or a remnant of the old world of status that sets the 'familial, paternal, natural, private sphere apart from the conventional, civil, public world of contract and capitalism' (Pateman 1991: 23). More recently, much feminist energy has gone into displaying that women have the same capacities as men and are, therefore, entitled to the same freedom. Certainly, the ANC has taken the issue of women seriously. The ANC Women's League has existed since 1950 and in its 1994 constitution, rule 14 on Gender and Affirmative Action pronounces:

(i) In an endeavour to ensure that women are adequately represented in all decision-making structures, the ANC shall implement a programme of affirmative action, including the provision of quotas.

(ii) The method of such implementation shall be addressed in all ANC structures immediately and on a continuing basis (African National Congress 1994a: 12).

A statement of the ANC's National Executive Committee in 1996 emphasized the need for the Women's League to be strengthened so that it could reach out to women in the country at large. The ANC saw the Women's League as a central organization that was essential in the task of empowering women (African National Congress 1996a). Equally, it recognizes that women's emancipation is a long process and acknowledges that while the constitution guarantees fundamental rights to all women, the 'structural oppression of women in our society places obstacles to women exercising their rights' (African National Congress 1994b: 30). It also understands that women's rights to equality and dignity can be violated in the privacy of homes and family lives and, therefore, the party knows that domestic violence must be addressed. White believes that feminists and their supporters in the ANC have won some remarkable battles, for example that 'one third of all names on the party's national and provincial electoral list had to be women and that they had to be distributed on the lists in such a way that a third of them would be elected' (White 1995b: 35–6). For the first time black women are political representatives. Inevitably, there will be distinctions among women on urban/rural lines, but as Cheryl Carolus says: 'The most important aim we must achieve in the next generation is to raise women's aspirations' (Carolus interview, 1996).

## Youth Day

On 16 June 1976 school students in Soweto organized a peaceful protest to demonstrate against the use of Afrikaans as a medium of instruction in black schools. Whilst this policy was the focus issue for the protest, the demonstration formed part of the overall struggle against the system of apartheid. The government responded by sending in heavily armed forces with clear and specific instructions to shoot to kill. The armed forces did as they were instructed and opened fire at the protesters. Thirteen-year-old Hector Peterson became the first victim of the shootings (see Figure 5.1). The events of that day caught the attention of the whole world. The United Nations Security Council condemned the South African government for the use of violence against demonstrators. A resolution was passed condemning apartheid as 'a crime against the conscience and dignity of mankind that seriously disturbs peace and security' (ANC Youth League 1996). The activities of 16 June 1976 marked a very important contribution by the young in the national liberation struggle. As the ANC Youth League explains: 'Soon after the violent attacks on the student protesters by security forces, students from other parts of the country joined in solidarity actions' (*ibid.*). Scores of youths who were involved in organizing the protests on 16 June were arrested and detained under the Internal Security Act. Others were charged under the Terrorism Act. The detentions and harassment of student leaders and other community leaders did not deter the young from working towards national liberation and many joined the ANC in exile.

In 1977 a number of organizations, including the South African Student Organisation and the South African Students Movement, were banned. The late 1970s saw the formation of the Congress of South African Students and Azanian Student Organisation, which subsequently changed its name to South African National Student Congress (SANSCO). In 1991 the South African Student Congress was formed. Youth involvement in the struggle against apartheid increased in the 1980s with mass action led by student bodies and local youth organizations taking place in schools, universities and colleges and in townships. By 1986 the system of apartheid education almost collapsed when all black educational institutions throughout the country were affected by mass action aimed directly at challenging the system. The day, 16 June, is now South African Youth Day and a designated public holiday: 'It is a demonstration that the government recognises the importance of its young people and values their contribution to the reconstruction and development of the country' (*ibid.*). The public holiday is seen

**Figure 5.1**   June 16: South African Youth Day

# June 16

# South African
# Youth Day

# A tribute to the youth

Published by ANC Youth League
51 Plain Street, Johannesburg

---

**Table 5.3**　16 June: Youth Day, A Day for Every Youth

---

Every young person should on this day feel free to make known their issues and aspirations. This can be done in various ways:

(a) Find out what activities are organised by various youth groups in your areas and attend, also take your friends with you;
(b) Get guest speakers to address your youth group or school on the meaning of 16 June and why it is important.
(c) Write letters to newspapers on why June 16 is important to you or your youth group and what your ambitions as a young South African are, or what you think of nation building and reconciliation.
(d) Link up with youth from other cultural and religious groups and exchange views on their expectations for the future.
(e) Speak to older people and ask them to tell their story of where they were and what they thought about the events of this day in 1976.
(f) Organise cultural, sporting and other activities to celebrate this day.

---

*Source*: *South African Youth Day: A tribute to the youth*, ANC Youth League, 1996

---

as a recognition of the participation of the young and the role they played in opposing apartheid, but the ANC also instructs the young on what activities might take place on that day, as Table 5.3 makes clear.

Clearly, 1976 was a momentous time for the young and a period of great politicization, and their involvement in the campaign for change must be acknowledged. However, during the early 1990s much discussion emerged on what was called the 'lost generation' and the problem of young people. Jeremy Seekings states that in mid-1992, there emerged a renewed 'panic' around 'youth' (Seekings 1995). When the CODESA 2 talks became dead-locked and the ANC withdrew because of the government's inability to stop the continuing violence, the *Sunday Times* coined the phrase 'the lost generation of youth', with references to 'undisciplined township youth, the lost generations of 1976 and the following years' (*ibid.*). It was also presumed that the ANC was not able to control the youth: the ANC is 'being dragged along helplessly by township youngsters whom it cannot control' (*ibid.*). Meanwhile, the *Sowetan* newspaper expressed anxiety about the effects of the deepening schooling crisis: 'The fruits of liberation and freedom, now within our grasp, will be extremely bitter if we produce another "lost generation" . . . But this time we will have only ourselves to blame' (*ibid.*). After the elections in 1994 the ANC commissioned research to discover whether or not there was a 'lost generation'. The findings revealed that the young had suffered from a lack of education, which was directly related to the disruption caused by their struggle against apartheid. Consequently, their educational attainments were barely beyond those of an elementary grade: the educational attainment levels of ten-year-olds. Equally, poverty levels were high and a sense of 'active resistance against the state' had been inculcated over the years (Polgieter interview, 1996).

## Youth employment

If not a 'lost generation' as such, then clearly there exists a youth 'problem' that the government has to address. Of the rural population 11 million are aged between 16 and 30 years, which represents nearly 25 per cent of the entire South African population. In 1996 unemployment levels were standing at 55 per cent among young male blacks. Young black men also figured prominently in crime figures. A 1994 ANC statement on the young makes sobering reading: 'The young have been severely disadvantaged by the system of apartheid. As a result many young people face a bleak and hopeless future with little prospects of securing meaningful employment or overcoming a plethora of social and economic difficulties they have to contend with' (African National Congress 1994b: 31). The new democratic government of South Africa now has to deal with the consequences of the youths' struggle against apartheid.

The *Sowetan* reported that there was one issue upon which almost all South Africans, of whatever colour or political affiliation, agree and that is the problem of youth unemployment. Attempts must be made to provide employment for the young (*Sowetan*, 21 June 1994). One of the strategies used to increase employment opportunities for young people is the stimulation of self-employment and small business development. The young have to understand the principles of entrepreneurship and be able to pass this knowledge on to others. But as Pemmy Majodina, the Treasurer-General of the ANC Youth League, states: 'Transformation will be a slow progress' (Majodina interview, 1996). However, there is some evidence of young black entrepreneurial activity. A World Bank study found that the owners of micro-enterprises, those with five or fewer workers, tend to be concentrated in the lower age brackets, with 35 per cent being less than 30 years of age (see Table 5.4). As unemployment tends to be high among this group, the World Bank believed that the connection between unemployment and the creation of micro-enterprises was reinforced.

However, the report asserted that 'the educational level of microentrepreneurs indicates the alternatives open to them, as well as the ability of individuals to manage their business properly' (World Bank 1993: 18). About 30 to 40 per cent have too little education, less than Standard 4 – the level of a ten-year-old – to be functionally literate. Depending on the quality of education, the level of functional literacy could be even lower. However, the study found that on the positive side, about two-thirds of the microentrepreneurs surveyed were functionally literate and could, therefore, potentially keep records and receive formal training.

97

**Table 5.4**  Black micro-enterprises in South Africa, 1992

| Age in years | % of owners | Cumulative % |
|---|---|---|
| 16–20 | 2.0 | 2.0 |
| 21–30 | 33.2 | 35.2 |
| 31–40 | 32.9 | 68.1 |
| 41–50 | 18.2 | 86.3 |
| 51–60 | 8.6 | 94.9 |
| 61 and older | 5.1 | 100 |

*Source*: *Characteristics of and Constraints Facing Black Businesses in South Africa*, World Bank, 1993

**Table 5.5**  Educational level and monthly turnover of black micro-entrepreneurs in South Africa, 1992

| Educational level | % of owners | Cumulative % | Monthly turnover (rand) | Number of firms |
|---|---|---|---|---|
| No education | 8.5 | 8.5 | 1106.38 | 48 |
| Less than Standard 4 | 18.7 | 27.2 | 1111.96 | 102 |
| Standards 4–6 | 33.8 | 61.0 | 1237.00 | 185 |
| Standards 7–9 | 29.8 | 90.8 | 1540.52 | 163 |
| Standard 10 | 7.6 | 98.4 | 2484.55 | 42 |
| Post-school education | 1.6 | 100 | 985.55 | 9 |

*Note*: The sample size is 549 firms. On average, children are ten years old when they enter Standard 4; they have completed five years of schooling and are functionally literate. On completing Standard 8 children are 16 years old. Standard 10, also called Matric, represents the completion of formal education. The exchange rate in 1997 is around 6.8 rands = £1.
*Source*: *Characteristics of and Constraints Facing Black Businesses in South Africa*, World Bank, 1993

A strong positive correlation exists between education and turnover. Micro-entrepreneurs who have achieved a Standard 10 (level for 18-year-old) level of education have an average turnover of nearly twice that of those who have completed only Standard 8 (level for 16-year-old), which is the status of 80 per cent of micro-entrepreneurs. The World Bank maintains that remedial education in basic numeracy and literacy has a potentially strong role to play in improving the capacity of micro-enterprises and should form the basis of further business training. Those entrepreneurs who have received post-secondary schooling have less turnover than uneducated ones, mainly because running a small business is often a short-term survival strategy rather than a long-term commitment. Table 5.5 shows the educational level and monthly turnover of black entrepreneurs.

During 1995, the organization IDASA instituted a process designed to explore such questions as: What will the future hold for young people in Cape Town in 2005? What will the job market offer? What will young people value? How will the choices we are making now impact on the lives of the next generation? Young people were given the task of developing a set of future scenarios of what might happen in ten years' time. Four scenarios developed. First, the 'Dark Forests' scenario depicted a society unable to deal with the weight of its past, lacking in direction and account-ability, suffering poor leadership, struggling for resources and a grow-ing crime rate. Ongoing conflict in the political, economic and educational spheres contributes to a cycle of chaos, mismanagement and disillusionment. In this scenario, a fractured and divided youth lack hope and nurse mutual distrust and resentment. The 'Rocky Mountains' scenario explores a society that highlights individualistic values and achievements but fails to address the inequalities between groups. High-achieving youth have good oppor-tunities but the less able remain undervalued and marginalized. The 'Deep Oceans' scenario points to a society in which democratic systems are work-ing but insufficient attention is paid to citizen responsibilities, which may threaten their long-term survival. Cape Town has become the 'Hollywood of Africa' with a strong international and individualist culture. Youth are largely apolitical. Finally, the 'Blue Skies' scenario envisions a society that has 'successfully developed the capacity and skills to share responsibility. A strong democratic and transparent government is complemented by high levels of public participation in social and political issues. Effective educa-tion programmes have led to a broad understanding of the Constitution, respect for the Bill of Rights and a culture of active citizenship and account-able leadership' (*Democracy in Action*, 15 December 1995).

It is interesting that these scenarios were centred on Cape Town because the Western Cape is largely seen as being atypical on ethnic and social grounds from the wider South Africa. Yet according to Febe Polgieter, the emphasis now is on getting 'black, coloured and white youth to find com-mon ground' (Polgieter interview, 1996). She explains that over the past three or four years young Afrikaaners have been challenging their own polit-ical/religious leadership. These attitudes have been expressed in two ways: either the Afrikaaner youth become more right-wing, or they become alien-ated from society as a whole. As such, they become distanced from their families but not assimilated into the wider black society. There is a disloca-tion and unemployment among white youth (*ibid.*). Equally, some attempt has been made to find commonalities between the IFP Youth League and the ANC Youth League and united rallies have been held. Majodina believes that 'young people must unite under one national anthem' (Majodina inter-view, 1996). The literature celebrating 16 June as a public holiday proclaims it as 'a day for all the youth of South Africa. It is not an anti-Afrikaans day. The youth must actually use this day to promote non-racialism and patriot-ism' (ANC Youth League 1996).

**Table 5.6**  Aims and objectives of the ANC Youth League (ANCYL)

---

*The ANCYL shall:*

1. strive to rally the youth of our country to support and unite behind the ANCYL and actively participate in the struggle to create a non-racial, non-sexist, united democratic and prosperous society;
2. support and reinforce the ANC in the attainment of the goals of the National Democratic Revolution;
3. ensure that the youth make a full and rich contribution to the work of the ANC and to the life of the nation;
4. champion the general interests and rights of the South African Youth in the socio-economic and political life of the country;
5. promote unity and patriotism among the youth;
6. promote the creation of a broad, non-aligned pioneer movement and fight for the rights of children as enshrined in the UN Declaration on Children Rights;
7. strive and work for the educational, moral and cultural upliftment of the youth;
8. promote gender equality in all spheres of life, especially among the youth;
9. promote among the youth the spirit of international solidarity, peace and friendship with other nations.

---

*Source*: Constitution of the ANC Youth League as amended at the 19th National Congress, Durban, March 1996

## ANC Youth League

The ANC Youth League was formed in 1944 and its membership is open to all youth aged between 14 and 35 years of age. Acknowledging that the League has been seen as a 'training ground' for ANC leadership, the broad definition of 'youth' is not without complications. For a start, given the high fertility rate of teenage women, it is quite feasible that by the age of 35 a woman could have a number of children, and perhaps grandchildren. Also, at the age of 35 a number of men would be married with children and responsibilities of their own. To place men and women in early middle-age in the same category as post-pubescent teenagers is clearly inappropriate and anomalous in the new South Africa. These definitions of youth may have been meaningful during the apartheid period and the ANC's years of exile, but they are virtually unsupportable now that the government is obliged to have policies which deal with the 'young'. These contradictions were not fully understood by the leadership of the Youth League, who stressed that 'youth needs to be integrated into the wider national economy' (Polgieter interview, 1996). But which youth: young teenagers at school, school leavers, unemployed 20-year-olds, pregnant and nursing mothers, women who have teenage children, men who are also fathers, the list is as contradictory and unwieldy as it is long. In order for government policies to be effective they have to focus on specific targets. Youth crime has not really been addressed fully, although punishment for under-18-year-olds may be changed (*ibid.*). In 1994 the ANC stated that youth policy should clearly set out concrete programmes to address the problems of youth, with specific emphasis on job creation and entrepreneurship, a national youth service programme, education and training especially aimed at out-of-school youth, and programmes addressing social issues, such as substance abuse, AIDS, abuse, teenage parenthood and crime and delinquency (African National Congress 1994b: 31) (see Table 5.6). Perhaps inevitably, there is simply too much to consider under the general term 'youth'. This, in turn, inevitably restricts the efficacy of government policies.

The Youth League has 1077 branches nationally and is funded by the ANC. Although the League is a separate organization, its policies are guided by the ANC, who would like the League to be strengthened (Majodina interview, 1966). The extent to which South Africa can overcome the profound effects of the struggle against apartheid and transform the country into 'a truly non-racial, democratic and prosperous society' remains one of the central challenges of the twenty-first century (ANC Youth League 1996). What is important, however, is for the nation to adopt the flexibility and willingness to acknowledge the suffering and sacrifices of the past whilst also maintaining the momentum to move into the future. It is a difficult task, but women and the young must help show the way.

# SIX

# Local democracy and electoral processes

The first non-racial South African municipal elections were held on 1 November 1995. The Local Government Transition Act of 1993 made provision for the establishment of non-racial transitional metropolitan councils, transitional local councils, local government co-ordinating committees, sub-regional councils, district councils and transitional councils for rural areas (see Figure 6.1). According to Nelson Mandela, a legitimate and efficient democratic local government would cement democracy in South Africa. The country needed local government to work together with civil society in order to serve the needs of communities (*RSA Review* 1995: 30).

The municipal elections were seen as a gateway through which active relationships could be developed and maintained between elected representatives and respective communities. Active relationships, for example, could be created by establishing forums to provide an arena for public debate on local issues. However, the ideal of democratic and legitimate local government structures does not end simply because municipal elections have taken place. It will be determined by how active the relationships between elected representatives and the community are and how effectively such relationships can be maintained. Yet in order for those elections to take place, certain procedures had to be followed. There had previously been a crisis of legitimacy in local government which had crippled many communities, with poor quality of services or their complete collapse in many areas. Equally, the de-racialization of the divided South African society and the normalization of the social fabric of communities could take place, in effect, only at the local level. In short, as Nelson Mandela stated: 'the local government elections are a continuation of April 27 because there cannot be full democracy without democratic local government' (African National Congress 1994b: 8).

## Local government procedures

Under the terms of the Local Government Transition Act (1993) transitional councils were established and their areas of jurisdiction demarcated before

**Figure 6.1**  Structure of Government, Provincial and Local Constitution 1993

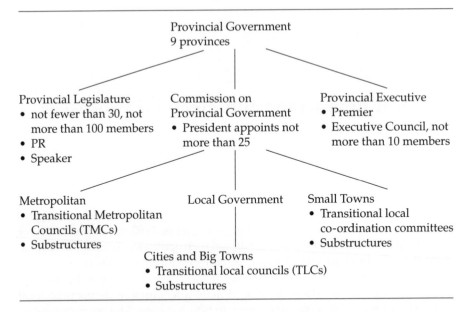

Provincial Government
9 provinces

Provincial Legislature
- not fewer than 30, not more than 100 members
- PR
- Speaker

Commission on Provincial Government
- President appoints not more than 25

Provincial Executive
- Premier
- Executive Council, not more than 10 members

Metropolitan
- Transitional Metropolitan Councils (TMCs)
- Substructures

Local Government

Small Towns
- Transitional local co-ordination committees
- Substructures

Cities and Big Towns
- Transitional local councils (TLCs)
- Substructures

*Source*: South Africa Yearbook 1995

the municipal elections were held. Johnston and Spence maintain that the 1993 Act was a 'hurried piece of legislation' that was passed by the old regime 'in the closing stages of the protracted negotiation process' (Johnston and Spence 1995). According to the Act the premier of a province could demarcate an area of jurisdiction only after the written representations of transitional councils and the advice and written recommendations of the local government demarcation board had been considered. As Figure 6.1 demonstrates, within the Transitional Metropolitan Councils (TMCs) and the Transitional Local Councils (TLCs), substructures are organized. In the case of the Greater Johannesburg Transitional Metropolitan Council (GJTMC) there are four Metropolitan Substructures (MSSs), divided into Western, Northern, Southern and Eastern MSSs. Both the TLCs and TMCs are divided into wards. The number of wards into which a transitional authority is to be demarcated is determined by the number of seats allocated to the transitional authority. Where a transitional authority contains areas covered by former white local authorities, coloured and Indian management committees, and areas covered by former African local authorities, each of these areas must be allocated 50 per cent of the total number of wards in the transitional authority (*RSA Review* 1995: 36). The Local Government Demarcation Board provides the provincial governments with recommendations for the boundaries of the wards. These recommendations are based on the following criteria:

- population figures in the area;
- topographical and physical features of the area;
- accessibility and availability of premises for voting stations.

The certified voters' roll for a transitional authority is divided into wards, and each ward into voting station areas. There had to be a least one voting station in each ward and a maximum number of voters per voting station has been set. In the former African local authority areas, there had to be sufficient voting stations so that no more than 2500 registered voters were within each voting station area and thus on the voters' roll for each voting station. In other areas, there had to be sufficient voting stations so that no more than 4000 registered voters were within each voting station area and therefore on the voter's roll. The number of voters per voting station in rural areas was less than 2500.

In each province the Member of the Executive Council (MEC) for local government determined the number of seats in each transitional authority and in each of its wards. An equal number of seats had to be allocated to each ward. Traditional leaders will be *ex officio* members of the transitional authorities and must be taken into account when determining the number of seats to be allocated to a transitional authority. In the Transitional Local Councils (TLCs) in non-metropolitan urban areas, and in the Transitional Metropolitan Substructures the seats included both those for wards and those for party representatives. Forty per cent of the representatives had to be elected through proportional representation by all the voters registered in the transitional authority. Voters voted for the party of their choice, although parties were not restricted to political groups and included any local organization, body or voluntary association that had objectives and purposes related to local government. Seats were allocated to each party according to the proportion of the total votes it received, and filled in priority order from the list of party members proposed as candidates by each party. Sixty per cent of the representatives were elected directly from candidates standing in each individual ward, by the voters registered in that ward. Separate ballot papers were issued in order that voters could distinguish between the two processes.

In the six Transitional Metropolitan Councils (TMCs) in the country members were elected as follows. Forty per cent of the representatives were elected through proportional representation by all the voters registered in the metropolitan urban council area. Voters chose the party of their choice and seats were allocated to each party according to the proportion of the total vote it received, filled by candidates from the list system. Sixty per cent of the representatives were appointed by the TMSs. Each of these substructures were allocated a number of seats according to its proportion of the total number of registered voters within the TMC area. Each substructure had to have at least one representative on the TMC. In short, voters outside metropolitan areas had two votes, one for an individual candidate to represent a specific ward and another for a political party. However, in metropolitan areas such as Greater Johannesburg, voters had a third vote to be exercised for a political party, which would make up 40 per cent of the TMC seats. The remaining 60 per cent of TMC seats went to MSS representatives elected by ward representatives on the various MSSs. As such, the MSSs are able to keep a check on the TMC as their representatives make up the bulk of the council (*The Star*, 23 January 1995).

For the ANC these transitional councils provided a bridge between the former apartheid system and democratic local government (African National Congress 1994b: 29). Recognizing that in traditional authority areas, chiefs are *ex officio* members of the transitional authority, a resolution was passed at the 1994 conference noting that traditional leaders must be (a) above partisan party politics, (b) involve themselves in a drive for peace and development and (c) serve their whole community (*ibid.*). The TMC in Johannesburg recognized that although organizations change from the 'outside' when restructuring takes place, real change has to happen on the 'inside'. Transformation takes place when people commit themselves to a new culture and a new way of doing things (*GTMC Perspective*, Johannesburg, May 1996). For decades, under the apartheid system, local government had been characterized by bureaucratic inefficiency and inequality in service delivery standards. Local government employees were voiceless, working in a hierarchical organization, characterized by a culture of control, fear and disempowerment. To help people move from this old culture towards new, participative, service-oriented administrations, special training sessions and forums for discussion and communication were established where seminars, workshops and open sessions on local government changes could take place. The Johannesburg TMC presented some ideas on how local government employees could change the old culture of the workforce and forge a new approach:

- Treat everyone as you would like to be treated yourself.
- Eliminate cynicism about the future. Be positive.
- Learn to trust and be trusted.
- Eliminate fear, it stops people from being creative.
- Build a team in your organisation – we all have a common goal: to make this city a better place.
- Look for common ground instead of focusing on diversity.
- Seek out every area for self-development.
- Take personal responsibility for everything you do.
- Take pride in your work and your organisation.
- Don't underestimate the importance of small changes. Little things: a positive attitude, a friendly greeting, listening patiently, half-an-hour's extra effort, all help to make change happen. (*ibid.*)

Developing people skills, changing attitudes and transforming local government into 'a learning organisation which invests in its workforce and helps create a different culture takes time but that is what real transformation is about' (*ibid.*). It is clear that real transformation does not simply take place because an administration changes its name or boundaries – it happens when people, black, white and coloured commit themselves to a new culture and a new way of doing things (*ibid.*).

## Registration and nomination

Nomination day had to be set 40 days before the election day with each TMS within TMC areas agreeing the same day. Applications for the registration of political parties had to be received by the returning officer at least 18 days before nomination day. The application had to include, among other information, the party's list of candidates for the proportional representation election and the symbol to be used against the party's name on the ballot paper. If the application did not conform with requirements, the returning officer had to advise the party of the defects in order that any necessary amendments could be made. Political parties whose applications for registration had been accepted were announced by the returning officer on the afternoon of nomination day. A list of these parties, their distinguishing symbols and their candidates had to be published by the returning officer within 21 days of election day (*RSA Review* 1995).

Nominations of persons as candidates in a ward election had to be received by the returning officer for the transitional authority at least 18 days before nomination day. The candidate had to be qualified to be nominated and the nomination had to be supported by 2 per cent of the number of voters on the voters' roll for the ward. The ward candidate could propose a symbol to be placed against his or her name on the ballot paper. Then the same procedure was followed as for political parties. Although candidates for a ward election could not be nominated in more than one ward, a person could be nominated for a ward election and also be a candidate on a party for a proportional representation election. But the person could not be elected to both these positions, the place on the party list being lost if the candidate was elected as a ward representative.

Initially, the registration of voters was scheduled to take place over a 90-day period, commencing in all the provinces except the Eastern Transvaal and KwaZulu Natal on 27 January 1995 and ending on 28 April 1995. In the Eastern Transvaal registration commenced on 26 January 1995 with the original deadline set on 28 April 1995. In KwaZulu Natal the 90-day period started on 3 February 1995 and the original deadline was 3 May 1995. Due to slow registration the government decided to extend the registration period in all provinces for five weeks to 5 June 1995. This extension was made possible by separating the delimitation of wards from the completion of voters' rolls for the election. The original idea was to use the level of registration as the basis for the delimitation of wards. However, because of delays in elector registration, population figures from the Department of Home Affairs and of the Central Statistical Service were used. Every South African who wished to vote on 1 November 1995 had to register as a voter in order that his/her name could be included in the voters' roll for the area in which he/she was eligible to vote. If a person's name was not on the voters' roll he/she was not allowed to vote. There were a number of reasons why the registration of voters was required. In the local government elections, representatives were elected to represent what, in a national and provincial context, were relatively small geographic areas. Voters' rolls were a prerequisite to enable only voters who were eligible to vote within each of these small specific areas to elect their local representatives democratically. Registration also provided a control measure to ensure that only those qualified to vote in the election were able to cast a vote. It also assisted in providing effective service to voters in that it made it easier to determine the number of voting stations required, their location and the quantity of election material.

A person qualified to register as a voter for a transitional authority if he/she was:

- a South African citizen or had been granted permanent residency in South Africa;
- 18 years of age or older; of sound mind, and possessing valid South African identity documents, or a temporary identity certificate or valid travel documents or a book of life issued by the former homelands of Transkei, Bophuthatswana, Venda or Ciskei;
- not a prisoner sentenced without the option of a fine following conviction for murder, robbery with aggravating circumstances and rape, or for attempting to commit these offences; or a person detained under drug dependency, prevention and treatment laws;
- 'ordinarily resident' in that transitional authority or liable to pay rates, rent, service charges or levies to that transitional authority.

Each transitional authority appointed a voters' roll officer who was responsible for the administration of the registration of voters in that authority. In rural areas where there are very few existing local government administrative structures, provincial governments appointed agents to administer registration and election processes. Each person was allowed to register only once in a single transitional authority. Should a person qualify to register both on the grounds of residence and on the grounds of liability for payment of rates, rent, service charges or levies, he/she had to choose only one of these addresses for which to claim registration. In exceptional circumstances, where an applicant claimed to be 'ordinarily resident' at both these addresses in a single transitional authority, he/she had to decide which residence to choose. Applicants had to be able to attend the voting station in the area in which they were registered in order to be able to vote on election day. Table 6.1 shows how information was given to the Johannesburg electorate in the media.

At the close of the registration period on 5 June 1995 the voters' roll officer in each transitional authority had to prepare a preliminary voters' roll, listing alphabetically all applicants whose claims for registration as a voter had been accepted. This list was then made available for public

**Table 6.1**  Your questions about municipal voting answered

| Question | Answer |
| --- | --- |
| Can I use a passport to register? | No, only a valid ID document can be used |
| If I have a business in Greater Jo'burg and live in Pretoria can I vote in both areas? | No, voters can only vote within one ward |
| Can I choose where I wish to vote? | No, voters can only vote in the ward in which they ordinarily reside |
| As a ratepayer, am I automatically registered? | No, the onus is on the voter to ensure they have been registered |
| Can I, as a migrant worker, vote at my family home? | No, registration takes place where voters ordinarily reside |
| Can I cast my vote from my holiday destination overseas? | No, there will be no special votes and voters will have to be present in their wards on the day of voting |

*Source*: *The Star*, 23 January 1995

inspection for 14 days at the offices of the transitional authority. If a person believed the he/she was entitled to be on the voters' roll it was possible to lodge a claim for registration. Equally, during this period it was possible for any person to object to the inclusion of another person on the roll and that objection would have to be presented at a Revision Court hearing.

A Revision Court consisted of three persons, appointed by the transitional authority. More than one court could be appointed. The court was able to consider all objections to the names of persons being included on the voters' roll and any matter concerning a claim for registration. The preliminary voters' roll could then be amended to give effect to the decisions of the Revision Court. The electoral roll used for the election was certified by the presiding officer of the court. Each transitional authority had to establish an Election Committee whose functions included the resolving of disputes between electoral roll officers and other parties. Also, it could adjudicate on any dispute over the use of symbols for candidates or parties on ballot papers.

## Voter education

In a sense, although the rules, regulations and processes for the local government elections of 1995 were meticulous, there was one essential feature upon which the introduction of electoral suffrage depended: voter education. Precise instructions about how to vote for the Constituent Assembly had been presented to the electorate by the ANC (see Figure 6.2) and before

**Figure 6.2** How to make your X for freedom step-by-step

# HOW TO MAKE YOUR X FO

## 1 Vote for a Constituent Assembly

The elections will be for a Constituent Assembly (CA)

The CA is a body where all the different parties will be represented. The number of people each party will have in the CA will depend on how many people vote for it.

The party with the highest number of votes will have the most number of people in the CA.

The CA will draw up the new constitution

For us to get rid of apartheid once and for all we must have a new constitution. All the laws of a country are based on the constitution. For us to have a democratic country we to must have a democratic constitution. If the ANC has the highest number of people in the CA it will be able to draw up a democratic constitution.

**MAKE YOUR X FOR FREEDOM**

## 2

If you are 18 years and older then you must make sure you have an identification document (ID). The ID book will be one of those used. You will also be able to get a voter card by using a baptismal or birth certificate.

## 5

The voting booth is a special place where you can make your X for freedom. Your vote is secret. No one will be able to see who you are voting for.

## 6

| AFRICAN DEMOCRATIC MOVEMENT |
| AFRICAN NATIONAL CONGRESS |
| CONSERVATIVE PARTY |
| DEMOCRATIC PARTY |
| NATIONAL PARTY |

You must make your X on the ballot form you want. You must make the X only once. No one can tell afterwards which organisati for. Your name will not appear on the form.

*Source*: ANC Youth League, *Horizon* No. 2, 1993

# FREEDOM STEP-BY-STEP

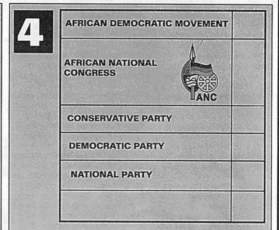

| | | |
|---|---|---|
| **AFRICAN DEMOCRATIC MOVEMENT** | | |
| **AFRICAN NATIONAL CONGRESS** | ANC | |
| **CONSERVATIVE PARTY** | | |
| **DEMOCRATIC PARTY** | | |
| **NATIONAL PARTY** | | |
| | | |

On the day of the elections you must go to your nearest voting station. That is the place where you will be making your X for the ANC. You must take your ID to the voting station and show it to the officials there.

The officials will check to see if you have voted already. You will be given a form to fill in. This is called the ballot form. It has the names of all the parties on it. With this form you must go to the voting booth.

e party
block.
u voted

You must then put your ballot form into the ballot box where it will be kept locked-up. It will only be opened by a member of the Independent Elections Commission.

You will then have ink put on your hand. This is so everyone votes only once. Then the Independent Elections Commission will count all the votes.

Table 6.2   Voters reached by radio, TV and the press

|  | All South Africans | Black South Africans |
|---|---|---|
| Radio | 68% | 78% |
| Radio & TV | 87% | 90% |
| Radio, TV & Press | 88% | 91% |

*Source*: Moller and Hanf 1995: 8

the 1994 election the media brought voter education messages to a large number of potential voters throughout the country. The headlines in the 1994 *Let's Vote* voter education manual were: 'Find out what is going on \ Listen to the radio \ Watch television \ Read the newspapers \ Go to meetings \ Ask people to explain things to you' (Moller and Hanf 1995: 7). Radio and TV both played an extremely important role in voter education at that time but as Moller and Hanf point out, the messages reached different groups of voters, with radio reaching a larger proportion of black voters and television reaching larger proportions of coloured, Indian and white voters. Perhaps inevitably, radio broadcasts in African languages reached more black voters than broadcasts in English or Afrikaans. Table 6.2 shows the percentage of voters reached by radio, TV and newspapers. As Table 6.3 indicates, newspapers brought voter education to smaller numbers of voters, 41 per cent, which is partly related to high levels of illiteracy rates within the country as a whole.

Voter education materials took different forms. Oral presentations and pamphlets were the most widespread methods of communicating voter information to more than 60 per cent of the electorate. A variety of films, videos, role playing, mock elections and workshops were presented. Comic books and picture books were widely used, especially among black audiences. Yet as Moller and Hanf suggest, more active forms of media presentations were favoured by younger and better educated black voters, whilst comic books on voting found greater appeal among illiterate voters. Political parties played a role in the education campaign, although the ANC was considered to be the most active political agency. In fact, Nelson Mandela announced to the ANC National Conference in 1994 that the party's 'emphasis on voter education had served the ANC well in the April election' (African National Congress 1994b: 8). In table 6.4 respondents were asked had they received voter information from political parties and clearly the 78 per cent registered for the ANC far exceeds the percentages for other parties. A number of resolutions on local government were passed at the 1994 ANC National Conference including one which recognized the need to establish 'democratic, non-racial and non-sexist local government throughout South Africa' (*ibid.*: 29).

**Table 6.3**   Sources of voter information (all voters)

| Media | Total % | Black % | Coloured % | Indian % | White % |
|---|---|---|---|---|---|
| *Radio* | 68 | 78 | 51 | 66 | 49 |
| *African Langs | 51 | 77 | 11 | 8 | 4 |
| *English/Afrikaans | 31 | 20 | 50 | 65 | 47 |
| | | | | | |
| *TV* | 66 | 61 | 79 | 89 | 72 |
| *English/Afrikaans | 46 | 31 | 75 | 88 | 70 |
| *African Langs | 41 | 57 | 26 | 22 | 10 |
| Watch TV on weekdays | 72 | 61 | 86 | 92 | 95 |
| | | | | | |
| *Newspapers* | 41 | 37 | 42 | 70 | 46 |
| Read daily newspapers | 39 | 34 | 50 | 58 | 49 |
| | | | | | |
| *Personal Network* | | | | | |
| Family | 57 | 63 | 60 | 60 | 39 |
| Friends/Neighbours | 54 | 64 | 61 | 55 | 26 |
| Work/School | 25 | 28 | 26 | 27 | 16 |
| Church | 22 | 28 | 21 | 12 | 6 |
| | | | | | |
| *Extended Network* | | | | | |
| Political Party | 43 | 54 | 36 | 28 | 18 |
| Voter education | 36 | 49 | 26 | 13 | 9 |
| Trade Union | 6 | 8 | 6 | 6 | 1 |

*Source*: Moller and Hanf 1995

**Table 6.4**   Voter education by political parties
(all South Africans)

| | |
|---|---|
| African National Congress | 78% |
| National Party | 10% |
| Inkatha Freedom Party | 5% |
| Democratic Party | 2% |

*Source*: Moller and Hanf 1995

In Moller and Hanf's study all respondents were asked the question: 'Of what you learned about voting, which information was very important or useful to you?' (Moller and Hanf 1995: 17). The responses are outlined in Table 6.5.

The secrecy of the vote was identified in 1994 as a particularly important component of the electoral process by all South Africans. However, the fact

**Table 6.5**  Useful voter information (all voters)

| | Total % | Black % | Coloured % | Indian % | White % |
|---|---|---|---|---|---|
| My vote is secret | 80 | 94 | 78 | 78 | 45 |
| I can vote for whom I please | 76 | 83 | 83 | 79 | 54 |
| My right to vote or not | 68 | 75 | 77 | 64 | 48 |
| How to vote: procedures at polling station | 64 | 79 | 74 | 65 | 21 |
| Which documents entitle me to vote and how to get them | 54 | 69 | 70 | 62 | 11 |
| The difference between the first and second ballot | 49 | 61 | 43 | 65 | 20 |
| I can vote for the same or different parties on the two ballots | 42 | 46 | 41 | 56 | 29 |

*Source*: Moller and Hanf 1995: 17

that it is the most important factor for black voters, 94 per cent (Table 6.5), has been seen as partly explaining the extremely slow registration of many black voters for the local government elections in 1995 ('Blacks reluctant to register for election', *The Citizen*, 26 January 1995). According to a survey conducted by the Community Agency for Social Enquiry (CASE) many black voters believed that by registering for the local elections they would be jeopardizing their secret ballots. The Cape-based organization Project Vote commissioned CASE to survey 15 focus groups within black, Asian and coloured populations in November and December 1994. The CASE study, led by Dr David Everatt, found that voters saw the registration process as 'violating the secrecy of the ballot'. They could not understand why the procedures of the 1994 election were not good enough for the local elections. Indeed, some older people were afraid of giving their names and addresses (Everatt 1995). Everatt saw these attitudes as almost inevitable given the stress placed on the secrecy of the ballot during the voter education campaign before the April 1994 election. At that time the *Let's Vote* manual stated: 'Remember: Your vote is a secret. Nobody will know who you vote for. Nobody can see who you vote for. You can vote for any party you want. If people ask you who you are going to vote for, you do not have to tell them' (Moller and Hanf 1995: 25). In fact, with levels of intimidation reportedly running very high, secrecy was of the utmost importance (Mzizi interview, 1996). In Moller and Hanf's study, '65 per cent or two-thirds of black voters indicated that they kept their vote secret' (Moller and Hanf 1995: 26).

The Local Government Elections Task Group co-chairman, Khehla Shubane, expressed scepticism at the study's other general findings, that is,

**Table 6.6**  Is voting in local government elections important?

|  | Total % | African % | White % | Coloured % | Indian % |
|---|---|---|---|---|---|
| Voting is important | 71 | 74 | 69 | 62 | 67 |
| In between | 10 | 10 | 8 | 12 | 14 |
| Waste of time | 16 | 13 | 21 | 17 | 18 |
| Don't know | 4 | 4 | 3 | 9 | 0 |

*Source*: IDASA 1996c

**Table 6.7**  Will local government elections make things better?

|  | Total % | African % | White % | Coloured % | Indian % |
|---|---|---|---|---|---|
| Better | 69 | 76 | 48 | 62 | 64 |
| No difference | 18 | 14 | 28 | 21 | 31 |
| Worse | 7 | 4 | 19 | 6 | 2 |
| Don't know | 7 | 7 | 4 | 12 | 4 |

*Source*: IDASA 1996c

there appeared to be confusion among sections of the black electorate about local government structures and elections and a level of discontent about the pace of change since April 1994 (*The Star*, 26 January 1995). In fact, an IDASA survey presented some extremely contradictory findings, with high percentages being scored on questions such as: Is voting in local government elections important? and Will local government elections make a difference? (See Tables 6.6 and 6.7).

Looking at black African responses, 74 per cent felt that voting in the local government elections was important and 76 per cent believed that the elections would make things better. It would be difficult to make a more stark contrast with the CASE findings. Yet when the time came for voting in the November 1995 local elections the turnout rate was 38 per cent as against an 86 per cent turnout rate in April 1994 (IDASA 1996c; Johnson 1996: 304). Table 6.8 outlines the voter turnout in all provinces with the exception of KwaZulu Natal. The voter turnout table was based on figures released by the Local Election Task Group(LETG) but as IDASA points out there can be different interpretations of the figures depending on which percentage is being considered. The LETG tended to emphasize voter turnout as a percentage of registered voters which gives a figure of 67 per cent at its highest in the Western Cape and 50 per cent at its lowest in Mpumalanga. Alternatively, if the turnout is seen as a percentage of eligible voters, it

**Table 6.8**   Voter turnout in local elections 1995

| Province | Actual voter turnout (number) | Voter turnout as % of registered voters | Voter turnout as % of eligible voters |
|---|---|---|---|
| Western Cape | 339 068 | 67% | 60% |
| Northern Cape | 219 373 | 64% | 55% |
| Eastern Cape | 1 254 235 | 46% | 35% |
| North West | 641 948 | 46% | 38% |
| Free State | 575 654 | 49% | 38% |
| Gauteng | 1 774 539 | 48% | 36% |
| Northern Province | 763 617 | 44% | 38% |
| Mpumalanga | 565 218 | 50% | 36% |
| Total | 6 133 652 | 48% | 38% |

*Source*:  IDASA 1996c

is much lower at 60 per cent for the Western Cape and only 36 per cent for Mpumalanga. The total turnout rate is either 48 per cent or 38 per cent, depending on how it is viewed. However, it is recognized that voter registration was low, more than 8 million, some 35 per cent of the country's estimated 23.4 million eligible voters failed to register by the closing date (*Africa Today* November/December 1995).

The *Let's Vote* 1994 education manual exhorted people to vote: 'It is very important to vote \ Everybody should vote \ This is our chance to build a new South Africa', and the electorate responded with enthusiasm (Johnson and Schlemmer 1996: 304). Most analysts would tend to agree that the most obvious measure of the success of a voter education campaign is a high electoral turnout (*Africa Today* 1995: 17). This certainly occurred in 1994, but what can be said of the poor turnout in 1995? Was it a failure of voter education? Well, first, the issue is not so straightforward as it initially may appear. It must be remembered that the voter education campaign before the April 1994 elections was conducted during periods of violence and widespread intimidation in some regions. In fact, a month before the elections, 'operation access' was launched to ensure that voters could be reached in areas dominated by a single party' (Moller and Hanf 1995: 21). As such, a pamphlet campaign was started in remote areas and in districts where there was political opposition to voter education. By April 1994 more than 90 per cent of the electorate had received some form of voter education (*ibid.*). Yet there were still bomb scares, racial violence and division. In fact, the four-year transition period from February 1990 to April 1994 has been seen as a time of 'unprecedented political violence' (*Africa World Review* 1995: 5). According to Cheryl Carolus: 'Two weeks before the 27 April 1994 I was not sure that the elections would take place at all' (Carolus interview,

**Table 6.9**  Motivations to vote in the 27 April 1994 elections
(black and white voters)

|  | All voters % | Black voters % | White voters % |
|---|---|---|---|
| I wanted to support my party | 97 | 98 | 94 |
| I felt proud to take part in the first elections for all South Africans | 91 | 97 | 74 |
| I am sure my vote was secret | 91 | 92 | 87 |
| When you get the opportunity to vote, you should use it | 89 | 88 | 91 |
| I knew the voting procedures well | 84 | 81 | 92 |
| There were enough monitors and security personnel at the voting station | 89 | 89 | 88 |
| There were no security problems | 86 | 84 | 89 |
| There were many voters at the polling station and I had to wait a long time | 63 | 77 | 32 |
| I had to travel a long way but I went to the polls anyway | 30 | 39 | 12 |

*Source*: Moller and Hanf 1995: p34

1996). So it would be misleading to present a picture of a calm and peaceful political environment before the 1994 elections. As Johnson and Schlemmer state, a number of voters anticipated the election with 'worry and anxiety' (Johnson and Schlemmer 1996: 106). Yet 86 per cent of the electorate participated in that historic occasion and cast their votes. Moller and Hanf surveyed the motivations of voters as outlined in Table 6.9. They found that the majority of black and white voters wanted to support their party but for black voters, pride in participating in their first elections was equally important (Moller and Hanf 1995: 34).

So why was there a dramatic drop in the turnout rate for the local government elections in November 1995? The Project Vote director, Fr Michael Weeder, pointed to some deficiency in voter education when he predicted: 'South Africa's first democratic local election could be doomed to a low voter turnout . . . without the necessary resources and attention in voter education' (*The Citizen*, 26 September 1995). CASE director, Dr David Everatt, said that media campaigns to encourage registration would have to explain the purpose of local government elections (*ibid.*). In a sense, it seems ironic that whilst the ANC was emphasizing local, democratic, non-sexist and non-racial modes of political participation and other commentators were pointing to the need for a high voter turnout in the local elections in order to establish a 'culture of democracy', ordinary members of the community were seemingly uncertain as to what 'local government' actually was. As one Sowetan male expressed: 'We can't go and vote when we hardly know

**Table 6.10**   Percentage of vote (by party)

| Party | % of the vote |
|---|---|
| African National Congress | 66.37 |
| National Party | 16.22 |
| Freedom Front | 4.03 |
| Democratic Party | 3.15 |
| Pan Africanist Congress | 1.42 |
| Inkatha Freedom Party | 0.71 |
| African Christian Democratic Party | 0.59 |
| Ratepayer Associations | 2.16 |
| Others | 3.18 |

*Source*: Johnston and Spence 1995

**Table 6.11**   Distribution of seats nationwide (by party)

| Party | % of seats |
|---|---|
| African National Congress | 63.78 |
| National Party | 16.43 |
| Freedom Front | 1.93 |
| Democratic Party | 0.75 |
| Pan Africanist Congress | 0.35 |
| African Christian Democratic Party | 0.03 |
| Ratepayer associations | 4.29 |
| Other parties | 6.14 |
| Independent candidates | 8.53 |

*Source*: Johnston and Spence 1995

who to vote for ... We need to know them (the candidates) and each one must tell us what he is going to do for us' (African Nation Congress 1994b; *Africa Today* 1995: 17). Nevertheless, as Johnston and Spence assert, the results of the 1995 elections indicated that 'although South Africa has a functioning multiparty system, the ANC is very much the dominant party' (Johnston and Spence 1995) (see Tables 6.10 and 6.11).

## Analysis of the 1995 local elections

One of the many anomalous aspects to emerge from the 1995 local elections was the disparity in survey responses. In the IDASA survey, when respondents were asked on election day, 'Did you vote?', over 70 per cent of people reported that they had voted. As Paul Graham reports: 'Even allowing for over-reporting of socially desirable behaviour, it is hard to reconcile this

figure with the Local Election Task Group's report of a 38 per cent turnout.'
He argues that this might be explained by closely examining the accuracy
of the national census figures and/or the accuracy of electoral rolls (IDASA
1996a: i–ii). During the 1994 electoral campaign, the *Let's Vote* voter education manual, when dealing with the issue of intimidation, stated: 'You do
not have to answer any questions from anyone about how you are going to
vote. If someone forces you to give an answer, you do not have to tell them
the truth' (Moller and Hanf 1995: 25). It could be possible that an element
of confusion may have arisen in the interpretation given to this section by
voters. When this section is taken together with the emphasis on the secrecy
of the ballot, it may be that these two factors were unintentionally muddled. Hence, when voters were questioned in surveys as to whether they
had voted or not, they may have given a wrong answer. In fact, other public
opinion surveys have detected 'a large lie factor' in respondents who 'disguise their preferences' when questioned about voting intentions (KwaZulu
Natal Briefing No. 2, May 1996 in Johnson and Schlemmer 1996). As Paul
Graham states: 'Shortly before the elections, indications were that the majority of voting age South Africans were planning to vote, some 84 per cent.
Yet after the elections were over, the official voter turnout was not much
better than a third of the voting age population' (IDASA 1996c: i).

For Graeme Gotz of the Centre for Policy Studies, the fact that voters
were hesitant to register was not surprising: 'Without a clear and stable image
of government to buy into, what point was there to expose oneself to the
perplexities and potential risks of putting one's name on a roll' (Gotz 1995:
13). He believes that the local government elections were undermined by
'a lack of capacity and confusion over the role of government'. These disadvantages were combined with an 'insensitivity' that alientated potential
voters (*ibid.*). Certainly, the CASE study suggested there was not an appropriately focused message getting over to the voters, or as Paul Graham puts
it, 'the stuff of elections was missing' (Everatt 1995, IDASA 1996c). Graham
argues that non-partisan information about the importance of voting in community elections dominated the media, a campaign which was constructed
by the advertising company Saatchi and Saatchi. Yet 'party campaigning,
getting out the vote activities and candidate information were all limited'
(*ibid.*). Gotz maintains that the very act of registering and voting displays
trust in a political system which has the 'potential to improve lives' (Gotz
1995). This was not made apparent to the electorate before the local elections. As the IDASA survey makes clear: 'In the final weeks preceding the
elections, about one-third of respondents could not tell us the name of any
candidates standing in their area' (IDASA 1996c: ii). The parties failed to
mobilize or stimulate interest among voters.

On balance, the IDASA survey indicated that there were two fundamental reasons for the low turnout: first, lack of specific technical knowledge about the elections and second, a lack of interest in the campaign (see
Tables 6.12 and 6.13). Whilst Table 6.13 shows there would appear not to be

**Table 6.12**  Do you feel confident that you understand the voting
system for the local elections?

|  | Total % | African % | White % | Coloured % | Indian % |
|---|---|---|---|---|---|
| Very confident | 30 | 26 | 37 | 41 | 29 |
| Confident | 31 | 31 | 32 | 24 | 39 |
| Not very confident | 25 | 27 | 20 | 22˙ | 24 |
| Not confident at all | 12 | 13 | 8 | 10 | 8 |
| Don't know | 2 | 3 | 3 | 3 | 0 |

*Source*: IDASA 1996c

**Table 6.13**  Interest in the 1995 campaign

|  | Total % | African % | White % | Coloured % | Indian % |
|---|---|---|---|---|---|
| Very much interested | 15 | 17 | 11 | 15 | 10 |
| Somewhat interested | 38 | 39 | 41 | 35 | 29 |
| Not much interested | 45 | 43 | 47 | 50 | 59 |
| Don't know | 2 | 1 | 1 | 0 | 2 |

*Source*: IDASA 1996c

exceptionally high levels of interest in the local elections, there is a combined total of 53 per cent in the 'very' and 'somewhat interested' categories.
Equally, Table 6.12 shows 61 per cent of the respondents answered that
they were 'confident' or 'very confident' that they understood the voting
system for the elections. IDASA believe these figures to be low, although a
rating of 61 per cent in terms of confidence might be viewed as relatively
high. In terms of 'interest' in the elections, a racial breakdown is necessary,
as Indian respondents registered lower 'interest' figures than 'non-interest'
rates: 39 per cent against 59 per cent.

Apart from the electorate's uncertainties about the campaign, there were
organizational problems which had to be overcome, that is, the inexperi-
ence of task groups which had been hastily established to run the elections,
together with management inadequacies (Gotz 1995: 12–13). In the Gauteng
area, it was alleged that 14 ballot boxes were lost during the elections (Mzizi
interview, 1996). Van Zyl Slabbert, co-chairman of the Task Group for the
Local Government Elections, considered the difficulties confronting the project some four months before the elections actually took place and admitted
that in future campaigns 'new mechanisms' would have to be created in
order to process elections (*The Star*, 11 July 1996). However, for Johnston and
Spence, the fact that the elections took place at all 'represented a triumph of

hope over experience' once it became clear that devising a 'fair, legitimate and efficient system of local government was a mammoth task' (Johnston and Spence 1995).

## Reconstruction and Development Programme

Prior to the local elections the ANC stressed the importance of local government in forging socio-economic progress. Nelson Mandela stated at the 1994 National Conference that 'local government is the arms and legs of the Reconstruction and Development Programme (RDP)'. A resolution was passed that all local governments were to establish RDP offices and standing committees in their councils and that an integrated campaign for socio-economic transformation be launched (African National Congress 1994b: 29). The RDP originally described itself as 'an integrated socio-economic framework aimed at building a democratic, non-racial and non-sexist community' (*RDP Vision* 1995). It was originally the creation of the ANC, SACP, COSATU, the South African National Civics Organisation (SANCO) and the national Education Co-ordinating Committee. It contained six basic principles which underpinned its political and economic philosophy:

1. The programme had to be integrated and sustainable.
2. Development was not about the delivery of goods to a passive citizenry. It was about active involvement and growing empowerment.
3. It must ensure peace and security for all. There must be a national drive for peace and endemic violence must be combated. Action must be taken against drug-trafficking, gun-running, lawlessness, abuse of women.
4. RDP must embark upon nation-building. Observe respect and protection for minorities. 'Unity in diversity' is the slogan.
5. Improve infrastructure, extend modern and effective services.
6. Through democratisation, people should participate in decision-making. Government must be accountable. Special attention must be paid to the empowerment of women in general and of black, rural women in particular (*ibid.*).

The RDP grouped into major policy areas:
- meeting basic needs of the people
- developing human resources
- building the economy
- democratising the State and South African society
- implementation of programmes (*Infospec* 1994)

Meeting the basic needs of the people essentially meant jobs, land, housing, water, electricity, telecommunication, transport, a clean and healthy environment, nutrition, health care and social welfare. It was hoped that people would be involved in these programmes by participating in deciding where infrastructure should be located, by being employed in its construction, and by being empowered to manage and administer these large scale pro-grammes (*ibid.*). The developing human resources policy area included education from primary to tertiary level, from child care to advanced scien-tific and technological training. It was also concerned with training and the empowerment of youth so they could be enabled to reach their true poten-tial. Building the economy had to focus on certain aspects: linking recon-struction and development, industry, trade and commerce, resource-based industries, upgrading infrastructure, and labour and working rights. Past policies of labour exploitation and repression had to be redressed and the imbalances of power between employers and workers corrected. Democrat-ization of the state was an essential component and it was concerned with the Constitution, the Bill of Rights, the administration of justice, the role of the police and security forces, civil society and local, provincial and national government (*RDP News*, January 1995).

In order for the RDP to be implemented, specific structures had to be in place. Their functions would include:

1. Managing policy and determining spending priorities.
2. Co-ordinating resources and actions.
3. Establishing legislature, procedural, institutional and financial frame-works to ensure the implementation of policies.
4. Ensuring adequate funding of integrated programmes and that re-sources reach targeted communities.
5. Conflict management.
6. Ensuring a stable macro-economic policy environment (*ibid.*)

As such, the RDP would be involved with the economy, job creation, hous-ing, public transport, health care and emergency services, natural resources, welfare and land. The practical implementation of such policies always pre-sented difficulties, although attempts were made through the Community Development Project to promote information about a range of issues, includ-ing the redistribution of land. However, in a study of township economic infrastructures, Coetzee and Naude point to the financial costs and fiscal subsidies that would be necessary in order to vastly improve disadvantaged communities (Coetzee and Naude 1995). After the 1994 elections, the RDP almost became a political mantra and every policy had to be considered within the framework of RDP. An RDP Fund was established but it quickly appeared that the costs of funding such a venture could be exhorbitant, although an initial budget of R2.5 billion had been set aside for Presidential projects. However, complaints began to be made that the RDP had become a bureaucratic organization. Communities were asked to present business plans to the RDP, which for ill-educated rural dwellers was simply imposs-ible. In a section of the RDP newsletter, devoted to informing groups how to apply for money, long and tortuous procedures had to be followed. There were 36 Presidential Lead Projects which focused on the provision of water, child feeding schemes, free medical care for pregnant women and children under five years of age and the provision of electricity. People were instructed to apply within those areas but they could not apply directly to the national RDP offices. Initially, they had to go, with their business plans, to a provincial co-ordinator. If the provincial co-ordinator approved the application, it would be referred to the provincial cabinet for approval. If the application gained the approval of the cabinet, only then could it be referred to the RDP office (*RDP News*, October 1995; Barnes 1996). By January 1995 all local communities had been encouraged to develop their own Reconstruction and Development Programmes and to set their own priorities. According to *RDP Vision* this meant that all aspects of society should be examined to ensure that:

- waste is eliminated
- resources are redirected
- people pay for what they receive to the best of their ability
- no racial and gender inequities occur
- communities participate in programmes and accept ownership of those programmes (*RDP Vision* 1995)

By shifting the focus of the RDP to the local level and by channelling resources to the various departments dealing with housing, education and so on, a death knell was sounded for programme: 'The RDP became no longer significant' (Wessels interview, 1996). By April 1996 the RDP office was dismantled, with some commentators believing it collapsed under the weight of its own 'grand vision' (Caliguire 1996). The programme had failed to meet both the public's expectations and its own stated goals. Caliguire argues that the most notable area of failure was in housing. Initially, the construction of one million houses within five years was the target set. In two years the government built 15 000 houses. In a sense, the RDP could never fully reach its objectives: they were over-ambitious from the beginning. However, it was useful as a means of galvanizing attention and interest in the economy and social redress during the post-election transitional period. Nevertheless, the profound socio-economic problems the RDP raised remain unresolved and confront local and provincial government.

## Post-1995 local government

Irrespective of the low turnout for the 1995 elections, those who were elected had to confront and deal with pressing, basic issues. Loretta King, Councillor on the Southern Metropolitan Substructure in Soweto, outlined the council's development framework. The supply of electricity had been provided to 80 per cent of homes, and the next policy was to promote shops and light industry to complement indigenous cottage industries. A clean-up scheme had been introduced and a community-based refuge clearance programme was running (King interview, 1996). Councillor Sophie Masite, the Mayor of Soweto, spoke of the need to ultimately desegregate the community, but for the next three years until 1999 there had to be a process of 'visible change' (Masite interview, 1996). People clearly needed services, but it was important for the local community to learn to take responsibility and to attempt to govern themselves. It was essential that the community worked together. She was very pleased with the 'community policing forums' which had been established in order to control crime. There also had to be a process of economic empowerment, in that the economic base of the community had to be built up. Yet Sophie Masite readily recognized the need to have an organized rates system and to institute an understanding within the community that services had to be paid for. As such, the executive committee of the council of Soweto had introduced a Rates System Account, which allowed people to pay something towards their rates on a regular basis (*ibid.*). The executive committee comprises eleven people, three of whom are women and the ANC is the majority party. There was a time in the past, said Masite, that black women felt themselves not to be equal but now they were 'very strong in the new South African democracy'.

The Mayor of Pietermaritzburg-Msunduzi, Omar Latiff described the problems facing his council: 'We have essentially two cities: one with all the infrastructure; the other with no services, no water, no lights, no parks. It's time to bridge that gap' (*Democracy in Action*, 1 September 1996). He was pleased that the position of mayor was no longer a figurehead position and that as an executive post the mayor could take direct responsibility for ensuring the council delivered to the electorate. The problems facing Omar Latiff are not dissimilar to those confronting other local governments: arrears and non-payment for services partly caused by an unemployment rate of 50 per cent (*ibid.*). Aggrey Klaaste believes that the majority of South Africans will remain poor for the immediate future (*The Sowetan*, 10 June 1996). Attempting to rebuild a community culture which recognizes that rents and rates must be paid is an exceptionally difficult issue for local government, especially as 65 per cent of people in black townships are not paying for their services (Johnston and Spence 1995).

National government set up a R30 million (£5 million) Masakhane Campaign aimed at encouraging communities to pay for services. The word 'Masakhane' means 'Let us build each other' in Nguni. When the campaign was launched by the Minister of Housing in May 1995 there were optimistic statements: 'The Masakhane Campaign is about participation, responsibility, community spirit, transformation, a better life for the people through the efforts of the people assisted by the government and business' (*RSA Review* 1995). The campaign aimed at accelerating the delivery of basic services and housing and stimulating economic development by promoting the resumption of payment for rents, rates and bond instalments. However, the boycotts make it very difficult for the partnership between government and the private sector to bring improved services to townships. In fact, non-payment for services has been singled out as the one factor that could destroy local government (*ibid.*).

The campaign was scheduled to end in December 1995, but the results were so poor that the cabinet decided to extend its life span. Critics of the campaign maintain that it has failed to involve local democratic structures (Ngwema 1996). As Khela Shubane asserts: 'What is absolutely clear is that there just isn't any political reason for people to continue boycotting payment. If people don't pay for services, the responsible authority must ensure that they don't receive services' (*The Star*, 11 January 1995). Yet collection procedures have to be organized and people must be clear in their own minds exactly what they are paying for. As Sipho Ngwema points out, ignorance among residents has to be combated. People often have not understood the distinction between services and rents and are uncertain as to what services actually are. One interviewee stated: 'I will never pay for water. We have drunk free water for years', without realizing that water had to be purified or that the main water supply system had to be maintained (Ngwema 1996). Inadequate institutional capacity complicates the situation further: 'Even if I don't pay, nothing will happen to me' (*ibid.*). Rate strikes took place in the affluent areas of Johannesburg and Pretoria in 1996 as residents protested against what they saw as arbitrary increases in their rates. Without consultation, the problems with non-payment or rate-strikes will continue. Yet the Masakhane Campaign organizers have recognized the need to communicate 'face to face' with local communities. Equally, the mayors of 14 major cities and towns across the country have pledged their support for the campaign and their commitment to popularize it through workshops and discussion: 'The Masakhane campaign depends on the strategic partnership between government, labour, the private sector and individuals in their communities' (*ibid.*). However, the campaign has raised questions about the need for stronger legal powers and a greatly improved administrative structure, which could assist in encouraging payment.

One of the key aspects of building a democracy is educating people in the basic procedures of democratic governance: voting and elections. In essence, promoting and encouraging participation through the ballot box is one step towards developing a democratic culture. Local government can sometimes seem the Cindarella of electoral politics, yet at its best it can serve the interests of local communities in a far more direct and accountable manner than national government. Local government in South Africa is under probation: seen as only partially legitimate in terms of low voter turnout rates; facing immense socio-economic problems within its communities particularly in rural areas; restructured councils previously tarnished by the brutality of apartheid are struggling to confront misunderstanding among their local residents. But as Sophie Masite, the Mayor of Soweto, stated: 'All people are South Africans now and they must work together in their communities' (Masite interview, 1996).

# SEVEN

# Political economy

For the past 50 years, through the system of apartheid and separate development, economic policies favouring the white majority interacted to form an economy characterized by serious structural weaknesses. Equally, these deficiencies created a deep divide between the affluence of a privileged few alongside the extensive poverty and social deprivation of the majority. The dominant interests of the apartheid period were the small number of large corporate groups, most with roots in the mining industry. Until the early 1990s, four mining groups controlled 80 per cent of the Johannesburg Stock Exchange, with Anglo-American Corporation and De Beers owning half the value of shares quoted (Overseas Development Institute 1994b). The ANC asserts that the economic legacy of apartheid featured levels of 'inequality, unemployment, economic disempowerment of the majority and the concentration of ownership by large conglomerates' (African National Congress 1994b). Therefore, it sought to 'transform' the economy and numerous resolutions were passed at its 1994 national conference, including promoting black economic empowerment, developing a policy on direct investment and engaging in a policy of fiscal discipline, all of which was couched in the language of the RDP (*ibid.*: 24).

## Problems facing the 1994 government

The RSA *White Paper*, published in September 1994, noted in its first paragraph: 'South African society is in need of transformation and renewal . . . following centuries of oppression and decades of formal apartheid' (RSA 1994). However, the *White Paper*'s approach to the economy was not interventionist. It provided more emphasis on the processes of development than on providing specific targets for key economic indicators. It also confirmed that programmes had to be financed in ways that were neither inflationary nor likely to create balance of payments difficulties. It was clear that both the NP and the ANC had moved away from their respective beliefs in state intervention in the economy and were moving towards a more market-oriented

127

**Table 7.1**  Economic facts

| | |
|---|---|
| Population: | 41.4 million (1995) |
| Population growth: | 2.5% per year (1991–95) |
| Area: | 1.2m sq km |
| Fiscal year: | Begins 1 April |
| Currency: | Rand |
| | R3.63 = $1(average 1995) |
| | R4.36 = $1 (27 May 1996) |
| Gross Domestic Product (GDP): | R484 billion (1995)/$134 billion (1995) |
| GDP per head: | $3224 (1995) |
| GDP growth: | 0.1% per year (1991–95) |
| | 3.3% (1995) |
| Inflation: | 11.3% per year (1991–95) |
| | 8.7% (1995) |

*Source*: Economic Intelligence Unit 1996

approach (Overseas Development Institute 1994a). In a sense, there was a contradictory element in the short-lived RDP, which combined a commitment to meeting the population's 'basic needs', thereby potentially implying strong state intervention and radical redistribution of wealth, whilst also acknowledging and accepting the mechanisms of the market. A profile of the basic needs in South Africa which confronted the Government of National Unity in April 1994 was formidable, as Table 7.2 demonstrates.

Table 7.2 does not include educational deficiencies, levels of unemployment, access to basic infrastructure such as roads and telecommunications, access to basic services such as postage, refuse collection, street lighting, recreational facilities and so on. Conrad Barberton points out that the 'government would have its work cut out if it wished to make any impact on meeting "basic needs". In fact, the extent of the poverty in South Africa could easily absorb all the government's time and resources' (Barberton 1995: 6). Historically, both the ANC and the NP had different approaches to economic and social policy, although they both shared the conviction that the state should intervene substantially in economic life. Under the apartheid system, the NP guided the economy, and the ANC in exile advocated radical change in the management and ownership of the economy, including outright nationalization and radical redistribution of wealth, including land. However, in the mid-1980s South Africa became exposed to the views of the IMF and World Bank who sought to influence economic thinking in a more *laissez-faire* position. Equally, with the demise of the Soviet Union and the dysfunction of the command economy the ANC began to shift its position on the pace and direction of social and economic change.

In essence, both the NP and the ANC have shifted away from policies of state intervention in the economy. From the mid-1980s the then government

**Table 7.2**   Profile of basic needs in South Africa, 1993

*Nutrition*
- 25 per cent of children under the age of five suffer from stunting as a result of chronic malnutrition, i.e. 3.37 million children.
- Malnutrition affects physical development as well as mental development, thus placing children at a disadvantage for the rest of their lives.

*Water*
- Nearly 25 per cent of South African households do not have access to piped water while only 40 per cent actually have water laid on to their homes.
- Only 17.5 per cent of all African households have access to piped water in their homes:
    (a) 33 per cent have to fetch water from other sources, such as rivers, streams, dams, springs or boreholes.
    (b) 7.7 per cent of African households in rural areas have piped water in their homes.
    (c) 40 per cent of African households in metropolitan areas have piped water in their homes.
- Over 99 per cent of all white and Indian households have water laid on.

*Energy*
- 45 per cent of all households in South Africa do not have access to grid electricity.
- 75 per cent of African households in rural areas are not connected to the national grid.
- Many households in rural areas are experiencing serious energy shortages due to the depletion of fuel wood stocks and because alternative energy sources are unaffordable.

*Housing*
- Just under one million households live in shacks in South Africa.
- Around 500 000 households live in hostels.

*Sanitation*
- 50 per cent of all households in South Africa have flush toilets:
    (a) nearly all white and Indian households have toilets.
    (b) 88 per cent of coloured households have toilets.
    (c) 34 per cent of African households have flush toilets.
    (d) 41 per cent of African households have pit latrines.
    (e) 6.5 per cent of African households have bucket toilets.
    (f) 16 per cent of African households have no form of toilet.

*Health*
- Life expectancy:
    (a) 73 years for whites.
    (b) 60 years for African.
- Infant mortality rate for children under 5 years:
    (a) Range from 36.9 per cent per 1000 births for all mothers of 15–19 years of age, to 81.1 per cent per 1000 births for all mothers of 45–49 years of age.
    (b) For African mothers 30–34 years of age: 85.1 per cent per 1000 births.
    (c) For white mothers 30–34 years of age: 2.2 per cent per 1000 births.

\* compiled from the South African Living Standards and Development Survey October 1993
*Source*: Barberton 1995

began to expose the economy more to the discipline of the market. By the elections in 1994 there was a consensus that a mixed economy was the appropriate way forward. The focus of the economy was on achieving high rates of growth with economic policies that encouraged the inflow of private foreign investment. A 'letter of intent' was signed with the IMF in which the government agreed the need to hold the budget deficit in check (Overseas Development Institute 1994a). An accord was signed by the ANC and the NP giving the Reserve Bank more autonomy, provided there was 'regular consultation between the governor and the minister of finance' (*ibid.*). Although nationalization remains part of the agendas of both COSATU and the SACP, the ANC in government has managed to evade commitment.

In any case, since the 1980s it is generally acknowledged that the economic performance of South Africa was poor (Lewis 1994). Per capita income had dropped by at least 15 per cent in real terms, and there was no growth in total employment, with unemployment rates among the economically active black population exceeding 50 per cent in urban areas. Ratios of both investment and saving to national income fell dramatically and there were substantial capital outflows every year since 1985 through a combination of capital flight and debt repayment. Further, urban migration put great pressure on both housing and infrastructure, and protection levels to manufacturing industry were high. The productivity of new investment had been continually falling, mainly because of the direction of investment to 'strategic' industries which the government considered to be important in order to combat sanctions, and the other related costs of maintaining the apartheid system (*ibid.*). The end of apartheid, then, presented 'a major opportunity to launch South Africa onto a new, higher path of growth and development' (Scott 1995: 199). Yet this growth would be impossible without the involvement of foreign investment in terms of trade, capital and technology inflows as well as knowledge, information and skills from abroad (*ibid.*). However, attracting foreign investment would not necessarily be easy because as Thomas Scott argues, the new government inherited 'a dualistic economic structure with a core modern formal industrial economy and a large underdeveloped Third World informal economy, the latter being characterised by chronic poverty and high unemployment' (*ibid.*: 200). The modern industrial economy has also suffered from a lack of international competition and technological renewal during the apartheid years. Equally, the structures of South Africa's large conglomerates are extremely complex in that there are pyramids, where a holding company owns 50 per cent of another holding company, which owns 50 per cent of yet another. As the *Business Day* puts it, 'not only are there conglomerates within conglomerates, there are also intricate feedback loops, whereby subsidiaries of subsidiaries own shares in the parent company' (*Business Day*, 25 September 1996). The inventiveness of such arrangements had 'more to do with power than industrial logic and helped a small number of families and insurance groups extend their influence throughout South African industry' (*ibid.*). This situation began to

**Table 7.3**   Exports and imports

| Major exports (1994) | % of total | Major imports (1994) | % of total |
|---|---|---|---|
| Unclassified (gold) | 36.2 | Machinery & equipment | 33.0 |
| Base metals | 13.2 | Transport equipment | 14.9 |
| Jewellery (diamonds) | 11.4 | Base metals | 4.5 |
| Total | 60.8 | Total | 52.4 |

*Source*: Economic Intelligence Unit 1996

unravel in 1996 with the mutual life insurer Sanlam dismantling two conglomerates it controlled, Gencor and Malbak, and preparing for possible conversion into a publicly listed company. Anglovaal is also reorganizing and replacing its traditional mining houses, which held stakes in a series of quoted mines but often extracted more value through management contacts, with two new mining groups which will manage their own assets. These old corporate structures, sustained under apartheid, are inefficient in that their long chains of command breed bureaucracy and elaborate control structures deter outside investors (*ibid.*). Under the apartheid system South African business was protected from foreign competition and exchange controls are still in operation. In fact, one senior executive of an international investment company asserted that South Africa must 'drop exchange controls'.

As Table 7.3 demonstrates, over 60 per cent of all South Africa's exports are in the category of gold, diamonds and base metals, which emphasises the country's dependence on those commodities. Kaizer Nyatsumba believes that one of the difficulties for the government, partly resulting from this industrial structure, is the role played by COSATU in economic policy-making. Certainly, given the historical inequalities, there is considerable sympathy for trade unionism within the country, but some regard the labour movement as a labour aristocracy in a vast hinterland of unemployed people (Nyatsumba 1996a). COSATU defends itself against this accusation by claiming that the benefits which accrue to its membership filter through to their less advantaged extended families. Certainly, this claim can be verified in Table 7.11 which outlines the extent to which the unemployed depend upon the assistance of working relatives. Of course, it is possible to regard employment as a form of quasi-welfare system, but large companies and international markets tend not to do so. The focus of their attention is profitability, productivity and viability in export trade (Table 7.4). Labour practices which obstruct those objectives are seen as damaging irrespective of the domestic financial imperatives which may confront the labour force.

In 1996, the National Union of Mineworkers and the Chamber of Mines reached agreement on wages and working conditions in South Africa's

**Table 7.4**  Markets and suppliers

| Leading markets (1994) | % of total | Leading suppliers (1994) | % of total |
|---|---|---|---|
| Switzerland | 6.7 | Germany | 16.7 |
| UK | 6.6 | USA | 11.6 |
| USA | 4.9 | UK | 11.6 |

*Source*: Economic Intelligence Unit 1996

collieries and gold mines, thus averting a potential strike. The union represented 194 000 employees and initially demanded an average 25 per cent increase. However, during negotiations the NUM acquiesced in favour of the restructuring of the miners' provident fund. Thomas Ketsise, a union official, said 'Employers have been contributing more in developing white workers than black workers, but this agreement established parity between white and black workers on training, retirement and death benefits' (*Pretoria News*, 12 September 1996). The preamble to the agreement stated: 'Inequalities cannot be addressed without the implementation of practical steps to correct the past by changing the future' (*ibid.*). Jabulani Sikhakhane sees the decision made by Anglo American Corporation and the NUM to plan a review of all work and management practices at Anglo's five gold mines, in order to improve productivity and secure jobs, as a radical move that could present challenges to both the company and the workers (*Business Report*, 18 September 1996).

## The National Economic Development and Labour Council (NEDLAC)

Nyatsumba believes that in an ideal situation the labour movement should see itself as a social partner to the government and business, for an adversarial relationship between the three is not in the long-term interest of the country. In fact, perceptions of an unstable labour market could affect the attractiveness of South Africa for foreign investment (*The Star*, 11 September 1996). Of course, corporatist structures are in place under NEDLAC, which some analysts believe is a major innovation (Webster 1996) (Table 7.5).

Webster maintains that NEDLAC is an important representative organization. NEDLAC was launched on 18 February 1995, and its founding document describes its character as 'a representative and consensus-seeking body where the parties to the council will seek to reach agreement through negotiation and discussion based on proper mandates' (*Business Report*, 5 June 1996). It is a statutory body and was passed by parliament, under the terms of the NEDLAC Act in 1994 after some six months of negotiation. Viewed broadly, NEDLAC is a negotiating body consisting of the govern-

**Table 7.5**   Corporatist structure

*NEDLAC*
Business organizations
Government representatives
Trade unions
*plus 5 community delegations*
Women's groups
Youth groups
Civic groups
Rural organizations
Disabled groups

*Source*: Webster 1996

ment and other social partners. Its aim is to bring about agreements on all social and economic policy issues. The NEDLAC Act states that the organization must:

- Strive to promote the goals of economic growth, participation in economic decision-making and social equity;
- Seek to reach consensus and conclude agreements pertaining to social and economic policy;
- Consider all significant changes to social and economic policy before it is implemented or introduced in parliament;
- Encourage and promote the formulation of co-ordinated policy on social and economic matters. (*ibid.*)

The government must implement agreements that have been reached within NEDLAC, and business and labour are expected to bear the responsibility of making agreements work. NEDLAC includes business, labour and government representatives and also has a community delegation which represents five sectors: women, youth, civics, the rural constituency and the disabled. The potential advantage of an agreement-making body such as NEDLAC is that it commits parties to co-operation. Each of the parties has a responsibility and a contribution to make. It also indicates that conclusive agreements will be implemented but it does not intend to replace the government's authority or the autonomy of the trade unions or business organizations. If agreements cannot be reached after a reasonable period, each party is free to do what it feels is in its best interest. Equally, the government may proceed with the implementation of legislation. Productivity is a key issue, but it is a matter not only concerning labour productivity but also the productivity of capital in terms of providing training, workplace improvements and a more integrated approach to technology.

Webster maintains that the community dimension of NEDLAC empowers civic organizations, women and so on and, therefore, it should not be regarded as simply a tripartite structure on the lines of labour–business–government. However, SANCO has criticized NEDLAC for not including civic associations fully into the agreement-making process and consequently marginalizing their interests (see Chapter 4). NEDLAC held a summit in 1996 to consider its first 15 months in operation and it resolved to streamline its structures and processes in order to become more effective. It prioritized certain essential points:

- To evaluate, improve and strengthen the process of social dialogue and agreement-making and to build confidence and trust in the Nedlac process at all levels;
- To enhance the agreement-making function of Nedlac by improving its co-ordination and capacity to deal with matters and set negotiations at the appropriate level of detail;
- To work towards developing a strategic framework which captures the requirements and challenges of economic development;
- To focus and prioritise issues on the agendas of the Nedlac chamber;
- To structure the policy formulation process to ensure that all parties substantively participate and are afforded adequate time to consult on policy issues, while also setting deadlines for the consideration of issues;
- To develop a structured relationship with the parliamentary process;
- To strengthen the capacity of the constituencies by improving access to, and the utilisation of, information and resources, including existing public resources;
- To ensure consistent and effective representation of delegates in Nedlac structures to allow for substantive dialogue to take place. (*Business Report*, 5 June 1996)

There seems to be a recognition by both business and labour that NEDLAC is an appropriate forum for discussion, but they have to establish some common ground in order to forge any agreements. Both COSATU and the South African Foundation, which represents 50 of the largest business groups in the country, have differing visions of future economic growth. The foundation argues that the way forward is through private enterprise, minimal government interference in the economy and full-scale privatization. COSATU, on the other hand, has argued against privatization and the restructuring of parastatals, believing that job creation should be an absolute priority. Some commentators want NEDLAC to engage in some straight analysis and acknowledge that a fundamental change in all people's attitudes to work is needed: 'Employment, money and freedom from poverty cannot be seen as rights . . . they are privileges to be worked towards.' The component parts of NEDLAC have turned the organization into a 'talking shop', willing to discuss new processes but less able to initiate any new ideas (*Business Report*, 10 June 1996).

Nevertheless, Webster believes the greatest threat to the new South Africa lies in the fact that less people are benefiting from the change of government and more people are suffering – or what he terms the 'losers' and 'winners' of democracy. He sees the 'winners' as the rising black business class and organized labour; the 'losers' are the youth underclass who are largely unemployed and ill-educated, the large rural population and the white working-class, who now no longer have access to the state. Therefore, as losers constitute a potential threat to society, the only way to consolidate democracy in South Africa is for the government to give some form of benefit to the 'losers'. This benefit would come from a 'strong, interventionist state' which would be involved in social and economic programmes and work-creation schemes (Webster 1996). Other analysts confirm that what South Africa needs is a 'social-democratic pact between business, labour and key state bureaucracies'. Such a pact would involve genuine co-determination in the private sector, negotiated wage constraints and limited price increases. According to Adam and Moodley, labour and business must see themselves more as partners in rebuilding a new nation: 'An affluent economy with high social wages and stable industrial relations is the goal, not the pre-condition of a social-democratic vision' (Adam and Moodley 1993).

Yet if 'capitalism is back in fashion' and market mechanisms triumph, then a cosy corporatist arrangement between business, labour and the government may not necessarily be sustainable. Strong links continue to exist between the ANC, COSATU and the SACP. Of COSATU's 2 million members, the Communist Party is 'very influential' (Cronin interview, 1996). Nelson Mandela announced in 1996 that the party would never part with the SACP and that there remained a powerful common purpose linking the alliance between the three organizations (*The Star*, 26 June 1996). Whatever that purpose is, it is certainly not expressed in government economic policy. While Jeremy Cronin complains of the ANC's approach to economics, the response of COSATU to the question of privatization has been a difficult one.

The issue of privatization has been on the political agenda since Nelson Mandela returned from a state visit to Germany and pledged to implement the policy (*Business Report*, 10 June 1996). In fact, one industrial analyst claimed that the ANC was more free-market oriented in its short term of office than the National Party (Cargill in *Business Report*, 6 June 1996). Stella Sigcau, the Minister of Public Enterprises, referred to privatization as 're-structuring' because, she argued, the 'economy had to be seen in a broader context' (*RSA Review*, June 1995). As the provision of transport by the government was so essential, it was important to discover the extent to which Transnet was capable of supplying an effective and affordable service to all sectors of the economy. Only then could the government identify whether certain industries needed to be privatized or part-privatized (*ibid.*). When the ANC announced its plans for partial or complete privatization of bodies including Suna Air, Transkei Airlines, Telkom and South Africa Airlines in December 1995, the unions held a one-day strike in protest. COSATU claimed it had reacted so militantly because of ideology, the fear of job losses and the lack of consultation. COSATU's initial response to privatization, then, was fiercely antagonistic. However, the government reportedly informed COSATU that if it failed to accept privatization their alliance could split (*Business Report*, 12 September 1996). COSATU decided to organize a three-day meeting to discuss the issue. Subsequently, labour and the government signed the National Framework Agreement, which provides guidelines and principles under which privatization can take place (*ibid.*). Eventually, COSATU declared itself to be 'not completely opposed to the privatisation of certain industries'. Exceptions should be made, however, for those industries which are 'concerned with people, for example, electricity, communications, etc.'. Nevertheless, COSATU admits that some industries would benefit from the private sector in terms of financial resources and technology (*Business Report*, 18 September 1996).

Plessey SA, the main operating arm of Plessey, the telecommunications and electronics company, secured a R30 million Telkom contract for the supply of prepaid smart-card telephones. Analysts suggested that the sale of 30 per cent of Telkom would raise around R10 billion. According to the Standard Bank, privatizing saleable state assets could raise R100 billion against a government debt of around R280 billion (*Business Report*, 10 June 1996). The ABSA Bank asserted that 'tangible progress' would have to be made with privatization and the proceeds 'wisely utilised' (ABSA Bank Quarterly 1996). Of course, there have been 'trickle down' effects from the process of electrification. The new electricity connections by Eskom are estimated to have created 1268 new businesses, thus creating around 5000 new jobs. These opportunities have been made possible because of the stimulation given to the sales of electrical appliances. In 1995, Eskom connected 313 000 homes, 4 per cent above target, and estimates that for every 100 new connections, there are between 10 and 20 'micro' business start-ups (*African Analysis*, 14 June 1996).

## Reorienting the economy

Reorienting the economy is not simple and straightforward. Trade liberalization places a heavy burden on companies to restructure quickly. If this takes place in an inflexible labour market with an artificially strong exchange rate and relatively high tax rates, the desired effect of an efficient and globally competitive industrial sector may not be achieved (Nedcor Economic Unit 1996). Brian Kahn argues that one of the ironies of transition in South Africa is the degree to which the liberalization of the economy has been accepted as a policy option aimed at stimulating economic growth through an outward-oriented approach: 'If we compare the current thinking of the present government with ANC economic policy proposals at the time of its unbanning, the transformation is truly remarkable' (Kahn 1996: 1). Yet, as he concedes, there are still strong elements within the ANC worried about the workings of the free market. In any case, liberalization and deregulation in a country that has been protected is bound to raise

**Table 7.6** Exchange control liberalization alternative:
Scenario 1 – relaxed phase

| Process | Preconditions | Possible impacts |
| --- | --- | --- |
| Relaxation on foreign direct investment abroad.<br>Asset swaps on institutions.<br>Relaxation of controls on individuals. | Sustained increase in foreign exchange reserves.<br>Sustained increase in long-term capital inflows.<br>Orderly response to previous phases. | Orderly response, outflows matched by inflows. Little impact on exchange rates or interest rates.<br>Relaxation results in boost of international confidence resulting in net capital inflows. This would put pressure on the rand to appreciate, which could be offset by increasing the pace of liberalization. OR<br>Large net capital outflows. Pressure on the rand to depreciate and upward pressure on interest rates. The net outflows could result in a slowdown of liberalization process. |

*Source*: Kahn 1996

uncertainties from labour and business. Business groups, although in favour of a free trade environment, are nevertheless cautious about tariff reform. Greater competition could inevitably lead to business failures and a consequent increase in unemployment. Investment analysts stress that South Africa must drop exchange controls which will, in turn, permit individual sectors of the economy to take off, but many businesses within the country feel threatened by the prospect. Tables 7.6, 7.7 and 7.8 show the possible exchange control alternatives and their possible impact on the economy. However, as Kahn points out, political stability and stable macro-economic policies still remain important preconditions for a stable process of liberalization. Any increase in levels of violence and political uncertainty would leave the country susceptible to sudden outflows of capital.

High savings rates, macro-economic stability and an educated workforce are seen as vital components in the process of encouraging entrepreneurial activity (World Bank 1993). The South African government is attempting to address these issues as outlined in its 1996 statement on macro-economic policy, which was aimed at realizing the potential of the economy. The Finance Minister, Trevor Manuel, recognized that major constraints on growth and job creation existed: 'The level of domestic savings and reserves are

**Table 7.7**  Exchange control liberalization alternative:
Scenario 2 – the Big Bang approach

| Process | Preconditions | Possible impacts |
|---|---|---|
| All controls suddenly lifted. | Sustained increase in reserves and long-term capital inflows. Macro-economic and political stability. | Large net capital outflows. Impact effect: depreciation of the rand and rising interest rates. In the medium term, either: (i) High credibility that reforms will not be reversed: once portfolio readjustment is completed, rand stabilizes at levels above that of the initial effect. (ii) Low credibility: large and unsustainable capital outflows. Exchange rate depreciates, interest rates and foreign debt rise to unsustainable levels. The reform process is then reversed. OR Large-scale inflows (international confidence affected). |

*Source*: Kahn 1996

**Table 7.8**  Exchange control liberalization alternative:
Scenario 3 – no further lifting of controls and possible tightening

| Preconditions | Possible impacts |
|---|---|
| Escalating violence and political instability. Lower credit ratings. Rising budget deficit. Rising inflation. Significant increase in international debt ratios. | A slowdown of capital inflows and possible net outflows. Will require higher interest rates to reduce the current account deficit. If there are net capital outflows, current account surpluses will have to be maintained at the expense of lower economic growth. |

*Source*: Kahn 1996

low, the economy suffers from the lack of skilled workers, many sectors are uncompetitive and the labour market is fragmented' (*The Star*, 14 June 1996). The balance of payments also remained a structural barrier to accelerated growth. The lack of sustained long-term capital inflows had made the economy too reliant on short-term capital flows. Equally, unemployment remained the biggest challenge the country faced. The government's policy did not envisage a minimum wage across the whole economy; instead it sought to set minimum wages according to appropriate standards by sector and area. Exchange control would be liberalized but not immediately abolished. New measures included: relaxing foreign investors' access to domestic credit; insurance companies, pension funds and unit trusts would now be able to obtain foreign assets of up to 10 per cent of their total assets and would be allowed foreign currency transfers; corporate exporters could offset their imports with the proceeds of their exports and tariff reform would continue. A series of inducements to encourage investment in the manufacturing sector included tax holidays for certain kinds of investment, particularly those with a labour-intensive bias (Nedcor Economic Unit 1996).

In 1995 South Africa achieved an economic growth rate of 3.3 per cent. High consumer confidence and a demand for durable and semi-durable goods led to an increase in real private consumption expenditure, which exceeded the growth in real personal disposable income. Private consumption, then, was partly financed by an expansion of credit at the cost of domestic saving (South African Reserve Bank 1996). Within the banking system the number of credit card transactions increased by 17.3 per cent and the number of electronic magnetic tape transactions rose by 13.5 per cent (Nedcor Economic Unit 1996). This is partly due to the increased availability and use of shop credit cards. The agricultural sector of the economy grew considerably, 82.3 per cent in real terms. This improvement resulted from an increase in the supply of livestock for slaughtering, the lowering of import tariffs on agricultural goods, a mild winter and reforms in the marketing of agricultural products. Whilst gold production was disappointing, other mining activity, particularly iron ore and chrome, continued to show some growth. The Reserve Bank felt that the economy performed 'extremely well' during 1995 (South African Reserve Bank 1996). However, the upturn in economic activity was not accompanied by employment growth, although the potentially inflationary consequences of the increase in labour remuneration were absorbed partially by a strengthening of labour productivity, which reduced unit labour costs.

In June 1996 the government took a policy stand with the introduction of a major macro-economic strategy, titled Growth, Employment and Redistribution (GEAR), which aims to double annual real GDP growth to around 6 per cent by the year 2000. The emphasis in GEAR is placed on market forces, with the government playing a reduced economic role. The reform of the labour market is identified as a crucial factor in creating a more flexible employment environment if new jobs are to be created. However, inevitably

COSATU is resistant to any proposals which it feels will undermine current practices. As Sam Shilowa, Secretary-General of COSATU, asserted, 'We will lobby, fight, convince, negotiate, twist around, do everything possible for our position' (Shilowa 1997). In a sense, COSATU's position is compromised within the political arena, for although there are former COSATU members who are currently sitting as MPs, it was agreed at the time of the election that they would forfeit their accountability to COSATU in favour of the ANC. Therefore, many openly support new employment legislative proposals (*ibid.*). In any case, the ANC National Conference in 1997 gave its support, in a carefully-worded resolution, to the policy of GEAR: 'The conference acknowledges the need for the basic objectives of macro-economic stability and that GEAR provides a basis for that stability' (*The Star*, 19 December 1997). Nevertheless, since 1994, economic growth, or as some term it, jobless growth, has not led to a significant increase in employment opportunities and has focused attention on the nature of unemployment in South Africa.

## Unemployment

The South African Institute of Race Relations (SAIRR), with major support from a number of corporations including the Anglo American and De Beer's Chairman's Funds, Iscor, Caltex and Nasionale Per and MarkData (Pty), instituted an investigation of the nature of unemployment in South Africa. Unemployment has been estimated by government and business to be in the region of 33 per cent but a review by the International Labour Organisation (ILO) suggested that official statistics 'may significantly over-estimate the unemployment rate' (South African Institute of Race Relations 1996).

The ILO considered a rate of 20 per cent would be more realistic. These contradictions prompted a study of the extent to which those who are classified as unemployed are, in fact, operational in the 'informal sector'. In a sense, unemployment figures in most advanced industrial countries can be massaged upwards or downwards, or calculated differently, so it perhaps is not surprising that South Africa's record might contain discrepancies. Estimates of unemployment were not based on the population census of 1991, which has been widely recognized as unreliable, but on large household surveys conducted by the Central Statistical Service (CSS). As SAIRR states, these define an unemployed person 'as someone of 15 years and older who was not in paid employment or self-employment for five hours or more in the week preceding the survey, who was available for employment, who took steps to find work or who wanted to take up employment or self-employment' (*ibid.*). The surveys conducted by SAIRR with MarkData attempted to allow for 'hidden' employment by eliminating persons who

**Table 7.9** Proportions of people claiming to be unemployed with money to spend personally on a range of typical purchases (unemployed respondents)

| | African | | Coloured | Indian | White |
| --- | --- | --- | --- | --- | --- |
| | Seeking work | Not seeking work | | | |
| *Have money for*: | | | | | |
| Food | 87% | 78% | 95% | 100% | 87% |
| Clothing | 72% | 63% | 81% | 83% | 37% |
| Transport | 78% | 72% | 75% | 100% | 48% |
| Entertainment (cigarettes/ liquor etc.) | 76% | 69% | 84% | 100% | 82% |
| Accounts/hire purchase | 69% | 65% | 86% | 94% | 56% |
| Family/household needs | 82% | 70% | 89% | 100% | 88% |

*Source*: South African Institute of Race Relations 1996

claimed to be unemployed but who also admitted to having personal earnings. By making this adjustment, a reduction of 10 per cent could be made to the employment figures. By February 1996 the survey changed the emphasis from income to expenditure and asked how much money the respondent had spent on himself/herself over the past month on food, clothing, transport, entertainment, payment of accounts and on family or household needs. Table 7.9 illustrates the responses to these questions.

SAIRR point out that the percentages in Table 7.9 include all respondents who stated that they spent something on those commodities irrespective of whether they could remember how much expenditure, and demonstrate that some two-thirds or more of the unemployed have access to resources. Table 7.10 shows the median amounts spent by respondents who have some money to spend. The study indicates that 'those people who are or claim to be unemployed include a large proportion who are not in desperate circumstances' (*ibid.*). The expenditure of those who are unemployed appears to be around the same level as the expenditure of those employed in low-level unskilled employment.

SAIRR believe it is 'impossible to reconcile this pattern of expenditure with the status of real unemployment in a poor society' (*ibid.*). However, the study also looked at where these resources were coming from. As Table 7.11 indicates, the extent of dependence upon employed family members is 'very substantial'. So there is a clear knock-on effect of unemployment on the resource base of the entire family. Equally, the study found that some of those who claimed to be 'unemployed' were not without work. Some 15 per cent of white and Indian 'unemployed' are indicated as working in the informal sector, and this figure rises to 21 per cent among Africans and 30 per cent among coloured people.

**Table 7.10**  Median expenditure per month on a range of items by the unemployed who spent some money (Rand)

| | Unemployed Respondents | | | | | Employed in low-level unskilled work |
|---|---|---|---|---|---|---|
| | African | | Coloured | Indian | White | |
| Median expenditure personal | Seeking work | Not seeking work | | | | |
| | R | R | R | R | R | R |
| Food | 129 | 89 | 198 | 345 | 68 | 137 |
| Clothing | 112 | 298 | 101 | 61 | 38 | 132 |
| Transport | 33 | 37 | 25 | 70 | 100 | 41 |
| Entertainment | 25 | 21 | 20 | 41 | 37 | 32 |
| Accounts | 151 | 90 | 221 | 214 | 578 | 154 |
| Family/Household | 264 | 536 | 304 | 1293 | 1263 | 273 |
| Total expenditure | 714 | 1071 | 869 | 2024 | 2084 | 769 |

*Source*: South African Institute of Race Relations 1996

**Table 7.11**  Means of survival of household member unemployed longest

| | African | Coloured | Indian | White |
|---|---|---|---|---|
| Depends on other members of family | 71% | 57% | 71% | 68% |
| Borrows money | 2% | – | 5% | – |
| Does odd jobs | 16% | 26% | 15% | 13% |
| Sells items | 4% | 2% | – | 2% |
| Begs or washes cars | 1% | 2% | – | – |
| Grants or insurance | 2% | 12% | 8% | 8% |
| Savings | 1% | – | – | 6% |
| Other | 1% | 1% | – | 2% |
| Cannot survive | 3% | 1% | – | – |

*Source*: South African Institute of Race Relations 1996

White respondents have the largest access to savings, grants and un-employment insurance, while African and Indian communities are more dependent on their families. However, when the survey posed the question of how much money unemployed respondents were able to earn in a month, irrespective of how they had responded to other questions, the findings changed significantly (see Table 7.12).

**Table 7.12**  Unemployed household members
earning more than r100 per month

| | |
|---|---|
| African | 35.0% |
| Coloured | 38.0% |
| Indian | 41.7% |
| White | 66.5% |
| All unemployed | 36.5% |

*Source*: South African Institute of Race Relations

Notwithstanding the facts that respondents may not be entirely honest and that the difficult issues of criminality and begging, both of which are clearly prominent in parts of South Africa, were excluded from the survey, the study maintains: 'the overall impression gained from these results is that there must be very substantial earning activity among the unemployed and quite sufficient to warrant scepticism regarding South Africa's official rates of unemployment' (*ibid.*). Hidden employment may also act as a disincentive for people to accept low-wage, labour-intensive public works, job-creation schemes or for jobs with low entry-level wages. Clearly, as SAIRR conclude, the picture of unemployment in the country is far more complex than had previously been considered. The extent of income-earning capacity among the 'unemployed' may suggest an element of entrepreneurial activity that is being actively promoted. An NGO in Johannesburg, Junior Achievement, has begun running business programmes at schools in order to encourage young South Africans to run their own businesses when they leave. They have the opportunity to gain experience of marketing a product, managing financial records and dealing with people. A number of organizations have contributed to training programmes including Johannesburg Consolidated Investments Limited Chairman's Fund, who made a donation of R260 000 to initiate training courses in self-employment. As Pat Molise, the head of the Institute of Personnel Management, stated the black African community needs to know and understand more about the basics of business (*Business Report*, 10 June 1996).

## Black entrepreneurship

Much attention has been focused on the development of black African entrepreneurship, although a World Bank study suggests there are a number of complex constraints. Micro-enterprises and other businesses in the informal sector have limited access to markets because business premises are scarce and poorly located. Entrepreneurs themselves are hampered by poor education and lack of skills or technical expertise. They also face a range of

**Table 7.13** Most important problems facing black micro-enterprises* (%)

| Constraints | At start-up | At time of survey |
|---|---|---|
| Crime and Violence | 4.4 | 7.2 |
| Getting a Licence | 1.8 | 0.2 |
| Inadequate premises | 18.0 | 15.7 |
| Lack of finances | 22.5 | 9.4 |
| Problems with law enforcement authorities | 10.5 | 6.6 |
| Unfavourable business conditions | 32.0 | 51.2 |
| Cost of doing business | 12.7 | 20.3 |
| Poor market conditions | 19.3 | 30.9 |
| Other | 10.8 | 9.7 |

* Those employing less than five people
*Source*: World Bank 1993

institutional barriers including a lack of access to financing. Potentially more worrying is the fact that these enterprises have difficulty growing or improving their services because they do not have access to broader markets or network opportunities in the formal sector (World Bank 1993). Table 7.13 indicates that the range of difficulties confronting micro-enterprises changes over time, in that some may lessen, for example, the initial lack of venture finance may ease, but problems with crime and violence increase.

The World Bank believes that enterprise constraints must be countered by government policy and legislation. An effective lobby representing black sector enterprises is needed to articulate the concerns of entrepreneurs to policy-makers. The lack of education and skills must be met in initial training drives, which concentrate on basic literacy and numeracy skills, basic accountancy methods and basic technical training. Certainly, there have been moves to establish black enterprise capacity, under the Kagiso Trust and NAIL, but funding has been in short supply from the traditional banking sector. Access to formal lenders is scarce until the firm exceeds five employees and has been in existence for three to five years. Only 20 have received credit and the major sources of funding are rotating savings clubs as well as the savings of the owner and of friends and family. Equally, lack of operating capital is a problem among new firms (World Bank 1995). More recently discussions have centred upon the trade union sector contributing towards venture capital. The World Bank emphasizes the need for new financial intermediaries to be developed with small start-up loans, circa R2000/US$350/£200 being made available by NGOs or community-based organizations (World Bank 1993, World Bank 1995). Under apartheid, blacks were restricted to operating a narrow range of businesses, mainly township-based retail enterprises. They were prohibited from operating in white areas. Now, competition is intense and largely confined to the low-income black market. Inadequate business premises and tenure arrangements are also an inheritance of the apartheid years because whites controlled the allocation of all formal business sites. Seventy-one per cent of micro-enterprises are operated in the home and of those who do operate outside the home, half do not have permission to occupy their site (World Bank 1995).

However, despite these constraints, the World Bank feels there is evidence of dynamic growth among black firms. Among micro-enterprises, light manufacturing in particular is identified as having above average incomes, employment and growth. They also employ on average three to five people compared to the sector average of two. The World Bank predicts that by the time of the new millennium, 'emerging enterprises enjoying access to support and finance will increase from 25,000, around 1 per cent of the total emerging small business population of 2.5 million, to at least 250,000'. The percentage of commercial bank assets invested in emerging and small enterprises should double to 10 per cent (World Bank 1995). Certainly, there is optimism among a number of analysts and bankers about the future direction of the South African economy, with predictions that economic growth will continue, inflation will be controlled and the rand will stabilize (*ibid.*, South African Reserve Bank 1996, Economic Intelligence Unit 1996). Nevertheless, all these forecasts are predicated on key assumptions: first, that there will be continuing political stability under an ANC-led government and second, that a 'skills crisis', resulting from improvements in training and education lagging behind an increasing growth rate, can be avoided. In a sense, the danger of this situation is already recognized. Cheryl Carolus admits that levels of educational attainment are so low that even if more jobs became available certain sections of the black community would be unable to take them (Carolus interview, 1996).

Currently, former public sector white labour has shifted into the private sector as more black labour is absorbed into government and parastatals (Economic Intelligence Unit 1996). On 1995 figures, 18 of the 36 department director-general posts and 51 deputy director generalships have been filled by black personnel. Lower down the scale, 133 black employees were in chief-director posts, and 260 in director positions. Fears that the state bureaucracy would expand are largely unfounded. An increase in the employment of 1.24 million people in 1994 rose to 1.25 million in 1995 although the quarterly wage bill fell from R11.5 billion in June 1994 to R10.76 billion in 1995 (*Africa Analysis*, 5 April 1996). Nevertheless, formal employment growth will not necessarily increase in traditional areas, as 'the struggle between capital and labour comes at the expense of productive labour absorption, potentially condemning most of the next generation to the informal sector' (Economic Intelligence Unit 1996). In other words, jobs in mining and manufacturing will no longer be guaranteed. If skilled black trade unionists

**Table 7.14**  Demographic trends, total population
(41.4 million) (1995)

| Age profile | % of total population 1994 |
|---|---|
| 0–18 | 47% |
| 18–64 | 45% |
| 65+ | 8% |

*Source*: Economic Intelligence Unit 1996

**Table 7.15**  Economic forecast 1995–2000 (real % change)

|  | 1995 | 1996 | 1997 | 1998 | 1999 | 2000 |
|---|---|---|---|---|---|---|
| *Real % change* | | | | | | |
| GDP | 3.3 | 3.8 | 2.5 | 3.5 | 4.0 | 3.5 |
| Private consumption | 4.9 | 3.5 | 2.5 | 4.5 | 5.0 | 2.5 |
| Government consumption | 0.3 | 0.5 | 0.5 | 1.5 | 1.0 | 1.0 |
| Gross domestic investment | 10.4 | 6.0 | 5.0 | 8.0 | 10.0 | 7.5 |
| Exports of goods and services | 8.1 | 8.0 | 6.0 | 5.2 | 4.5 | 5.3 |
| Imports of goods and services | 17.1 | 8.7 | 6.5 | 8.5 | 8.5 | 7.0 |
| *Income* | | | | | | |
| GDP ($bn) | 133.6 | 128.9 | 136.0 | 147.8 | 157.7 | 175.1 |
| *Inflation (%)* | | | | | | |
| Consumer prices | 8.7 | 8.2 | 8.5 | 8.5 | 9.3 | 9.5 |
| Average wage rate | 13.5 | 15.0 | 14.5 | 13.0 | 14.0 | 12.0 |
| *Financial indicators* | | | | | | |
| Exchange Rate R:$ | 3.63 | 4.22 | 4.45 | 4.60 | 4.90 | 5.00 |
| Prime Lending Rate % | 17.9 | 18.7 | 17.5 | 16.0 | 16.5 | 18.0 |
| *External trade ($bn)* | | | | | | |
| Merchandise exports | 27.9 | 30.6 | 32.5 | 35.1 | 37.3 | 38.6 |
| Merchandise imports | –27.1 | –28.8 | –30.7 | –35.0 | –36.8 | –37.8 |
| Trade Balance | 0.7 | 1.8 | 1.9 | 0.0 | 0.6 | 0.8 |
| Invisibles credits | 5.6 | 6.0 | 6.6 | 6.3 | 6.7 | 7.1 |
| Invisibles debits | –9.9 | –10.4 | –10.8 | –11.1 | –11.6 | –11.9 |
| Invisibles balance | –4.3 | –4.4 | –4.2 | –4.7 | –4.9 | –4.9 |
| *Foreign debt* | | | | | | |
| Total debt ($bn) | 30.8 | 34.3 | 37.4 | 41.2 | 45.5 | 50.6 |
| % of GDP | 23.1 | 26.6 | 27.5 | 27.9 | 28.9 | 28.9 |

*Source*: Economic Intelligence Unit 1996

are regarded as the 'winners' now, unproductive workers in an increasingly capitalizing sector will find themselves 'losers' and without employment. In this scenario, black enterprise initiatives are vital but so are other socio-political factors, such as a decisive fall in population growth and the uncoupling of COSATU from the ANC. There is little doubt that the economy of South Africa will change and develop over the next decade (Table 7.15) and this process will have to be recognized by all sections of society. South Africa's economic future and its ability to steer itself away from the inequities of the past crucially depend on the ability and commitment of its own people to work together to build a future.

# EIGHT

# Conclusion

The first universal elections held in April 1994 heralded a new democratic age for the majority of South Africans. The moving spectacle of people exercising their right to vote in multi-party elections for the first time stirred international opinion and focused attention firmly on the country's democratic transition. Nelson Mandela spoke of the need to emancipate people from the scourges that confronted them – 'poverty, disease, ignorance and backwardness' – in order that they could move towards the great issues of the moment: 'peace, stability, democracy, human rights, co-operation and development' (*The Star*, 8 May 1994). People were never to be deprived of their humanity again (Carolus interview, 1996). Yet, beyond the emotion, the transfer of power has been described as a 'rite of passage' (Welsh 1994). Both President Mandela and F. W. de Klerk recognized that a process of reconciliation had to commence before any elections actually took place and all parties agreed to share power in a government of national unity. This form of consociationalism, then, marked the early transitional period. Since 1994 it has been repeatedly recognized that the democratization process is 'a long one', especially given the deep contradictions and complex problems facing the country (Carolus interview, 1996). That democracy has been connected to development and the resolving of severe socio-economic problems is not surprising, but it does present the government with enormous difficulties.

## Democracy and development

By raising the question of development, the spectre of 'modernization' re-enters the discourse about democracy. Obviously, the asymmetrical nature of South Africa's development under apartheid has produced a first/third-world society: an industrialized, urban, technological society running in parallel with an impoverished rural hinterland. In fact, it is believed that taken as a whole, South Africa is a 'third world country'. Cheryl Carolus presents the paradox graphically when she observes that the highest percentage of deaths in white children is caused by drowning in swimming pools, whilst the predominant cause of death among black children is the result of dehydration due to lack of drinking water (*ibid.*). In the past, liberal democracy was seen as co-terminous with economic advancement, yet, as Adrian Leftwich points out, a new orthodoxy now prevails, which sees democracy as part of the process of development, that is, countries will not develop appropriately if they do not embrace some form of liberal democratic political expression (Leftwich 1996). However, the promotion of economic growth can inflict social costs and pressures upon those who struggled against the former regime. Tom Lodge asserts: 'Labour may not view increased government expenditure on the needs of the rural poor – primary health care, clean water and electrification – as adequate compensation for curbing the wage claims of urban workers' (Lodge 1996: 204). Whilst Carolus speaks of the need for the ANC to raise people's socio-economic expectations, studies of other countries have pointed to the potentially destabilizing consequences for democracies unable to meet those needs: 'New interests are generated, new consciousness is kindled and new political and organisational capacities are acquired at the individual and group level. Demands multiply both for the right to participate and for tangible and symbolic benefits. If these are not met, institutions run the risk of breaking down with society lapsing into chaos' (Diamond, Linz and Lipset 1988: 34).

Although there is a general consensus that South Africa has made the transition from apartheid to democracy in a context of national reconciliation, few ignore the challenges that continue to present themselves to national, provincial and local government. The business community is critically poised to assist the process of democratic consolidation, yet at times the future direction of the government's economic policy is polarized between quasi 'socialist' forces and a more liberalizing, capitalist agenda. On *prima facie* evidence the economy has performed well since 1993, the GDP growing by 2.7 per cent in 1994 and 3.3 per cent in 1995. Between July 1994 and December 1995 more than R30 billion of foreign capital flowed into the country, ending a ten-year period when capital outflows averaged around R5 billion a year. Moreover, this economic recovery has occurred in the context of falling inflation. In fact, the country's 'substantial economy' has been pointed to as one of the reasons why the shift to democracy has been relatively easy. Yet there are nagging elements behind this apparently healthy facade. In the first instance, the economic growth is 'jobless growth', so unemployment figures remain discouragingly high. Equally, the currency value has collapsed by more than 20 per cent, foreign reserves are falling and the crime rate has soared. R. W. Johnson points to some debilitating aspects:

The justice system, public hospitals and significant parts of both the education and welfare systems are in a state of collapse. There is strong and ominous pressure upon the two key liberal institutions of the press and the universities, and the rule of law is unevenly observed. The government's instinctive urge to shovel dirt under the carpet means that there is an open door for the growth of corruption. The loss of professional manpower together with sometimes rash affirmative action policies threatens to undermine the viability of many public sector institutions. Unemployment is still growing hugely. Unless this tidal wave of unemployment can be turned back it is difficult to see how not just minimal welfare standards but public order and democracy itself can be maintained. (Johnson 1996)

Equally, schisms are developing between the alliance of the ANC, COSATU and the SACP on the issue of liberal economic policy. Elements within both COSATU and the SACP reject the argument that globalizing economic forces and international competition are, of necessity, forcing a new economic reorientation upon the country. There is, of course, no certainty that even if the country goes wholeheartedly down the path of free market liberalization more jobs will be created immediately or, indeed, that a number of jobs will not be lost. This uncertainty inculcates a degree of tension in the short to medium term between people's expectations and government policy. Although the South African Reserve Bank points encouragingly to the fact that the rise in employment recorded at the end of 1996 occurred entirely in the private sector, it recognizes that the rise was insufficient, at that time, to make any inroads on the total level of unemployment in the economy (South African Reserve Bank 1997).

There is much mockery on the traditional left of the so-called 'corporate comrades', that is, those former socialists who are now enamoured of capitalism. Yet the neo-corporatism of the National Economic Development and Labour Council (NEDLAC) is likely to increasingly be frustrated if the economy continues to move in a more liberal direction. Sam Shilowa, the influential trade union leader, asserts: 'It is inconceivable that the pre-1994 ANC could have come up with its present macro-economic strategy' (Shilowa 1997). And certainly, that clarion call of a liberalizing economy, privatization, has not only been introduced into the country, but has also been accepted by sections of the trade union community. As Johnson reminds us: 'It is already becoming hard to credit the heady days of 1990–1994 when men who are now besuited ministers marched in demonstrations declaring their faith in socialism and "people's power"' (Johnson 1996). But, in a sense, this is precisely what development is about. Policies must evolve through discussion, debate and opposition. That the SACP and sections of COSATU still favour a strongly interventionist state, continue to speak the language of Marxist analysis and criticize the government, is a sign that opposition can take place in a free and open society. Equally, there is nothing intrinsically wrong with democracy if the ANC/SACP/COSATU alliance splits. It has always been acknowledged that any move from an authoritarian state to a democratic government is likely to cause dislocation and ideological shifts, so a critique of the fact that former socialists now espouse capitalist sentiment is not a reflection that democracy is under threat. It is, quite the reverse, an indication that democracy is consolidating.

Within the context of development, however, greater challenges present themselves when resource allocation is considered. Largely because of the nature of transitional democracies, civic organizations have recently played a reduced role within South African society. Their ability to negotiate with the government has changed: either they have been co-opted into government positions or they feel marginalized and functionless. This development is not peculiar to the South African experience and has taken place in Latin American countries and southern Europe (O'Donnell and Schmitter 1986). Civil society has to reassess its role and redefine its identity, especially so in the socio-economic arena in order that it may access resources for poorer communities. Current intellectualizing about the 'development state' returns to the capitalist model that was outlined by the modernization school of thought in the past, for example: economic growth, a strong private sector, democratic norms, social differentiation, legitimate political institutions and capacity building (Leftwich 1996: 285). There is no reason why any of these features should be inappropriate for South Africa.

## Variants of democracy

Since 1994 variants of liberal democracy have been expressed within South Africa: first, consociationalism or power sharing, second, a legitimizing and participatory democracy and third, an emphasis on local democracy and citizenship rights and responsibilities. It is necessary to look at these in turn. Consociationalism lasted in a quasi formal sense until the National Party left government in 1996. It seemed a suitable form of democracy to adopt during the transitional phase, yet it had weaknesses. The role of opposition parties are less strong and the policy formulation process can become slow and unresponsive. Also, the power-sharing of those two years failed to adequately formalize the apportionment of power to the mutual satisfaction of the parties concerned. So, in a sense, it could only be regarded as a short-term expedient. The great emphasis placed upon legitimizing political institutions is quite understandable. Legitimacy is seen to result from public involvement or participation. The great media campaigns devoted to the writing of the constitution which resulted in around 2 million submissions from the public to the Constitutional Committee were promoted by government. Yet it is debatable whether these campaigns can merely be regarded as a public relations exercise or a very purposeful demonstration of participatory democracy. Certainly, this form of activity may encourage participation, but its legitimizing effects may be more apparent than real. It is as well to remember than only 35 per cent of respondents replied affirmatively when asked the question: 'Did ordinary people help to write the constitution?

whilst 65 per cent said no or were unsure (CASE 1996). A distinction should be drawn between the dissemination of information to the general population and what might be regarded as public mobilization, in that public education will increase political knowledge but it may not automatically increase participation.

This debate returns to the theoretical assumptions underpinning much of participatory theory, that is, that the very act of participation is somehow educative and politically significant. Greater participation in political spheres is seen as enhancing democracy, but mechanisms may be at play within a democratic state which affect citizen participation. At the time of the local elections in 1995 much stress was placed on the need for people to participate by, first, registering to vote and second, by actually casting a vote on election day. However, both registration and the turnout remained comparatively low despite a strong media campaign and exhortations to the electorate from political parties. The requirement in the local elections that voters should register initially was in distinct contrast to the 1994 elections. The procedures were different and the results varied with an 86 per cent turnout in 1994 and a 38 per cent turnout in 1995. Failures in voter education, fear of registration, concerns about the secrecy of the ballot, apathy, indifference and lack of knowledge could all have contributed to the low turnout rate, but do these suggest that South Africa's democracy is any less viable, simply because people, for one reason or another, failed to vote? These voting figures only seem significant because the ANC placed an enormous emphasis on 'local, democratic, non-sexist and non-racial' modes of political participation. Therefore, non-participation immediately appeared as opposition to democracy and the government when, in fact, it was more likely to be conditioned by a range of causal factors, social and economic. It is important to remember that participation must never be desired for its own sake or seen as intrinsically democratic. Although there is much talk of governance being open to the people in order that they may be 'carried along with the process of democratic change', the ultimate mark of liberal democracy is the freedom to choose to participate or not. Of course, poverty and ignorance among the electorate can distort those principles, but essentially in any democratic state the extent to which people participate should never be judged as a yardstick of democracy. The essential principle of a democracy is that the public be enabled to participate should they choose to do so, through effective channels of communication and civil society.

It is, perhaps, not irrelevant to observe at this point that the marches organized by SANCO against possible local government housing evictions received a somewhat muted response from government and were not regarded as meaningful signs of an increase in participatory democracy. Rather, these actions were seen as being largely misinformed and undesirable. The notion of citizen participation, then, is a two-edged sword in that it can be invoked by governments as a symbol of democratic involvement, but equally can be disregarded as wrongly focused, arbitrary and actually serving to deny the wider community and their elected representatives the right to make policy. The state defines participation in a particular, pragmatic and functional way and delineates the parameters in which it is to occur. Relations between government and civil society can at times be strained, particularly as the strictures of governmental responsibility forge a different perspective than that of organizations operating at grassroots level. It is the responsibility of government to collect rates and taxes from its citizenry in order to redistribute resources within the wider society. Equally, it is the responsibility of the citizenry to fulfil certain obligations. As a number of commentators agree, the so-called 'culture of entitlement' must be broken in order for a democratic culture and civic-mindedness to be established (interviews with Masite, Nhlapo, Rabaji, White, 1996).

Almond and Verba believe that the distinctive property of a 'civic culture' does not rest alone on participant orientation, but on the ability of society to reconcile activity with passivity. In other words, whilst citizens are enabled to play an activist role, that is, engaging in the political process, they can also display a passive, or parochial role, in their acceptance and allegiance to government. This mixture of roles serve to moderate the potential intensity of political participation with a measure of legitimacy and acceptance of political norms (Almond and Verba 1963: 19). According to IDASA national opinion polls 41 per cent of respondents are satisfied with democracy and 59 per cent are unsatisfied. This suggests that it may be too early to rely upon the idea of a strong societal 'democratic political culture'. This is especially true if we consider the responses to the question posed: What if democracy does not work? Only 47 per cent consider democracy to be always best, whilst 43 per cent favour a strong, non-elected leader and 10 per cent did not know (IDASA 1996a). These replies raise the spectre of both legitimacy and expectation. Seymour Lipset defines legitimacy as 'the capacity of a system to engender and maintain public confidence in its efficacy' (Lipset 1960: 77). With 91 per cent of interviewees seeing democratic change resulting in economic benefits to all, the expectations of government are great (IDASA 1996a). Certainly, many within the ANC have spoken of the need for the population to perceive 'a process of visible change' (interviews with Masite, Carolus, King, 1996). But this places great pressures on new democratic structures.

There is a generally accepted view that a stable democracy requires from the people a belief in the legitimacy of democracy which should be held at two levels. First, the general principle must be accepted that democracy is the best form of government possible. Second, the electorate must be able to evaluate their own democratic system, irrespective of any weaknesses or failures, as being preferable to any non-democratic order (Diamond 1994: 13). In part, these views derive from the performance of the government, not only in terms of socio-economic spheres but in other terms such as 'the capacity to maintain order, to govern with probity and transparency, to maintain a rule of law and otherwise to respect and preserve the democratic rules of the game' (*ibid.*). Despite the low electoral turnout in the 1995 local elections, there is a clear level of optimism about accountable local democracy and the role it can play in meeting people's expectations. Sophie Masite, the Mayor of Soweto and local councillors have upbeat views and programmes about community issues. They believe that local democracy can actually be taken to the people in a practical and potentially life-enhancing way, with community policing forums, refuse collection schemes, instalment systems for rate and service payments, the promotion of light industry, the organization of savings schemes and the increasingly raised profile of women as political practitioners. A large number of women from very different backgrounds have been elected as local councillors; some women are professionally trained, while others are simply engaged in domestic labour. Local government is, in many ways, at the sharp end of the political system, in that it confronts deprivation, poverty and neglect. Yet at its best it can serve the interest of local communities in a far more direct, accountable and effective manner. The key aspects of building a democracy are manifold and involve not only the education of people in the basic procedures of governance, that is voting and elections, but also the encouragement of individual and community self-confidence.

## The dominant party

According to Steven Friedman of the Centre for Policy Studies, it has become 'almost a conventional wisdom to assume that the ANC will monopolise government for a considerable period' (Friedman 1996). It is generally recognized that parties are critical forces in the construction of new political institutions and much attention has focused on post-independent states where liberation movements have confronted the challenges of governmental office (Apter 1967, Huntington 1967, Ottoway 1991). The ANC's 1994 constitution declares its primary aim and objective: 'To unite all the people of South Africa, Africans in particular, for the complete liberation of the country from all forms of discrimination and national oppression' (Africa National Congress 1994a: 4). Presenting itself as a broad popular front, or a loose coalition, may have strengthened the ANC organizationally during the transitional period following the 1994 elections. However, parties need some degree of institutional autonomy, that is, a defined sense of self-direction and clear boundaries marking them off from other institutions and movements (Randall 1988: 179).

Whether a liberation movement can resist the temptation to define and discipline itself as a political party in the long-term is debatable. As democracy consolidates, the functions, orientations and influences of political parties become more important in that programmes and plans need to be clearly outlined. Certainly, the organizational structure of the ANC is democratic, but the ideological polarization of those sitting on the National Executive

Committee is wide. Currently there is great discussion of the role to be played by opposition parties in South Africa, and it is widely held that in order for opposition to be effective there must be some possibility that it could take power, if not alone, then in some form of coalition. On demographic grounds all parties will have to attract black support if they are to be potent as oppositionist forces. The National Party is anticipating the possibility of having a black leader within the next ten years and although the party has low expectations of attracting black votes in the elections of 1999, it is looking forward to the 2004 elections. Some members of the party are concerned that the NP will lose voter support if it is seen to discriminate against the emergence of a black and coloured leadership. Equally, the Inkatha Freedom Party is seeking to be the main opposition force. It sees its role as a 'black party' as being fundamental to its potential success. Yet, there are several critiques of the IFP position: on the one hand, analysts suggest that when Chief Buthelezi goes the party is unlikely to succeed, whilst on the other, some believe that the party will increase its support, particularly if Buthelezi's successor is of a more liberal disposition (interviews with Cornwall, Hyden, 1996). The IFP itself has differing views of its relationship with the NP, some elements seeking a closer relationship while others see the NP as fragile and likely to collapse.

Friedman sees no essential difficulties with party-dominant systems, chiefly on the grounds that they are functioning democracies: 'There is regular and open electoral contest, opposition parties are free to organise and civil liberties are, at least in the main, respected' (Friedman 1996). Maurice Duverger maintains that an intermediate system of democracy often follows a transition from an authoritarian regime, during which a 'ruling party' dominates: 'Many parties may flourish in the country but one of them is so much stronger than the others that they cannot oust it from power nor hinder it much in its exercise of power.' Whilst the presence of other parties facilitates open criticism to be made of the state and the questioning of its acts, in elections, parliament, the press, public meetings and so on, the opposition can be 'very weak and the ruling party very powerful'. In this situation, the system almost approximates a single-party state (Duverger 1967: 111; Southall 1997). In a sense, the legitimacy and viability of oppositionist parties in South Africa are central to the trajectory of its democracy. Sections of the ANC argue that 'opposition parties represent the interests of the past' and the SACP asserts that 'competitive, multi-party politics is unlikely to sustain itself into the next millenium'. These views raise questions about the perceptions of pluralism adopted by the ANC/SACP alliance (interviews with Carolus and Cronin, 1996). If the IFP and NP are seen as illegitimate opposition parties because of their association with apartheid, then it is vitally necessary for more credible opposition parties to be formed. Liberal democracy can only exist if there is a willingness among all political organizations to support its basic principles. According to Friedman, the deligitimation of opposition parties is not automatically within the gift of dominant parties:

An excluded party's deligitimation is a function not only of its enemies' actions but of the cultural understandings of the mass public and . . . the way in which international and domestic conditions support or deny its basic view of reality. In other words, dominant parties cannot delegitimate the opposition by fiat; conditions must exist in which the electorate is open to delegitimation. (Friedman 1996)

This is, of course, absolutely true and underlines the fact that the major opposition groups within South Africa's new democracy are susceptible to deligitimization.

The ANC currently occupies a pre-eminent political position, but as Friedman makes clear, the fact that 'dominant party systems are democracies means they remain vulnerable to inevitable changes within society and politics and must retain flexibility of manoeuvre if they are to survive' (*ibid.*). As Edmund Burke stated, a state lacking the means of change is without the means of its conservation, and in a sense, this is equally true of political parties. Parties, of necessity, have to be dynamic in order to appeal to diverse and often fragmented populations. As increasing urbanization, improved literacy rates, an expanding and differentiated economy, continuing technological change and exposure to mass communications begin to become manifest within the wider South African society, there will be different levels and expressions of what James Coleman called 'interest aggregation' (Almond and Coleman 1960: 550). In other words, the focus of civic organizations will change and political parties will reconfigure themselves in order to fulfil a wider range of interests. The formation of the United Democratic Movement (UDM) may be a first sign of change. However, one very important development is the Public Funding of Represented Political Parties Bill, which intends to provide public support for 'represented' political parties, that is, parties that currently have MPs in either parliament or a provincial legislature. New parties such as the UDM will have to prove their public support by winning seats before they can gain access to any public funds. Inevitably, there are complaints of what is perceived as an inbuilt bias in the bill against new parties in favour of existing ones. Clearly, parties must demonstrate their viability in the political domain before qualifying for public support, but as the UDM cautions: 'If you want multi-party democracy you can't concentrate only on existing parties' (Mafenya 1997).

## Challenges to democracy

One of the major concerns in South Africa is that of youth, or what many have referred to as the 'lost generation'. On 1996/97 figures unemployment levels were estimated to be around 55 per cent among young black males. The dislocated schooling during the apartheid years, low educational attainment and lack of skills have placed jobs, education and training at the top of the government's priorities. However, the ANC Youth League, with its wide and unwieldy definition of youth as anyone aged between 14 and 35 years, appears to be insufficiently organized to meet the challenge. Although statements are made which assert that 'youth must be integrated into the wider national economy', remedial education in basic literacy and numeracy is a priority (Polgieter interview, 1996). Equally, the unresolved issue of violent crime continues to undermine the democracy. There is great pressure from civil society to motivate the government to do more against the rising crime rate. A National Crime Prevention document links crime and development and considers the socio-economic factors which give rise to criminality together with crime statistics. Although there are moves towards community policing and an emphasis placed on government, business and local communities to work together to combat crime, there are no immediate or easy solutions.

Another factor that has been commented upon is the ANC's ambivalent responses to criticism. The ANC's constitution enshrines the principle of freedom of speech and states that one of the rights of membership is 'to offer constructive criticism of any member, official or policy programme' (African National Congress 1994a). In a sense, it is the word 'constructive' that is open to interpretation, both within the party and the government. Although many feel that the ANC has been remarkably open, particularly in including foreigners in their discussions and public hearings on defence, education and other major aspects of policy, there are concerns that more recently the ANC at both organizational and governmental level views criticism as 'negative'. The ANC's NEC castigated ANC members 'who publicly criticise and challenge the organisation'. The NEC believed that such criticism 'weakened' the ANC and 'undermined democratic transformation' even though there had been clear malfunctions of policy. Criticism of the ANC was dismissed as either 'racism' or the result of 'a conspiracy'. These are worrying trends because they seemingly undermine the ANC's commitment to democratic expression. If it is true there is intimidation of ANC critics and opponents, an increasing intolerance of critical comment and a perceived marginalization of certain groups, for example coloureds in the Western Cape, then these are warning signs that bode ill for democratic development. It is crucially necessary for the ANC, as the dominant political force within the country, to demonstrate that it is completely scrupulous in its democratic instincts, responses and handling of criticism and opposition. One of the beneficial aspects of South Africa is its lively press, which in many respects acts as one of the standard-bearers of democracy. Crucially, therefore, the media must not be undermined.

The diversity of South African society and the polarization of the urban and rural communities remain a constant challenge to the government. Whilst the rural areas account for around 37 per cent of the total population and 47 per cent of the African population, the definition of rural can be problematic, in that it includes large resettlement areas and many migrants. A high, predominantly female population live in rural areas and these poorer sections of society will continue to present a challenge to the government in terms of their need for more economic resources. However, there is a feeling both within and outside South Africa that, notwithstanding all the difficulties, the democratic transition has gone comparatively well: free and fair elections have taken place and a multi-party competitive structure exists. As everyone agrees, the process of democratic change will be a long one, but perhaps more importantly, one that is 'focused on building the new, not reliving the past' (Carolus interview, 1996).

# Afterword

As South Africa approaches the end of its transitional phase and faces the elections of 1999 together with a new millenium, certain issues dominate the headlines: the economy, crime and corruption. These areas are viewed as presenting the greatest challenges to the country's young democracy. This section will examine and assess the potential of each issue to undermine reform and progress.

## Economy

It is generally accepted that the government's Growth, Employment and Redistribution (GEAR) macro-economic policy has been controversial, predominantly because the tripartite alliance of ANC, COSATU and SACP has not resolved its attitude towards the market economy. Although the 1997 ANC Conference witnessed the passing of a resolution upholding the basic objectives of GEAR, there have been numerous arguments in the National Assembly between various ANC ministers, with one demanding that the 'R of Redistribution be put back into GEAR' (Thabethe 1997). As Sam Shilowa of COSATU prepares to defend his workers' interests at all costs and parts of the SACP strain at the leash to escape capitalism, it is hardly surprising that commentators anticipate difficult negotiations. In certain quarters there has been no ideological shift away from the notion of some form of socialist, quasi-planned, egalitarian economy where the government will engage in job-creation schemes and become a major player in the economy. Despite the fact that a number of rural and urban dwellers do not expect to depend on the government, there continues to be an intellectual climate which is suspicious of capitalism. In part this is a result of the historical experience of apartheid, which was seen as coterminous with capitalism and operating against the interests of ordinary people. Of course, the ANC has expounded its own conception of democracy as being one that 'derives from its experience in struggle and from its humane and progressive outlook'. A central and leading role within that notion of democracy is placed with the working class who will assist the process of transformation (African National Congress 1994b).

One of the major criticisms of the government now is that it is reneging on its commitments to the 'working class', that is organized trade unionists, in the interests of an emerging black bourgeoisie. What role does the working class play in an increasingly liberalizing economy where flexibility in the labour market and the removal of past privileges are viewed as *sine qua non* with improving economic trends? This, of course, is the classic Marxist dialectic between capital and labour, but where does it fit in the new South Africa? There is the corporatist model of NEDLAC but that organization has become less efficacious and embracive in policy-making. Corporatism, in any case, can lead to a narrowing of sectional interests and operate against non-unionized labour, casual workers and those more marginalized, temporary and seasonal employees. According to Sipho Ngwema the public debate informing this ideological tussle is driven by the 'realpolitik' of the transition. In other words, events have overtaken ideology, or as Ngwema explains the dynamics of the government's shift in economic policy: 'The growth of a black middle class with interests counter to that of the majority, and the seeming end of any discourse on alternatives to capitalism within the boundaries of the nation state' (Ngwema 1997). Whether black middle-class interests are really antipathetic to those of other South African workers is debatable. To adopt a purely class analysis has the potential to create enormous tensions between people and to run against the very real desires of the population to improve their lives and those of their children. On the question of an alternative to capitalism, however, Ngwema is absolutely right and it is this factor which underscores much of the uneasiness felt about a liberalizing economy. In short, there appears to be no real choice of options, it's either capitalism or what? A command economy based on old Soviet lines or social democratic corporatism with an interventionist state?

The area of concern that inevitably and, indeed, not unnaturally focuses attention on the frailties of the market economy is the insistent issue of 'jobless growth'. Economic growth without concommitant falls in the number of unemployed further exacerbates the debate as economic strategy is seen as helping neither the poor nor the disadvantaged. Although, as Chapter 7 outlined, there are problems in assessing the exact number of people unemployed, this is obviously an issue that highlights the exigencies of an uncaring capitalist agenda ready and willing to treat labour simply as a factor of production or unit cost. Equally, further economic adjustment to both the business sector and to established trade union practices may very well result in job losses. The position in South Africa is stark: a highly-paid worker-elite overwhelmingly concentrated in increasingly capitalizing, specific industrial sectors; a large unemployed, unskilled workforce; and an established business sector which must bend to global initiatives. It is easy to see the contradictions confronting the government, but can the country reach that degree of economic flexibility without hurting the very constituency it purports to represent? Perhaps not in the short to medium term. And this is the great difficulty.

However, on an ideological front there may be signs of a change in prospect as certain government ministers now call for an abandonment of socialist rhetoric in favour of a process of democratizing capitalism (Mokaba 1997). It is only by coming to terms with a liberalizing economy, by in some way harnessing the dynamic of the private sector to society as a whole, that conditions may be created for wider and more inclusive economic success. Immediately after the election of Thabo Mbeki as ANC president, he announced that a national job summit was planned for 1998. Of course, the ANC's National Executive Committee was mandated by the ANC conference in 1997 to appoint a committee to develop a detailed economic transformation programme that would give priority to developing a job creation strategy. The 1998 job summit will provide an opportunity for 'South Africa's business sector to elaborate on concrete proposals about what it can do to create more jobs' (*Business Report*, 10 January 1998). More importantly, Mbeki emphasized that as corporate citizens the business community has as much interest in peace, stability and progress as any other citizen (*ibid.*). This is a significant point. Recently, ideas have emerged as to how private and public spheres can be connected in a meaningful way. Paul Hirst's notion of 'associative democracy' envisages new forms of 'economic and social governance' in which the economy is connected more firmly with 'the interests of a wide range of economic agents including . . . the consumer and the producer, the worker and the manager and so on' (Hirst 1994: 97; see Chapter 1). Democracy is conceptualized as a process of accountability for every community within society: political and economic, business and social, welfare and domestic, employed and unemployed. These ideas are not vehemently anti-capitalist – rather they seek a more engaged and involved business sector within broader society.

Regarding that other contentious issue, globalization, reports suggest that South Africa may be well placed to accrue some benefits from the crisis in South East Asia. Even President Mandela observed that at the time when the most vibrant economies in the world were being buffeted by storms, South Africa had performed relatively well, and urged everyone 'to join hands with a new determination – as big and small business, as government and society at large – to create more jobs' (*The Star*, 2 January 1998). Although exports to Asian markets might suffer, there is no doubt that stockbrokers and economists believe the country has the 'economic and financial strength to attract foreign investment as an emerging nation in 1998' (Magliolo, *Business Report*, 21 January 1998; *Economist*, 3 January 1998). South Africa has a tight fiscal and monetary budget and has achieved control over inflation and production pressures. Since 1994 the country has witnessed the break-up of the cement cartel, deregulation of the local petroleum industry and the gradual process of privatization of state-owned assets. The country's 'sound economic principles and political prudence' place it in a solid position to benefit from global inward investment (*ibid.*). If this forecast is accurate and South Africa does attract significant levels of foreign investment with the capacity to create jobs, it should be viewed as working to the country's advantage. But it might not be so straightforward. As one politician asserted at the 1997 ANC conference: 'a battle is looming for the soul of the ANC' (Mokaba 1997). Undoubtedly, the economy is at the heart of that struggle.

## Crime

It is practically impossible to spend any time in South Africa without becoming directly or indirectly aware of the issue of crime. Newspapers such as the *Johannesburg Star*, the *Sowetan* and the *Cape Times* devote large sections to reporting criminal activity. In fact, the Justice Minister, Dullah Omar, believes 'a terrible culture of violence and a breakdown of moral fibre' is partly responsible for the incidence of crime (*The Star*, 21 January 1998). He is not alone. Thabo Mbeki insists that communities must work with police to fight crime, Nelson Mandela asserts that crime must be overcome, and other cabinet ministers warn of the dangers crime presents to the economy as a whole. In fact, crime is seen as not only threatening the whole fabric of society, but also as serving to undermine the fledgling democracy itself. The situation seems dire but what are the facts and figures?

The Crime Information Management Centre (CIMC), as a component of the Detective Services, was established by the South African Police Service on 1 January 1996. The Centre, consisting of a head office and nine provincial offices, was tasked with the co-ordination, processing, analysis and interpretation of crime information and intelligence in order to facilitate the combatting of crime. The CIMC is responsible for research on crime, both tactical and strategic, in order that it may gain a wider understanding of the nature of crime. This information can then be utilized by both the police at grassroots level and the government in deciding upon effective strategic planning. Crime is divided into different categories and assessed on a regional basis. Clearly, criminal activity is an enormous subject and ranges from the highly organized, such as the crime syndicates that crystallized during the apartheid years, to the haphazardly instantaneous behaviour of the petty thief. However, for purposes of clarity this section will concentrate on a few specific types of crime: murder, robbery with violence, burglary of business and residential premises, the illegal possession of firearms/ammunition and drug-related incidents. The following tables display the number of cases reported in each region, the ratio per 10 000 of the population and the percentage difference in cases reported on a yearly basis as well as between 1994 and 1997.

Table A.1 charts the cases of murder reported since 1994 and it is clear there are disparities between the nine regions, with KwaZulu Natal, Gauteng and the Western and Eastern Cape among the highest. The figures which are interesting, and may run counter to general expectations, are the declining numbers registered for KwaZulu Natal, and the increase in the cases reported in the Western Cape. Respectively, these can be partly explained by the lessening of tensions between the IFP and ANC, and the greater preponderance of crime syndicate activity which contributes to the internecine conflict on the Cape Flats. Perhaps the figures which are most surprising are those for Guateng, which includes Johannesburg, Soweto and Pretoria. Since 1994 there has been a systematic decline in the reported cases of murder with a differential between 1994 and 1997 of –12.9 per cent. Of course, the figures are far too high, but on *prima facie* evidence they suggest that the incidence of murder in the region is declining rather than increasing. Mpulmalanga has the highest increase since 1994 and some analysts attribute this to political violence occasioned by the entry of the National Party into an area in which the ANC and IFP are major players. Certainly, there have been reports of a number of IFP and NP supporters being killed in fratricidal conflict (Claude 1997). This form of violence has profound implications for the growth of a real culture of democratic tolerance and undermines the whole principle of free political activity.

In respect of robbery with aggravated circumstances there has been a decline in all regions, although overall the number of cases reported in Guateng vastly outweigh all other areas (see Table A.2). If those figures are then considered with those for illegal possession of firearms and ammunition, which registers an increase of 19.2 per cent for the region, it may account for the heightened sense of criminal menace felt by the general public (Table A.5). Similarly, if the figures for common robbery and burglary attempts at residential premises are examined together, there is both a large rise and an increasing incidence in Guateng (see Tables A.7 and A.4 respectively). In fact, apart from the Northern Cape, there has been an increase in residential burglaries in all regions against 1994 figures whilst drug-related crime would seem to be increasing in only two regions, the Eastern Cape and Northern Province (see Table A.6). These figures indicate that although, in some instances, there is a relative decline in reported cases of serious crime, that is murder and robbery with aggravated circumstances, there is an increase in common robbery and burglary. Clearly, then, it is important to distinguish between a number of factors: the nature of the crime, for example serious, opportunistic, planned, organized, political; the motivation for the crime; and the regional dimension.

Justice Minister Omar raised the question of deterrence when he announced to the country that South Africa needed a total strategy to deal with crime. The introduction of capital punishment has been rejected, however,

**Table A.1**  Murder

| | Cases reported Jan–Sep | | | | Ratio per 10 000 of the population | | | | % Difference in cases reported | | | |
|---|---|---|---|---|---|---|---|---|---|---|---|---|
| | 1994 | 1995 | 1996 | 1997 | 1994 | 1995 | 1996 | 1997 | 1994/95 | 1995/96 | 1996/97 | 1997/94 |
| Eastern Cape | 3 120 | 3 261 | 2 938 | 3 109 | 48.5 | 50.3 | 45.0 | 47.3 | 4.5% | -9.9% | 5.8% | -0.8% |
| Free State | 967 | 959 | 876 | 924 | 35.5 | 34.5 | 34.4 | 31.9 | -0.8% | 1.8% | -5.3% | -4.4% |
| Gauteng | 4 618 | 4 243 | 4 205 | 4 022 | 67.2 | 60.2 | 58.1 | 54.2 | -8.1% | -0.9% | -4.4% | -12.9% |
| KwaZulu Natal | 6 199 | 5 669 | 4 880 | 4 372 | 72.9 | 65.1 | 54.7 | 47.8 | -8.5% | -13.9% | -10.4% | -29.5% |
| Mpumalanga | 762 | 814 | 982 | 931 | 26.1 | 27.1 | 31.7 | 29.2 | 6.8% | 20.6% | -5.2% | 22.2% |
| North West | 950 | 888 | 1 158 | 978 | 29.2 | 26.5 | 33.5 | 27.5 | -6.5% | 30.4% | -15.5% | 2.9% |
| Northern Cape | 386 | 445 | 456 | 394 | 52.4 | 60.0 | 61.1 | 52.4 | 15.3% | 2.5% | -13.6% | 2.1% |
| Northern Prov | 801 | 650 | 723 | 710 | 15.4 | 12.0 | 12.9 | 12.2 | -18.9% | 11.2% | -1.8% | -11.4% |
| Western Cape | 1 869 | 2 202 | 2 321 | 2 269 | 51.4 | 50.2 | 60.9 | 58.1 | 17.8% | 5.4% | -2.2% | 21.4% |
| Total | 19 672 | 19 131 | 18 539 | 17 709 | 48.8 | 46.4 | 44.1 | 41.0 | -2.8% | -2.6% | -5.0% | -19.0% |

*Source:* Crime Information Management Centre, South African Police Service, 1998

**Table A.2**  Robbery with aggravated circumstances

| | Cases reported Jan–Sep | | | | Ratio per 10 000 of the population | | | | % Difference in cases reported | | | |
|---|---|---|---|---|---|---|---|---|---|---|---|---|
| | 1994 | 1995 | 1996 | 1997 | 1994 | 1995 | 1996 | 1997 | 1994/95 | 1995/96 | 1996/97 | 1997/94 |
| Eastern Cape | 5 005 | 4 469 | 3 695 | 3 799 | 77.8 | 69.0 | 56.6 | 57.8 | −10.7% | −17.3% | 2.8% | −24.1% |
| Free State | 2 221 | 2 138 | 1 859 | 1 486 | 81.4 | 76.8 | 65.5 | 51.3 | −3.7% | −13.0% | −20.1% | −33.1% |
| Gauteng | 28 200 | 26 577 | 20 952 | 22 444 | 410.5 | 376.4 | 289.7 | 302.4 | −5.9% | −21.0% | 7.1% | −20.4% |
| KwaZulu Natal | 12 538 | 13 261 | 12 190 | 11 682 | 147.4 | 152.2 | 136.6 | 127.8 | 5.8% | −8.1% | −4.2% | −6.8% |
| Mpulmalanga | 2 918 | 2 714 | 2 767 | 2 628 | 99.9 | 90.3 | 89.4 | 82.5 | −7.0% | 2.0% | −5.0% | −9.9% |
| North West | 3 610 | 3 405 | 2 442 | 2 384 | 111.0 | 101.6 | 70.7 | 67.0 | −5.7% | 28.3% | −2.4% | −34.0% |
| Northern Cape | 461 | 729 | 509 | 276 | 62.5 | 98.2 | 68.2 | 36.7 | 58.1% | −30.2% | −45.8% | −40.1% |
| Northern Prov | 2 967 | 2 358 | 1 983 | 1 842 | 57.0 | 43.7 | 35.4 | 31.7 | −20.5% | −15.9% | −7.1% | −37.9% |
| Western Cape | 4 957 | 4 753 | 4 017 | 3 865 | 136.4 | 127.7 | 105.4 | 99.0 | −4.1% | −15.5% | −3.8% | −22.0% |
| Total | 628 77 | 60 404 | 50 414 | 50 406 | 156.1 | 146.3 | 119.4 | 116.6 | −4.0% | −16.5% | 0.0% | −19.8% |

*Source:* Crime Information Management Centre, South African Police Service, 1998

**Table A.3** Burglary (and attempts) – business premises

| | Cases reported Jan–Sep | | | | Ratio per 10 000 of the population | | | | % Difference in cases reported | | | |
|---|---|---|---|---|---|---|---|---|---|---|---|---|
| | 1994 | 1995 | 1996 | 1997 | 1994 | 1995 | 1996 | 1997 | 1994/95 | 1995/96 | 1996/97 | 1997/94 |
| Eastern Cape | 6 029 | 6 449 | 6 927 | 7 170 | 93.7 | 99.5 | 106.1 | 109.1 | 7.0% | 7.4% | 3.5% | 18.9% |
| Free State | 5 755 | 5 256 | 5 238 | 5 034 | 211.1 | 188.9 | 184.5 | 173.8 | -8.7% | -0.3% | -3.9% | -12.5% |
| Gauteng | 16 194 | 14 722 | 14 053 | 14 082 | 235.8 | 208.9 | 194.3 | 189.8 | -9.1% | -4.5% | 0.2% | -13.0% |
| KwaZulu Natal | 12 397 | 12 558 | 12 226 | 11 488 | 145.8 | 144.1 | 137.0 | 125.6 | 1.3% | -2.6% | -6.0% | -7.3% |
| Mpumalanga | 4 319 | 4 407 | 4 613 | 4 401 | 147.8 | 146.6 | 149.0 | 138.2 | 2.0% | 4.7% | -4.6% | 1.9% |
| North West | 5 403 | 4 658 | 4 974 | 4 901 | 166.1 | 139.0 | 144.0 | 137.7 | -13.8% | 6.8% | -1.5% | -9.3% |
| Northern Cape | 1 924 | 2 097 | 2 027 | 2 033 | 260.9 | 282.6 | 271.4 | 270.5 | 9.0% | -3.3% | 0.3% | 5.7% |
| Northern Prov | 4 043 | 3 480 | 4 355 | 4 781 | 77.7 | 64.5 | 76.0 | 82.3 | -13.9% | 22.3% | 12.4% | 18.3% |
| Western Cape | 11 034 | 11 039 | 11 347 | 11 625 | 303.7 | 298.7 | 297.7 | 297.8 | 0.0% | 2.8% | 2.4% | 5.4% |
| Total | 67 098 | 64 666 | 65 760 | 65 515 | 166.6 | 156.8 | 155.5 | 151.5 | -3.6% | 1.5% | -0.2% | -2.4% |

*Source*: Crime Information Management Centre, South Africa Police Service, 1998

**Table A.4** Burglary (and attempts) – residential premises

| | Cases reported Jan–Sep | | | | Ratio per 10 000 of the population | | | | % Difference in cases reported | | | |
|---|---|---|---|---|---|---|---|---|---|---|---|---|
| | 1994 | 1995 | 1996 | 1997 | 1994 | 1995 | 1996 | 1997 | 1994/95 | 1995/96 | 1996/97 | 1997/94 |
| Eastern Cape | 18 832 | 18 339 | 18 785 | 19 135 | 292.6 | 283.9 | 287.8 | 291.2 | -2.6% | 2.4% | 1.9% | 1.6% |
| Free State | 11 452 | 12 208 | 12 440 | 11 964 | 420.0 | 438.7 | 438.1 | 413.0 | 6.6% | 1.9% | -3.8% | 4.5% |
| Gauteng | 54 651 | 59 159 | 58 547 | 57 121 | 795.6 | 839.3 | 809.5 | 769.7 | 8.2% | -1.0% | -2.4% | 4.5% |
| KwaZulu Natal | 28 165 | 29 751 | 31 061 | 30 603 | 331.1 | 341.5 | 348.0 | 334.7 | 5.6% | 4.4% | -1.5% | 8.7% |
| Mpumalanga | 9 856 | 10 950 | 12 268 | 11 836 | 337.4 | 364.1 | 396.4 | 371.5 | 11.1% | 12.0% | -3.5% | 20.1% |
| North West | 9 320 | 9 617 | 10 811 | 11 423 | 286.5 | 286.9 | 313.0 | 321.0 | 3.2% | 12.4% | 5.7% | 22.6% |
| Northern Cape | 3 598 | 3 845 | 3 846 | 3 546 | 488.9 | 518.0 | 517.4 | 471.8 | 6.9% | 0.5% | -8.2% | -1.4% |
| Northern Prov | 6 541 | 7 630 | 8 772 | 8 566 | 125.0 | 141.4 | 156.6 | 147.4 | 16.6% | 15.0% | -2.3% | 31.0% |
| Western Cape | 25 568 | 27 613 | 27 999 | 29 045 | 703.8 | 742.0 | 734.6 | 744.0 | 8.0% | 1.4% | 3.7% | 13.6% |
| Total | 167 983 | 179 112 | 184 529 | 183 239 | 417.9 | 434.3 | 437.0 | 423.7 | 6.6% | 3.0% | -0.7% | 9.1% |

*Source:* Crime Information Management Centre, South African Police Service, 1998

169

**Table A.5** Illegal possession of firearms and ammunition

| | Cases reported Jan–Sep | | | | Ratio per 10 000 of the population | | | | % Difference in cases reported | | | |
|---|---|---|---|---|---|---|---|---|---|---|---|---|
| | 1994 | 1995 | 1996 | 1997 | 1994 | 1995 | 1996 | 1997 | 1994/95 | 1995/96 | 1996/97 | 1997/94 |
| Eastern Cape | 627 | 667 | 1070 | 1212 | 9.7 | 10.3 | 16.4 | 18.4 | 6.4% | 60.4% | 13.3% | 93.3% |
| Free State | 446 | 430 | 471 | 438 | 16.4 | 15.5 | 16.6 | 15.1 | -3.6% | 9.5% | -7.0% | -1.8% |
| Gauteng | 1853 | 2027 | 2108 | 2208 | 27.0 | 28.8 | 29.1 | 29.8 | 9.4% | 4.0% | 4.7% | 19.2% |
| KwaZulu Natal | 3245 | 3187 | 3346 | 2826 | 39.3 | 36.6 | 37.5 | 30.9 | -4.7% | 5.0% | -15.5% | -15.5% |
| Mpulmalanga | 417 | 385 | 507 | 467 | 14.3 | 12.8 | 16.4 | 14.7 | -7.7% | 31.7% | -7.9% | 12.0% |
| North West | 390 | 413 | 486 | 491 | 12.0 | 12.3 | 14.1 | 13.8 | 5.9% | 17.7% | 1.0% | 25.9% |
| Northern Cape | 52 | 116 | 119 | 119 | 7.1 | 15.6 | 15.9 | 15.8 | 123.1% | 2.6% | 0.0% | 128.8% |
| Northern Prov | 326 | 286 | 472 | 448 | 6.3 | 5.3 | 8.4 | 7.7 | -12.3% | 65.0% | -5.1% | 37.4% |
| Western Cape | 615 | 980 | 1282 | 1180 | 16.9 | 26.3 | 33.6 | 30.2 | 59.3% | 30.8% | -8.0% | 91.9% |
| Total | 7971 | 8491 | 9861 | 9389 | 20.0 | 20.6 | 23.4 | 21.7 | 5.2% | 16.1% | -4.8% | 16.3% |

*Source*: Crime Information Management Centre, South African Police Service, 1998

**Table A.6**  Drug-related crime

| | Cases reported Jan–Sep | | | | Ratio per 10 000 of the population | | | | % Difference in cases reported | | | |
|---|---|---|---|---|---|---|---|---|---|---|---|---|
| | 1994 | 1995 | 1996 | 1997 | 1994 | 1995 | 1996 | 1997 | 1994/95 | 1995/96 | 1996/97 | 1997/94 |
| Eastern Cape | 4 003 | 3 456 | 4 044 | 4 690 | 62.2 | 53.3 | 62.0 | 71.4 | -13.7% | 17.0% | 16.0% | 17.2% |
| Free State | 3 478 | 3 244 | 2 988 | 2 879 | 127.5 | 116.6 | 105.2 | 99.4 | -6.7% | -7.9% | -3.6% | -17.2% |
| Gauteng | 6 092 | 5 206 | 4 466 | 4 679 | 88.7 | 73.9 | 61.8 | 63.1 | -14.5% | -14.2% | 4.8% | -23.2% |
| KwaZulu Natal | 7 432 | 5 614 | 5 657 | 6 827 | 87.4 | 64.4 | 63.4 | 74.7 | -24.5% | 0.8% | 20.7% | -8.1% |
| Mpumalanga | 1 755 | 1 396 | 1 399 | 1 472 | 60.1 | 46.4 | 45.2 | 46.2 | -20.5% | 0.2% | 5.2% | -16.1% |
| North West | 1 875 | 1 978 | 1 984 | 1 761 | 57.6 | 59.0 | 57.4 | 49.5 | 5.5% | 0.3% | -11.2% | -6.1% |
| Northern Cape | 1 193 | 1 173 | 1 123 | 1 129 | 161.8 | 158.1 | 150.4 | 150.2 | -1.7% | -4.3% | 0.5% | -5.4% |
| Northern Prov | 1 179 | 882 | 1 018 | 1 376 | 22.7 | 16.3 | 18.2 | 23.7 | -25.2% | 15.4% | 35.2% | 16.7% |
| Western Cape | 9 204 | 8 648 | 7 443 | 8 113 | 253.3 | 232.4 | 195.3 | 207.8 | -6.0% | -13.9% | 9.0% | -11.9% |
| Total | 36 211 | 31 597 | 30 122 | 32 926 | 89.9 | 76.6 | 71.3 | 76.1 | -12.7% | -4.7% | 9.3% | -9.1% |

*Source:* Crime Information Management Centre, South African Police Service, 1998

171

**Table A.7** Common robbery

| | Cases reported Jan–Sep | | | | Ratio per 10 000 of the population | | | | % Difference in cases reported | | | |
|---|---|---|---|---|---|---|---|---|---|---|---|---|
| | 1994 | 1995 | 1996 | 1997 | 1994 | 1995 | 1996 | 1997 | 1994/95 | 1995/96 | 1996/97 | 1997/94 |
| Eastern Cape | 1 925 | 2 137 | 3 826 | 3 871 | 29.9 | 33.0 | 58.6 | 58.9 | 11.0% | 79.0% | 1.2% | 101.1% |
| Free State | 1 376 | 1 428 | 1 731 | 1 884 | 50.5 | 51.3 | 61.0 | 65.0 | 3.8% | 21.2% | 8.8% | 36.9% |
| Gauteng | 8 226 | 10 216 | 14 734 | 14 118 | 119.8 | 144.9 | 203.7 | 190.2 | 24.2% | 44.2% | -4.2% | 71.6% |
| KwaZulu Natal | 3 342 | 4 184 | 5 758 | 5 370 | 39.3 | 48.0 | 64.5 | 58.7 | 25.2% | 37.6% | -6.7% | 60.7% |
| Mpumalanga | 1 030 | 1 220 | 1 512 | 1 516 | 35.3 | 40.6 | 48.9 | 47.6 | 18.4% | 23.9% | 0.3% | 47.2% |
| North West | 1 431 | 1 449 | 2 664 | 3 019 | 44.0 | 42.2 | 77.1 | 84.8 | 1.3% | 83.9% | 13.3% | 111.0% |
| Northern Cape | 677 | 843 | 985 | 956 | 91.8 | 113.6 | 131.9 | 127.2 | 24.5% | 16.8% | -2.9% | 41.2% |
| Northern Prov | 1 224 | 1 245 | 1 718 | 1 765 | 23.5 | 23.1 | 30.7 | 30.4 | 1.7% | 38.0% | 2.7% | 44.2% |
| Western Cape | 4 149 | 4 645 | 5 160 | 5 342 | 114.2 | 124.8 | 135.4 | 136.8 | 12.0% | 11.1% | 3.5% | 28.8% |
| Total | 23 380 | 27 367 | 38 088 | 37 841 | 58.0 | 66.4 | 90.2 | 87.5 | 17.1% | 39.2% | -0.6% | 61.9% |

*Source*: Crime Information Management Centre, South African Police Service, 1998

**Table A.8**  Should there be one national police force or provincial
and city police forces? (%)

|          | Local police forces | Single national police force |
| -------- | ------------------- | ---------------------------- |
| All      | 50.9                | 36.7                         |
| African  | 60.0                | 37.1                         |
| White    | 55.2                | 36.7                         |
| Coloured | 43.3                | 30.2                         |
| Asian    | 50.2                | 45.4                         |

*Source*: MarkData cited in *Focus*, No. 7, May 1997, The Helen Suzman Foundation

despite some evidence of public demand for the reinstatement of the death penalty (*The Star*, 21 January 1998). The sensitivity of the policy of capital punishment, given the brutality of the apartheid years, is clear. Also the clause in the Bill of Rights which protects the right to life further diminishes it as a policy option. Yet the efficiency and effectiveness of anti-crime agencies is under question, and despite commitments in the White Paper on Defence to withdraw the South African National Defence Force (SANDF) from policing, they too are engaged in combating crime (Cawthra 1997). As Table A.8 reveals, there has been a major reversal of public opinion regarding federalizing the police. According to R. W. Johnson: 'Before the election, majorities took the centralist line in favour of a single national police force. Now there is a huge shift of opinion among all groups in favour of provincial and city police forces' (Johnson 1997). A local police force might be considered better able to work at grassroots level and to be more accountable to the community. Such organizations may also be considered to be potentially less susceptible to bribery and corruption.

Clearly, the rule of law must be observed by all members of the polity and the government obviously understands the damaging effects of crime on society. But it is important to return to the issue of citizens' rights and responsibilities. If sections of the public fail to recognize that democracy not only carries rights but also responsibilities and the observance of laws then the whole country is under threat. Although crime is one of the most pressing problems which all South Africans should fight, a recent study suggests that a racial divide has opened upon the law and order issue. MarkData carried out a survey in which voters were asked whether there was a low level of respect for law and order in the country: all non-Africans agreed emphatically but two-thirds of Africans denied this was so. One explanation for the African denial assumed that such an admission might be 'construed as a vote of no confidence in the first majority rule government' (Johnson 1997). Alternatively, other racial communities may feel they suffer a higher incidence of crime. However, one point is clear, black South Africans continue to be victims of crime, particularly those in business or employment. (See Chapter 7 for details of crime in black small businesses.)

**Table A.9**   Public opinion on corruption in public office (%)

|  | African | Coloured | Indian | White | Total |
|---|---|---|---|---|---|
| Officials are much less honest | 11 | 16 | 20 | 23 | 14 |
| Officials are much more honest | 12 | 10 | 12 | 3 | 10 |
| Officials help themselves | 52 | 55 | 63 | 71 | 56 |
| Officials help the people | 39 | 27 | 21 | 15 | 33 |
| Almost all officials engaged in corruption | 17 | 14 | 18 | 17 | 17 |
| Almost no officials engaged in corruption | 7 | 7 | 2 | 2 | 6 |
| A lot more corruption | 29 | 28 | 29 | 43 | 26 |
| A lot less corruption | 14 | 7 | 4 | 0 | 11 |

*Source*: IDASA 1996a

## Corruption

Another disturbing tendency which is attracting increasing attention is the incidence of political corruption. Political corruption is defined as 'the unsanctioned or unscheduled use of public resources for private ends' (Lodge 1997). This form of corruption can take place in various institutions of government and is 'constituted by transactions or exchanges of public resources and benefits between actors some or all of whom are officials or public representatives' (*ibid*.). Lodge poses the question: 'Has democratisation weakened or strengthened corrupt predispositions in South African government?' Certainly, it was widely recognized that former homeland administrations suffered from corrupt practices and by the 1980s 'political corruption was quite common in certain government departments too' (*ibid*.). More recently, however, there have been numerous reports of scandals such as the Sarafina affair, which resulted in the misappropriation of monies, of accusations of irregularities in pension payments, of fraud in the parastatal sector and, more worryingly, of bribery within the police force. In a 1995 survey 67 per cent of respondents were convinced that police force members accepted bribes (*ibid*.).

An IDASA study reveals that corruption in public office constitutes real and widespread public concern. Table A.9 illustrates the extent to which people believe in the honesty of public officials. Although there are disparities between African, coloured, Indian and white responses, all groups believe to varying degrees that officials help themselves, rather than the people. These replies are an appalling indictment of public service and cut to the very core of democracy. If there is a lack of popular trust in the probity of public office it behoves the government to demonstrate that it will root out any misdemeanours or corrupt practices irrespective of party political affinities. Otherwise a climate of endemic corruption will set in and gradually erode the democratic base of society. In a sense, the signs already exist as reports emerge of a commander of a Guateng anti-corruption unit being implicated in a bribery probe together with ongoing investigations into police conduct (*The Star*, 21 January 1998). As IDASA caution: 'Government officials or parliamentarians hoping to defend themselves by arguing that corruption is a concern only of the news media or NGO community, rather than the African majority, can find no solace in public opinion' (IDASA 1996a).

If there is one slightly optimistic aspect to this disturbing catalogue, it is that a vigilant media is shining a light into these dark corners of corruption and is prepared to discuss sensitive and controversial issues. This exposure, in turn, contributes to better public awareness and the increasing availability of information. Equally, it must be admitted that all countries suffer from incidences of bribery and corruption, and the ascent to power inevitably brings with it all the temptations of high public office. But in the final analysis, corrupt practices cannot be tolerated in any democratic society: 'There may be no more important challenge in building a new democracy than instilling among citizens a sense of trust, confidence and credibility in their government and in their elected representatives' (IDASA 1996a).

So what of the future for South Africa? The country is rightly proud of its achievements in breaking away from the shackles of the past. But hope, courage, probity and determination are all needed to meet the challenges of the long and hard road ahead. As Nelson Mandela announced: 'Sweat and toil are required to improve our lives and forge out unity as a nation' (Mandela 1998).

# Constitution of the Republic of South Africa 1996 – Constitutional principles

I. The Constitution of South Africa shall provide for the establishment of one sovereign state, a common South African citizenship and a democratic system of government committed to achieving equality between men and women and people of all races.

II. Everyone shall enjoy all universally accepted fundamental rights, freedoms and civil liberties, which shall be provided for and protected by entrenched and justiciable provisions in the Constitution, which shall be drafted after having given due consideration to inter alia the fundamental rights contained in Chapter 3 of this Constitution.

III. The Constitution shall prohibit racial, gender and all other forms of discrimination and shall promote racial and gender equality and national unity.

IV. The Constitution shall be the supreme law of the land. It shall be binding on all organs of state at all levels of government.

V. The legal system shall ensure the equality of all before the law and an equitable legal process. Equality before the law includes laws, programmes or activities that have as their object the amelioration of the conditions of the disadvantaged, including those disadvantaged on the grounds of race, colour or creed.

VI. There shall be a separation of powers between the legislature, executive and judiciary, with appropriate checks and balances to ensure accountability, responsiveness and openness.

VII. The judiciary shall be appropriately qualified, independent and impartial and shall have the power and jurisdiction to safeguard and enforce the Constitution and all fundamental rights.

VIII. There shall be representative government embracing multi-party democracy, regular elections, universal adult suffrage, a common voters' roll and, in general, proportional representation.

IX. Provision shall be made for freedom of information so that there can be open and accountable administration at all levels of government.

X. Formal legislative procedures shall be adhered to by legislative organs at all levels of government.

XI. The diversity of language and culture shall be acknowledged and protected and conditions for their promotion shall be encouraged.

XII. Collective rights of self-determination in forming, joining and maintaining organs of civil society, including linguistic, cultural and religious associations, shall, on the basis of non-discrimination and free association, be recognised and protected.

XIII. The institution, status and role of traditional leadership, according to indigenous law, shall be recognised and protected in the Constitution. Indigenous law, like common law, shall be recognised and applied by the courts, subject to the fundamental rights contained in the Constitution and to legislation dealing specifically therewith.

Provisions in a provincial constitution relating to the institution, role, authority and status of a traditional monarch shall be recognised and protected in the Constitution.

XIV. Provision shall be made for participation of minority political parties in the legislative process in a manner consistent with democracy.

XV. Amendments to the Constitution shall require special procedures involving special majorities.

XVI. Government shall be structured at national, provincial and local levels.

XVII. At each level of government there shall be democratic representation. This principle shall not derogate from the provisions of Principle XIII.

XVII:

1. The powers and functions of the national government and provincial governments and the boundaries of the provinces shall be defined in the Constitution.

2. The powers and functions of the provinces defined in the Constitution, including the competence of a provincial legislature to adopt a constitution for its province, shall not be substantially less than or substantially inferior to those provided for in this Constitution.

3. The boundaries of the provinces shall be the same as those established in terms of this Constitution.

4. Amendments to the Constitution which alter the powers, boundaries, functions or institutions or provinces shall, in addition to any other procedures specified in the Constitution for constitutional amendments, require the approval of a special majority of the legislatures of the provinces, alternatively, if there is such a chamber, a two-thirds majority of a chamber of Parliament composed of provincial representatives, and if the amendment concerns specific provinces only, the approval of the legislatures of such provinces will also be needed.

5. Provision shall be made for obtaining the views of a provincial legislature concerning all constitutional amendments regarding its powers, boundaries and functions.

The powers, boundaries and functions of the national government and provincial governments shall be defined in the Constitution. Amendments to the Constitution which alter the powers, boundaries, functions or institutions of provinces shall in addition to any other procedures specified in the Constitution for constitutional amendments, require the approval of a special majority of the legislatures of the provinces, alternatively, if there is such a chamber, a two-thirds majority of a chamber of Parliament composed of provincial representatives, and if the amendment concerns specific provinces only, the approval of the legislatures of provinces will also be needed. Provision shall be made for obtaining the views of a provincial legislature concerning all constitutional amendments regarding its powers, boundaries and functions.

XIX. The powers and functions at the national and provincial levels of government shall include exclusive and concurrent powers as well as the power to perform functions for other levels of government on an agency or delegation basis.

XX. Each level of government shall have appropriate and adequate legislative and executive powers and functions that will enable each level to function effectively. The allocation of powers between different levels of government shall be made on a basis which is conducive to financial viability at each level of government and to effective public administration, and which recognises the need for and promotes national unity and legitimate provincial autonomy and acknowledges cultural diversity.

XXI. The following criteria shall be applied in the allocation of powers to the national government and the provincial governments:

1. The level at which decisions can be taken most effectively in respect of the quality and rendering of services, shall be the level responsible and accountable for the quality and the rendering of the services and such level shall accordingly be empowered by the Constitution to do so.

2. Where it is necessary for the maintenance of essential national standards, for the establishment of minimum standards required for the rendering of services, the maintenance of economic unity, the maintenance of national security or the prevention of unreasonable action taken by one province which is prejudicial to the interest of another province or the country as a whole, the Constitution shall empower the national government to intervene through legislation or such other steps as may be defined in the Constitution.

3. Where there is necessity for South Africa to speak with one voice, or to act as a single entity – in particular in relation to other states – powers should be allocated to the national government.

4. Where uniformity across the nation is required for a particular function, the legislative power over that function should be allocated predominantly, if not wholly, to the national government.

5. The determination of national economic policies, and the power to promote interprovincial commerce and to protect the common market in respect of the mobility of goods, services, capital and labour, should be allocated to the national government.

6. Provincial governments shall have powers, either exclusively or concurrently with the national government, inter alia:

(a) for the purposes of provincial planning and development and the rendering of services; and

(b) in respect of aspects of government dealing with specific socio-economic and cultural needs and the general well-being of the inhabitants of the province.

7. Where mutual co-operation is essential or desirable or where it is required to guarantee equality or opportunity or access to a government service, the powers should be allocated concurrently to the national government and the provincial governments.

8. The Constitution shall specify how powers which are not specifically allocated in the Constitution to the national government or to a provincial government, shall be dealt with as necessary ancillary powers pertaining to the powers and functions allocated either to the national government or provincial governments.

XXII. The national government shall not exercise its powers (exclusive or concurrent) so as to encroach upon the geographical, functional or institutional integrity of the provinces.

XXIII. In the event of a dispute concerning the legislative powers allocated by the Constitution concurrently to the national government and provincial governments which cannot be resolved by a court on a construction of the Constitution, precedence shall be given to the legislative powers of the national government.

XXIV. A framework for local government powers, functions and structures shall be set out in the Constitution. The comprehensive powers, functions and other features of local government shall be set out in parliamentary statutes or in provincial legislation or in both.

XXV. The national government and provincial governments shall have fiscal powers and functions which will be defined in the Constitution. The framework for local government referred to in Principle XXIV shall make provision for appropriate fiscal powers and functions for different categories of local government.

XXVI. Each level of government shall have a constitutional right to an equitable share of revenue collected nationally so as to ensure that provinces and local governments are able to provide basic services and execute the functions allocated to them.

XXVII. A Financial and Fiscal Commission, in which each province shall be represented, shall recommend equitable fiscal and financial allocations to the provincial and local governments from revenue collected nationally, after taking into account the national interest, economic disparities between the provinces as well as the population and developmental needs, administrative responsibilities and other legitimate interests of each of the provinces.

XXVIII. Nothwithstanding the provisions of Principle XII, the right of employers and employees to join and form employer organisations and trade unions and to engage in collective bargaining shall be recognised and protected. Provision shall be made that every person shall have the right to fair labour practices.

XXIX. The independence and impartiality of a Public Service Commission, a Reserve Bank, an Auditor-General and a Public Protector shall be provided for and safeguarded by the Constitution in the interests of the maintenance of effective public service.

XXX:

1. There shall be an efficient, non-partisan, career-orientated public service broadly representative of the South Africa community, functioning on a basis of fairness and which shall serve all members or the public in an unbiased and impartial manner, and shall, in the exercise of its powers and in compliance with its duties, loyally execute the lawful policies of the government of the day in the performance of its administrative functions. The structures and functioning of the public service, as well as the terms and conditions of service of its members, shall be regulated by law.

2. Every member of the public service shall be entitled to a fair pension.

XXXI. Every member of the security forces (police, military and intelligence) and the security forces as a whole, shall be required to perform their functions and exercise their powers in the national interest and shall be prohibited from furthering or prejudicing party political interest.

XXXII. The Constitution shall provide that until 30 April 1999 the national executive shall be composed and shall function substantially in the manner provided for in Chapter 6 of this Constitution.

XXXIII. The Constitution shall provide that, unless Parliament is dissolved on account of its passing a vote of no-confidence in the Cabinet, no national election shall be held before 30 April 1999.

XXXIV.

1. This Schedule and the recognition therein of the right of the South African people as a whole to self-determination, shall not be construed as precluding, within the framework of the said right, constitutional provision for a notion of the right to self-determination by any community sharing a common cultural and language heritage, whether in a territorial entity within the Republic or in any other recognised way.

2. The Constitution may give expression to any particular form of self-determination provided there is substantial proven support within the community concerned for such a form of self-determination.

# Bill of Rights

## Rights

1. This Bill of Rights is a cornerstone of democracy of South Africa. It enshrines the rights of all people in our country and affirms the democratic values of human dignity, equality and freedom.
2. The state must respect, protect, promote, and fulfil the rights in the Bill of Rights.
3. The rights in the Bill of Rights are subject to the limitations contained or referred to in section 36, or elsewhere in the Bill.

## Application

The Bill of Rights applies to all law and binds the legislature, the executive, the judiciary, and all organs of state.

## Equality

Everyone is equal before the law and has the right to equal protection and benefit of the law.

Equality includes the full and equal enjoyment of all rights and freedoms. To promote the achievement of equality, legislative and other measures designed to protect or advance persons, or categories of persons, disadvantaged by unfair discrimination may be taken.

The state may not unfairly discriminate against anyone on grounds of race, gender, sex, pregnancy, marital status, ethnic or social origin, colour, sexual orientation, age, disability, religion, conscience, belief, culture, language and birth.

No person may unfairly discriminate directly or indirectly against anyone.

## Human dignity

Everyone has inherent dignity and the right to have their dignity respected and protected.

## Life

Everyone has the right to life.

## Freedom and security of the person

1. Everyone has the right to freedom and security of the person which includes the right:
• not to be deprived of freedom arbitrarily or without just cause;
• not to be detained without trial;
• to be free from all forms of violence from both public and private sources;
• not to be tortured in any way; and
• not to be treated or punished in a cruel, inhuman or degrading way.
2. Everyone has the right to bodily and psychological integrity, which includes the right:
• to make decisions concerning reproduction;
• to security in and control over their body;
• not to be subjected to medical or scientific experiments without their informed consent.

## Slavery, servitude and forced labour

No one may be subjected to slavery, servitude or forced labour.

## Privacy

Everyone has the right to privacy, which includes the right not to have:
• their person or home searched;
• their property searched;
• their possessions seized; or
• the privacy of their communications infringed.

## Freedom of religion, belief and opinion

1. Everyone has the right to freedom of conscience, religion, thought, belief and opinion;

2. Religious observances may be conducted at state or state-aided institutions provided that:
• those observances follow rules made by the appropriate public authorities;
• they are conducted on an equitable basis; and
• attendance at them is free and voluntary.
3. (a) This section does not prevent legislation recognising:
• marriages concluded under any tradition or a system or religious, personal or family law; or
• systems of personal and family law under any tradition or adhered to by persons professing a particular religion.
(b) Recognition in terms of paragraph (a) must be consistent with this section and the other provisions of the Constitution.

## Freedom of expression

1. Everyone has the right to freedom of expression, which includes:
• freedom of the press and other media;
• freedom to receive and impart information and ideas;
• freedom of artistic creativity; and
• academic freedom and freedom of scientific research.
2. The right in subsection (1) does not extend to:
• propaganda for war;
• incitement of imminent violence; or
• advocacy of hatred that is based on race, ethnicity, gender or religion, and that constitutes incitement to cause harm.

## Assembly, demonstration, picket and petition

Everyone has the right, peacefully and unarmed, to assemble, to demonstrate, to picket and to present petitions.

## Freedom of association

Everyone has the right to freedom of association.

## Political rights

1. Every citizen is free to make political choices, which includes the right:
• to form a political party;
• to participate in the activities of, or recruit members for, a political party; and
• to campaign for a political party or cause.

2. Every citizen has the right to free, fair and regular elections for any legislative body established in terms of the Constitution.

3. Every adult citizen has the right:

• to vote in elections for any legislative body established in terms of the Constitution, and to do so in secret; and

• to stand for public office and, if elected, to hold office.

## Citizenship

No citizen may be deprived of citizenship.

## Freedom of movement and residence

Everyone has the right to freedom of movement.

Everyone has the right to leave the Republic.

Every citizen has the right to enter, to remain in and to reside anywhere in, the Republic.

Every citizen has the right to a passport.

## Freedom of trade, occupation and profession

Every citizen has the right to choose their trade, occupation or profession freely. The practice of a trade, occupation or profession may be regulated by law.

## Labour relations

1. Every worker has the right to fair labour practices.

2. Every worker has the right:

• to form and join a trade union;

• to participate in the activities and programmes of a trade union; and

• to strike.

3. Every employer has the right:

• to form and join an employers' organisation; and

• to participate in the activities and programmes of an employers' organisation.

4. Every trade union and every employers' organisation has the right:

• to determine its own administration, programmes and activities;

• to organise;

• to bargain collectively; and

• to form and join a federation.

## Environment

Everyone has the right:
• to an environment that is not harmful to their health or well-being; and
• to have the environment protected, for the benefit of present and future generations, through reasonable legislative and other measures that:
(a) prevent pollution and ecological degradation;
(b) promote conservation; and
(c) secure ecologically sustainable development and use of natural resources while promoting justifiable economic and social development.

## Property

1. No one may be deprived of property except in terms of law and general application, and no law may permit arbitrary deprivation of property.
2. Property may be expropriated only in terms of law of general application:
• for public purposes or in the public interest; and
• subject to compensation, the amount, timing, and manner of payment, of which must be agreed, or decided or approved by a court.
3. The amount, timing and manner of payment of compensation must be just and equitable, reflecting an equitable balance between the public interest and the interests of those affected, having regard to all relevant factors, including:
• the current use of the property;
• the history of the acquisition and use of the property;
• the market value of the property;
• the extent of direct state investment and subsidy in the acquisition and beneficial capital improvement of the property; and
• the purpose of the expropriation.
4. For the purposes of this section:
• the public interest includes the nation's commitment to land reform, and to reforms to bring about equitable access to all South Africa's natural resources; and
• property is not limited to land.
5. The state must take reasonable legislative and other measures, within its available resources, to foster conditions which enable citizens to gain access to land on an equitable basis.
6. A person or community whose tenure of land is legally insecure as a result of past racially discriminatory laws or practices is entitled, to the extent provided by an Act of Parliament either to tenure which is legally secure, or to comparable redress.
7. A person or community dispossessed of property after 19 June 1913 as a result of past racially discriminatory laws or practices is entitled, to the extent provided by an Act of Parliament, either to restitution of that property, or to equitable redress.

8. No provision of this section may impede the state from taking legislative and other measures to achieve land, water and related reform, in order to redress the results of past racial discrimination.

## Housing

1. Everyone has the right to have access to adequate housing.
2. The state must take reasonable legislative and other measures, within its available resources, to achieve the progressive realisation of this right.
3. No one may be evicted from their home, or have their home demolished, without an order of court made after considering all the relevant circumstances. No legislation may permit arbitrary evictions.

## Health care, food, water and social security

1. Everyone has the right to have access to:
• health care services, including reproductive health care;
• sufficient food and water; and
• social security, including, if they are unable to support themselves and their dependants, appropriate social assistance.
2. The state must take reasonable legislative and other measures, within its available resources, to achieve the progressive realisation of each of these rights.
3. No one may be refused emergency medical treatment.

## Children

1. Every child has the right:
• to a name and a nationality from birth;
• to family care, parental care, or appropriate alternative care when removed from the family environment;
• to basic nutrition, shelter, basic health care services and social services;
• to be protected from maltreatment, neglect, abuse or degradation;
• to be protected from exploitative labour practices;
• not to be required or permitted to perform work or provide services that:
(a) are inappropriate for a person of that child's age; or
(b) place at risk the child's well-being, education, physical or mental health, or spiritual, moral or social development;
• not to be detained except as a measure of last resort, in which case, in addition to the rights a child enjoys under sections 12 and 35, the child may be detained only for the shortest appropriate period of time, and has the right to be:
(a) kept separately from detained persons over the age of 18 years; and

(b) treated in a manner, and kept in conditions, that take account of the child's age;
• to have a legal practitioner assigned to the child by the state, and at state expense, in civil proceedings affecting the child, if substantial injustice would otherwise result; and
• not to be used directly in armed conflict, and to be protected in times of armed conflict.
2. A child's best interest is of paramount importance in every matter concerning the child.
3. In this section, 'child' means a person under the age of 18 years.

## Education

1. Everyone has the right:
• to a basic education, including adult basic education; and
• to further education, which the state must take reasonable measures to make progressively available and accessible.
2. Everyone has the right to receive education in the official language or languages of their choice in public educational institutions where that education is reasonably practicable. In order to ensure the effective access to, and implementation of, this right, the state must consider all reasonable educational alternatives taking into account:
(a) equity;
(b) practicability; and
(c) the need to redress the results of past racially discriminatory law and practice.
3. Everyone has the right to establish and maintain, at their own expense, independent educational institutions that:
• do not discriminate on the basis of race;
• are registered with the state; and
• maintain standards that are not inferior to standards at comparable public educational institutions.

## Language and culture

Everyone has the right to use the language and to participate in the cultural life of their choice, but no one exercising these rights may do so in a manner inconsistent with any provision of the Bill of Rights.

## Cultural, religious and linguistic communities

1. Persons belonging to a cultural, religious or linguistic community may not be denied the right, with other members of their community, to:

• enjoy their culture, practise their religion and use their language; and
• form, join and maintain cultural, religious and linguistic associations and other organs of civil society.
2. This right may not be exercised in a manner inconsistent with any provision of the Bill of Rights.

## Access to information

1. Everyone has the right of access to:
• any information held by the state; and
• any information that is held by another person and that is required for the exercise or protection of any rights.
2. National legislation must be enacted to give effect to this right, and may provide for reasonable measures to alleviate the administrative and financial burden on the state.

## Just administrative action

1. Everyone has the right to administrative action that is lawful, reasonable and procedurally fair.
2. Everyone whose rights have been adversely affected by administrative action has the right to be given written reasons.

## Access to courts

Everyone has the right to have any dispute that can be resolved by the application of law decided in a fair public hearing in a court or, where appropriate, another independent and impartial forum.

## Arrested, detained and accused persons

1. Everyone who is arrested for allegedly committing an offence has the right:
• to remain silent;
• to be informed promptly of the right to remain silent, and of the consequences of not remaining silent;
• not to be compelled to make any confession or admission that could be used in evidence against that person;
• to be brought before a court as soon as reasonably possible, but not later than 48 hours after the arrest, but if that period expires outside ordinary court hours, to be brought before a court on the first court day after the end of that period;

• at the first court appearance after being arrested, to be charged or to be informed of the reason for the detention to continue, or to be released; and

• to be released from detention if the interests of justice permit, subject to reasonable conditions.

2. Everyone who is detained, including every sentenced prisoner, has the right:

• to be informed promptly of the reason for being detained;

• to choose, and to consult with, a legal practitioner, and to be informed of this right promptly;

• to have a legal practitioner assigned to the detained person by the state, and at state expense, if substantial injustice would otherwise result, and to be informed of this right promptly;

• to challenge the lawfulness of the detention in person before a court and, if the detention is unlawful, to be released;

• to conditions of detention that are consistent with human dignity, including at least exercise and the provision, at state expense, of adequate accommodation, nutrition, reading material, and medical treatment; and

• to communicate with, and be visited by, that person's:

(a) spouse or partner;

(b) next of kin;

(c) chosen religious counsellor; and

(d) chosen medical practitioner.

3. Every accused has a right to a fair trial, which includes the right:

• to be informed of the charge with sufficient details to answer it;

• to have adequate time and facilities to prepare a defence;

• to a public trial in an ordinary court;

• to have their trial begin and conclude without unreasonable delay;

• to be present when being tried;

• to choose, and be represented by, a legal practitioner, and to be informed of this right;

• to have a legal practitioner assigned to the accused by the state, and at state expense, if substantial injustice would otherwise result, and to be informed of this right;

• to be presumed innocent, to remain silent, and not to testify during the proceedings;

• to adduce and challenge evidence;

• not to be compelled to give self-incriminating evidence;

• to be tried in a language that the accused person understands or, if that is not practicable, to have the proceedings interpreted in that language;

• not to be convicted for an act or omission that was not an offence under either national or international law at the time it was committed or omitted;

• not to be tried for an offence in respect of an act or omission for which that person has previously been either acquitted or convicted;

• to the benefit of the least severe of the prescribed punishments if the prescribed punishment for the offence has been changed between the time that the offence was committed and the time of sentencing; and

• of appeal to, or review by, a higher court.

4. Whenever this section requires information to be given to a person, that information must be given in a language that the person understands.

5. Evidence obtained in a manner thàt violates any right in the Bill of Rights must be excluded if the admission of that evidence would render the trial unfair or otherwise be detrimental to the administration of justice.

## Limitation of rights

The rights in the Bill of Rights may be limited only in terms of law of general application to the extent that the limitation is reasonable and justifiable in an open and democratic society based on human dignity, equality and freedom, taking into account all relevant factors including:

• the nature of the right;

• the importance of the purpose of the limitation;

• the nature and extent of the limitation;

• the relation between the limitation and its purpose; and

• less restrictive means to achieve the purpose.

## States of emergency

1. A state of emergency may be declared only in terms of an Act of Parliament and only when:

• the life of the nation is threatened by war, invasion, general insurrection, disorder, natural disaster or other public emergency; and

• the declaration is necessary to restore peace and order.

2. A declaration of a state of emergency, and any legislation enacted or other action taken in consequence of that declaration, may be effective only:

• prospectively from the date of the declaration; and

• for no more than 21 days from the date of the declaration, unless the National Assembly resolves to extend the declaration. The National Assembly may extend a declaration of a state of emergency for no more than three months at a time. The first extension of the state of emergency must be by a resolution supported by a majority of the members of the National Assembly. Any subsequent extension must be by a resolution supported by at least 60% of the members of the Assembly. A resolution in terms of this paragraph may be adopted only following a public debate in the Assembly.

## Enforcement of rights

Anyone listed in this section has the right to approach a competent court, alleging that a right in the Bill of Rights has been infringed or threatened, and the court may grant appropriate relief, including a declaration of rights. The person who may approach a court are:

• anyone acting in their own interest;
• anyone acting on behalf of another person who cannot act in their own name;
• anyone acting as a member of, or in the interest of, a group or a class of persons;
• anyone acting in the public interest; and
• an association acting in the interest of its members.

## Interpretation of Bill of Rights

1. When interpreting the Bill of Rights, a court, tribunal or forum:
• must promote the values that underlie an open and democratic society based on human dignity, equality and freedom;
• must consider international law; and
• may consider foreign law.
2. When interpreting any legislation and when developing the common law or customary law, every court, tribunal or forum must promote the spirit, purport and objects of the Bill of Rights.
3. The Bill of Rights does not deny the existence of any other rights or freedoms that are recognised or conferred by common law, customary law or legislation, to the extent that they are consistent with the Bill.

# Representation and structures of government

## Proportional representation

South Africa's national and provincial legislatures are elected on the basis of PR, using the party list and proportional allocation seats system. This is based on the idea that the number of seats that a party occupies in the national and provincial parliaments should be in proportion to the number of votes it received in the elections. A party which wins 10 per cent of the votes in the national election should therefore occupy 10 per cent of the seats in parliament. The number of seats it occupies in each of the provincial legislatures depends on the proportion of votes it received in each of the provincial elections.

Who takes up the seats as MPs (Members of Parliament) and MPLs (Members of Provincial Legislature) on behalf of the parties is decided before the elections are held. Each party has to submit a party list of its candidates for each legislature that it is contesting in a fixed order of preference. If a party is allocated 20 seats on the basis of the proportion of votes it received in the national election, the first 20 people named on its national list become MPs. The number of MPLs each party is entitled to in each provincial legislature is proportional to the number of votes it received in each provincial election. The balance of power between the parties will remain the same until the next general election. If an MP dies, resigns or is expelled from the party, he or she will lose the seat and be replaced by the next person on the party list. Parties can, however, change the order of their lists and once a year, they are allowed to change the list by adding new people. The PR system prevents MPs from 'crossing the floor' to join other parties and gives the parties considerable power in enforcing party discipline. This is because seats in the legislatures are owned by the party not by the individual MPs.

## Comparison of proportional list system with constituency-based system

### PROPORTIONAL LIST SYSTEM

Voters can vote at any polling station in a general election, at any polling station in the province in which they are registered in provincial elections, and in the local area in which they are registered in local government elections.

Minority parties can win seats even if they do not have enough support to win any constituency, provided they have enough support across the entire electorate.

Representation in Parliament reflects overall support for parties across the electorate.

Only members of parties may win seats.

Parties hold seats, appoint members to take seats and have the power to take away seats. Any MP who resigns or is expelled from the party loses the seat. This gives parties central control over the selection of MPs and can be used to enforce party discipline.

Parties appoint members to take up vacant seats on the basis of party lists.

The balance of power remains constant because the number of seats allocated to each party stays constant between elections.

There are no constituency delimitation procedures to be manipulated.

### CONSTITUENCY-BASED SYSTEM

Voters must vote in their constituency area and can only do so if they appear on the voters' roll.

'Winner takes all/first past the post' – only candidates who have a majority in any single constituency can win seats. This favours large parties that have the resources to undertake large-scale campaigns. Minority interests are likely to be under-represented in such a system.

Representation in Parliament reflects the number of constituencies a party has won, regardless of the overall level of support for a party.

Independent candidates are eligible for election.

Individual MPs hold seats and can act as independents or 'cross the floor' to join other parties as they wish. Parties may nominate candidates, give them support during elections and discipline their members but do not have the power to take away their seats.

Individual candidates must contest by-elections to fill vacant seats.

The balance of power can change, depending on the results of by-elections and whether the political allegiance of MPs change.

The delimitation of constituencies can be manipulated to suit the interests of the ruling party.

MPs do not represent the voters of a specific constituency – they are appointed on the basis of party lists. The key shortcoming of PR is the fact that MPs do not represent, and are not accountable to, voters of a specific constituency. South African MPs are given constituency allowances to encourage them to work with their supporters on the ground in an attempt to overcome this problem.

MPs represent the voters in a specific constituency and are accountable to those voters.

*Source*: IDASA Parliamentary Pocketbook, Cape Town 1996

## National legislative authority

There are two categories of legislation, defined by a list of functions:
1. Laws which the national and provincial legislatures are jointly competent to pass; and
2. Laws which the provincial legislatures are exclusively competent to pass.

Parliament may amend the Constitution and it may pass legislation in category 1. It may not pass legislation in category 2 unless this is necessary to:
- maintain national security;
- maintain economic unity;
- maintain essential national standards;
- establish minimum standards for the rendering of services;
- prevent unreasonable action taken by a province which prejudices another province or the country as a whole.

A Bill which falls into category 1 must be passed by both houses before it can become an Act. If the houses are unable to agree, it is referred to a Mediation Committee to try to reach agreement. If the Mediation Committee is unable to agree within 30 days of the Bill having been referred to it, the NA (National Assembly) can pass the Bill into law on its own by a two-thirds majority.

With a Bill which falls outside category 1 the NA has the power to force a Bill through Parliament even if the National Council of Provinces (NCOP) rejects it or proposes amendments which the NA does not accept. Under these circumstances, the NCOP's power is limited to delaying the passage of the Bill while its objections and amendments are considered more carefully by the NA. If the Bill is an amendment to the Constitution which affects the NCOP or the provinces, it must be passed by both houses to become an Act. Any other amendments to the Constitution are not referred to the NCOP – they may become Acts when they are passed by the NA.

## National Assembly

The NA must consist of no fewer than 350 MPs and no more than 400. The various parties are represented in proportion to the number of votes they received in the 1994 national election as follows:

| | |
|---|---|
| African National Congress | 252 |
| National Party | 82 |
| Inkatha Freedom Party | 43 |
| Freedom Front | 9 |
| Democratic Party | 7 |
| Pan Africanist Congress | 5 |
| African Christian Democratic Party | 2 |
| TOTAL | 400 members |

*Source*: IDASA Parliamentary Pocketbook 1996

## National Council of Provinces (NCOP)

The NCOP is intended to ensure that provincial interests are represented in national parliamentary decision-making. It does this mainly by participating in the national legislative process and by providing a national forum for public consideration of issues affecting the provinces. The NCOP is made up of 90 members – one ten-member delegation for each of the nine provinces. Each delegation is made up of six permanent members and four 'special' delegates, which may include the premier of the province. Each province's delegation is generally proportionately representative of the political parties that contested the election in that province. Provision is made for municipal delegations to represent the interests of local government in the NCOP when necessary, but municipal representatives may not vote. The NCOP and any of its committees also have the power to summon anyone to give evidence or produce documents and may request any individual or institution to report to them. Each delegation has one vote and most decisions require five delegations to vote in favour of the motion. Amendments to the Constitution which affect the NCOP or the provinces must be supported by six of the nine delegations.

## The Mediation Committee

This committee will be convened when the NA and the NCOP cannot agree on a particular Bill. Unitl the new Constitution comes into effect, this role will be played by a joint sitting of the NA and the Senate. The Mediation Committee is made up of nine representatives from the NA, elected proportionally, and one representative from each of the nine provincial delegations to the NCOP. In order to come to a decision, at least five of the NA representatives and at least five of the NCOP representatives must support the decision. If the committee fails to agree, or if the committee's recommendations are unacceptable to either the NA or the NCOP, the Bill will lapse unless it receives the support of two-thirds of the NA in another vote.

## Parliamentary privilege

MPs and Cabinet ministers have freedom of speech in parliament and its committees. This means that they are able to say, produce or submit anything without having to worry about any legal consequences, subject to the rules and orders of Parliament and its committees. Anything that is said in parliamentary debates or questions is a matter of public record.

## Terms and sessions

An election is held every five years, although the President has the power to dissolve the NA and call an early election if a majority of members support the move, or if three years have passed since the last election. Parliament is in session for most of the year, and committee meetings may continue during the recess.

## Committees

Parliament delegates much of its most important work to parliamentary committees. Members of the public may present submissions to a committee, which means the views of citizens, including experts, can be heard in a parliamentary committee. There is a portfolio committee for every government department. Each portfolio committee consists of about 30 MPs and is responsible for shadowing a government department, for instance education, health or housing. The political parties are represented roughly in proportion to the number of seats they hold in the NA. The committees must monitor the government department they oversee and may investigate and make recommendations relating to any aspect of the legislative programme, budget, rationalization, restructuring, functioning, organization, structure, personnel, policy formulation or anything else they think is relevant. They may make inquiries and hear evidence and it is their duty to debate, amend and put forward proposals for legislation. They are potentially powerful bodies that have a crucial role to play in the legislative process. Each committee elects its own chairperson, although the majority party parliamentary caucus is effectively able to decide who will chair the committees and ensure that those candidates are elected. Only two of the 27 NA portfolio committees do not have an ANC chairperson.

## The President and the National Executive

The President and Cabinet together make up the executive body. Their task includes implementing national legislation, developing and implementing national policy, co-ordinating state departments and preparing and initiating legislation. The Cabinet consists of the President, Deputy-President and ministers. The Deputy-President and ministers are appointed by the President. All but two of the ministers must be members of the NA. The Cabinet is collectively and individually accountable to Parliament and members of the Cabinet must report regularly to Parliament. Deputy ministers may also be appointed by the President. The Cabinet may intervene in a province when a province does not fulfil its executive functions. It may assume responsibility to the extent necessary to maintain essential services, economic unity and national security. If the Cabinet intervenes in the affairs of a province, it must give notice of the intervention in the NCOP which must approve the intervention within 30 days of its first sitting after the intervention began, and must review the intervention regularly. If, by a majority vote, the NA passes a motion of no-confidence in the Cabinet, excluding the President, the President, the entire Cabinet and any deputy ministers must all resign.

## State institutions supporting constitutional democracy

Six independent institutions are established. They are to act without state interference and are to be directly accountable to the NA:
- The Public Protector (appointed for a non-renewable period of seven years) has the task of investigating improper conduct in state affairs. The only thing he/she may not investigate are court decisions.
- The Human Rights Commission is to promote respect for human rights and to monitor the observance of human rights in South Africa. Organs of state are required to report to it annually on the steps they have taken towards the realization of the rights in the Bill of Rights concerning housing, health care, food, water, social security, education and the environment.
- The Commission for the Promotion of Protection of the Rights of Cultural, Religious and Linguistic Communities is to promote tolerance and respect for the different groups in South Africa.
- The Commission for Gender Equality is to facilitate the attainment of gender equality.

- The Auditor-General audits and reports on the accounts of all national and provincial state departments and municipalities as well as on any institution funded from a national or provincial revenue fund or by a municipality or any institution that is authorized by law to receive money for a public purpose.
- The Electoral Commission manages all national, provincial and municipal elections.

*Source*: IDASA Parliamentary Information and Monitoring Service Cape Town 1996

# Structure of the ANC

At the 1997 Conference of the ANC, the executive positions were as follows:
President: Thabo Mbeki
Deputy-President: Jacob Zuma
Secretary-General: Kgalema Motlanthe
Chairpreson: Patrick Lekota

## Duties of the National Working Committee

(a) to carry out decisions and instructions of the National Conference and the National Executive Committee;
(b) to conduct the current work of the ANC and ensure that provinces and branches carry out the decisions of the ANC;
(c) to submit a report to each National Executive Committee meeting.
(*Source*: ANC Constitution: 12 as amended and adopted at the ANC Conference December 1994, Marshaltown)

## Provincial structures

The Provincial Conference shall:
(a) be held at least once every two years and more often if requested by at least one-third of all branches in the Province;
(b) be a delegates' conference attended by delegates chosen on a democratic basis by all branches in the region with representation in proportion to membership, with attention being paid to ensuring representation of areas where membership is reduced;
(c) be attended by members of the Provincial Executive Committee who shall have full voting and speaking rights as *ex officio* pariticants;
(d) be attended by representatives of the Women's League and Youth League with voting rights;

(e) carry out the decisions of the National Conference, the National Executive Conference and the National Working Committee;
(f) receive and consider reports by the Provincial Executive Committee;
(g) elect the Provincial Chairperson, Deputy Chairperson, Secretary, Deputy Secretary, Treasurer and other members of the Provincial Executive Committee who will hold office for two years;
(h) carry out and develop the policy and programme fo the ANC in the Province.
(*Source*: ANC Constitution 1994: 14–15)

## The Provincial General Council

• The Provincial General Council is the highest decision-making body in the region between Provincial Conferences.
• The Provincial General Council consists of all members of the Provincial Executive Committee and delegates representing branches in proportion to membership with a minimum of one delegate per branch.
• It shall meet a least twice a year.
• It shall on good cause shown be convened by the Provincial Executive Committee upon the request of one-third of the branches in the Province.
• Reports following meetings of the Provincial General Council shall be submitted to the Provincial Executive Committee and the branches.
• The Provincial General Council shall have the power to deal with any issue it deems necessary including the filling of vacancies on the Provincial Executive Committee provided they do not exceed 50 per cent of the Executive, subject always to policies and directives of National Conference.
(*Source*: ANC Constitution 1994: 15)

## Provincial Executive Committee

• The Provincial Executive Committee shall be the body responsible for carrying out the decisions of the Provincial Conference and Provincial General Council.
• It shall consist of the Provincial Chairperson, Deputy Chairperson, Secretary, Deputy Secretary, Treasurer and not more than 13 other persons elected by the Provincial Conference.
• The Women's League and the Youth League in the Province shall be represented by two representatives with full voting rights.
• The Provincial Executive Committee shall:
(a) meet as soon as possible after its election to elect the Provincial Working Committee and thereafter at least once a month;
(b) carry out the decisions of the Provincial Conference and the NEC;
(c) manage and control the funds and assets of the ANC in the Province;

(d) submit reports to the NEC Provincial Conference and Provincial General Council as often as is required, on the state of the organization, the financial position of the province, and such other matters as may be specified;

(e) appoint the regional organizer and staff as required;

(f) organize, establish and service branches in the Province and supervise the work of the regions in the Province;

(g) carry out the policy and programme of the ANC and do all things necessary to further the interests, aims and objectives of the organization;

(h) have the right to co-opt up to three persons subject to confirmation by the Provincial General Council.

(*Source*: ANC Constitution 1994: 15–16)

## Provincial Working Committee

• The Provincial Working Committee shall be a core group of the Provincial Executive Committee and shall consist of not less than one-quarter of its members, including the Chairperson, Deputy Chairperson, Secretary, Deputy Secretary and Treasurer of the Province.

• It shall perform the duties and functions of the Provincial Executive Committee to which it shall report.

• It shall meet at least once a week.

(*Source*: ANC Constitution 1994: 16)

The PEC is elected for a two-year term and is accountable to the NEC. There must not be more than 13 regions per province. Each region has a Regional Executive Committee, elected at the regional AGM, which will be an executive structure accountable to the Provincial Executive Committee. The region will be represented on the PEC by its Chair and Secretary. With the regions there are sub-regional structures which serve a co-ordinating rather than an executive function. The branches continue as executive structures accountable to the Regional Executive Committee. According to the 1994 Conference Report, the branches remain 'powerhouses of the organisation, where responsibility for the building of the organisation and the effectiveness of ANC activity must reside' (African National Congress 1994b: 16).

## Structure of ANC branches

Every member of the ANC shall belong to a branch, which shall be the basic unit of the organization. The branch shall:

(a) be registered;

(b) meet as provided for in the rules and regulations;

(c) be the place where members exercise their basic democratic rights to discuss and formulate policy;

(d) be the basic unit of activity for members;

(e) elect at an annual branch meeting a Branch Executive Committee, consisting of Chairperson, Deputy Vice-Chairperson, Secretary, Treasurer, and other committee members, consisting of not less than three and not more than seven persons;
(f) meet at least once per month.

The branch committee shall:
(a) meet as soon as possible after its election and choose a branch sub-committee to carry on the day-to-day affairs of the branch;
(b) carry out the publicity and organizational work in its area in furtherance of the policy, programme and decisions of the ANC;
(c) meet at least once per fortnight;
(d) submit reports on its work to the branch meeting and at least each month to the Regional Executive Committee;
(e) co-opt not more than three persons, if it considers it necessary to ensure greater representivity.
(*Source*: ANC Constitution 1994: 17)


# Membership rules of the ANC

1. Membership of the ANC shall be open to all South Africans above the age of 18 years, irrespective of race, colour and creed, who accept its principles, policies and programmes and are prepared to abide by its Constitution and rules.
2. Spouses or children of South Africans who have manifested a clear identification with the South African people and its struggle, may apply for membership.
3. All other persons who have manifested a clear identification with the South African people and their struggle and are resident in South Africa may apply for membership.
4. The National Executive Committee may, acting on its own or on the recommendation of branch or provincial executive committees, grant honorary membership to those men and women who do not qualify for membership under Rules 1, 2, or 3, but who have demonstrated an unwavering commitment to the ANC and its policies.
5. Applications for membership shall be considered by the branch committee where such exits, and by the provincial executive committee, if no branch committee exists. The branch committee, the provincial executive committee, or such interim structures as the Provincial Executive Committee or the NEC may create from time to time to decide on applications, shall have the power to accept or refuse any application for membership provided such acceptance or refusal shall be subject to review by the next higher organ of the ANC.

6. Membership cards shall be issued to registered members of the ANC and to persons whose application for membership has been accepted, subject to review as aforesaid, and, in all cases, subject to payment of the prescribed subscription.

7. On being accepted in the ANC, a new member shall, in a language he or she knows well, make the following solemn declaration to the body or person who received the application:

'I, [name], solemnly declare that I will abide by the aims and objectives of the ANC as set out in the Constitution and the Freedom Charter, that I am joining the organization voluntarily and without motives of personal gain or material advantage, and that I will participate in the life of the organization as a loyal, active and disciplined member.'

(*Source*: ANC Constitution 1994: 5)

## The character of the ANC

1. The ANC is a non-racial and democratic liberation movement.

2. The ANC is a democratic organization whose policies are determined by the membership and whose leadership shall be accountable to the membership in terms of the procedures laid down in the Constitution.

3. The ANC shall, in its composition and functioning, be non-racial, anti-racist and anti-sexist and against any form of tribalistic exclusivism or ethnic chauvinism.

4. While striving for the maximum unity of purpose and functioning, the ANC shall respect the linguistic, cultural and religious diversity of its members.

5. The ANC shall support the emancipation of women, combat sexism and ensure that the voice of women is fully heard in the organization and that women are properly represented at all levels.

6. The principles of freedom of speech and free circulation of ideas and information shall operate within the ANC.

7. Membership of all bodies of the ANC will be open to all men and women in the organization without regard to race, colour and creed.

8. The ANC co-operates closely with religious bodies in the country and provides, on an inter-faith basis, for the recognition of the spiritual needs of its many members who are believers.

(*Source*: ANC Constitution 1994: 5)

## Organizational structure of the ANC Youth League

1. National Congress
2. Extra-Ordinary Congress
3. National Executive Committee

4. National Working Committee
5. Provincial Congress
6. Provincial General Council
7. Provincial Executive Committee
8. Regional Congress
9. Regional Committee
10. Branches
11. Branch Congress
12. Branch Executive Committee
13. Branch General Meeting
(*Source*: Constitution of the ANC Youth League as amended at the 19th National Congress, March 1996, Durban)

The National Congress, which meets every two years, is the highest decision-making body of the ANCYL. The National Congress has the power to elect the President, the Deputy President, the Secretary-General, the Deputy Secretary-General, the Treasurer-General and 18 other members of the National Executive Committee. The President, the Deputy President and the Secretary-General of the League are *ex officio* members of the ANC National Executive Committee. The basic unit of the ANCYL is the branch and every member has to belong to a branch.

## Duties of ANC Youth League branches

The duties and functions of the branch shall be to:
1. ensure that the youth in a particular village, area, township, institution of learning, town or suburb are organized into the ANCYL;
2. encourage the youth to take an active part in all activities of the ANCYL;
3. mobilize all youth to participate in the general mass campaigns in the area;
4. prepare members to participate effectively in the formulation of ANCYL policies and programmes;
5. elaborate and implement the political education programme of the ANCYL;
6. encourage members to take an active interest in sports, arts and cultural activities;
7. encourage all youth above 18 years of age to join the ANC;
8. support and reinforce the local ANC branch.
(*Source*: ANC Youth League Constitution 1996)

# Interviews/meetings

Alant, Dr Theo, National Party MP, Cape Town, 13 June 1996.

Carolus, Cheryl, Deputy Secretary-General, African National Congress, Johnnesburg, 3 June 1996.

Chalker, Baroness, UK Minister of Overseas Development, The Royal Institute of International Affairs (RIIA), Chatham House, London, July 1994.

Cornwall, Richard, Head Current Affairs, Africa Institute of South Africa and Research Associate of the Institute for Security Studies, Midrand, 6 June 1996.

Cronin, Jeremy, Deputy Secretary-General, South African Communist Party, Johnnesburg, 3 June 1996.

Dlamini, Bonginkosi Provincial Youth Secretary, Inkatha Freedom Party, Gauteng Leadership, 6 June 1996.

Haines, Richard, University of Port Elizabeth, South Africa, 10 July 1995.

van Heerden, Frik, Member of Parliament, Republic of South Africa National Party, Cape Town, 13 June 1996.

Hyden, Professor Goran, Johannesburg, 10 June 1996.

King, Loretta, Councillor, Soweto, Southern Metropolitan Substructure, 3 June 1996.

Kotelo, Kenneth, Head Communications, Africa Institute of South Africa, Pretoria, 6 June 1996.

Leon, Peter, Leader of Democratic Party, Gauteng Legislature, Johannesburg, 4 June 1996.

Lodge, Professor Thomas, Department of Political Studies, University of Witwatersrand, 5 June 1996.

Majodina, Pemmy, Treasurer-General, ANC Youth League, Johannesburg, 6 June 1996.

Masite, Sophie, Mayor of Soweto, Southern Metropolitan Substructure, Johannesburg, 3 June 1996.

Msimang, Mendi, SA High Commissioner, RIIA, London, 13 December 1995.

Myeni, Musa, MP Inkatha Freedom Party, Johannesburg, 6 June 1996.

Mzizi, Gertrude, Member, Gauteng Legislature, Inkatha Freedom Party, 6 June 1996.

Ndlovu, Humphrey, Member, Gauteng Legislature, Inkatha Freedom Party, 6 June 1996.

Nhlapo, Pat, Personal Assistant to Mayoress of Soweto, Johannesburg, 3 June 1996.

Polgieter, Febe, Secretary-General of the Youth League, Johannesburg, 6 June 1996.

Rabaji, Chris, Ward Councillor, Soweto, Southern Metropolitan Substructure, 3 June 1996.

Radue, Ray, National Party Senator, RSA Cape Town, 13 June 1996.

Razak, Sam, Deputy Provincial Secretary, Inkatha Freedom Party, Gauteng Leadership Johannesburg, 6 June 1996.

Rubin, Helene, Principal, Anchor College, 7 February 1996.

Van Vuuren, Andre, Director-General, The Association of Law Societies of the Republic of South Africa, Pretoria, 4 June 1996.

Venter, Dr Dennis, Executive Director, Africa Institute of South Africa, Pretoria, 1996.

Wessels, Elizabeth, Africa Institute of South Africa, Pretoria, 25 September 1996.

White, Dr Caroline, Centre for Policy Studies, Johannesburg, 7 February 1996.

# References

ABSA Bank Quarterly 1996. *South African Economic Monitor* (July).

Adabunu, K. 1995. *Africa World Review*, May–September.

Adam, H. & Moodley, K. 1993. *South Africa International* **23**(4).

*Africa Today* 1995. (November/December).

*Africa World Review* 1995. November 1994–April 1995.

African National Congress 1994a. *Constitution*. Marshaltown: ANC Department of Information and Publicity.

African National Congress 1994b. *Strategy and tactics*, 49th National Conference.

African National Congress 1996a. *Annual statement of the National Executive Committee*. Johannesburg: ANC Publication.

African National Congress 1996b. *South African Youth Day*, Johannesburg: ANC Youth League.

African National Congress Youth League 1996. *South African Youth Day, a tribute to the youth*. Johannesburg: ANC Publication.

Ake, C. 1967. *A theory of political integration*, Princeton: Princeton University Press.

Almond, G. A. & Coleman, J. S. (eds) 1960. *The politics of developing areas*. Princeton, NS: Princeton University Press.

Almond, G. & Verba S. 1963. *The civic culture*. Princeton: Princeton University Press.

Apter, O. 1967. *The Politics of modernisation*. Chicago: University of Chicago Press.

Association of the Law Societies of the Republic of South Africa 1996. *Submission to the Constitutional Assembly, Supplement*. Pretoria.

Aybak, T. 1997. *The politics of citizenship and immigration in the new Europe*. Middlesex University Migrants Project.

Barberton C. 1995. *Prioritising prioritisation in government*. Capetown: IDASA.

Barnes, T. 1996. *Poverty alleviation*. Witswatersrand: University of Witswatersrand Discussion Paper.

Beinart, W. 1994. *Twentieth centry South Africa*. Oxford: Oxford University Press.

Berelson, R. 1970. Survival through apathy. In *Frontiers of democratic theory*, H. Kariel (ed.). New York: Syracuse University Press.

Berelson, R., Lazerfield, P. & McPhee, W. 1954. *Voting*. Chicago: University of Chicago Press.

Bernstein, A. 1994. NGOs and a democratic South Africa. *Development and Democracy* **7**.

Bernstein, H. 1983. *For their triumphs and for their tears. Women in apartheid.* London: South Africa IDAF.

Billy, A. 1996. Ground Down. *Democracy in action* **10**(5), 1 September.

Blondel, J. 1990. *Comparative government.* Hertfordshire: Philip Allan.

Blondel, J. 1995. *Comparative government.* Hertfordshire: Prentice Hall/Harvester.

Bossuyt, J. & Develtere, P. 1995. Between autonomy and identity: the financing dilemma of NGOs. *The Courier*, No. 152, July–August.

Bradley, P. (ed.) 1945. *A de Tocqueville 1805–1859. Writings on Democracy on America.* New York: A. A. Knopf.

Bratton, M. 1994. Civil society and political transitions. In *Civil society and the state in Africa*, J. Harbeson, D. Rothchild, Chazan, N. (eds). Boulder: Lynne Rienner.

Buijs, G. 1995. Risk and benefit as functions of savings and loan clubs: an examination of rotating credit associations for poor women in Rhini. University of Port Elizabeth: African Studies Association of South Africa.

Caliguire, D. 1996. Death of a dream. *Democracy in Action* **10**(3).

Cargill, J. 1996. *Business Report.*

CASE (Community Agency for Social Enquiry) 1996. *A new constitution for a new South Africa.* Cape Town Community Agency for Social Enquiry Publication.

Cawthra, G. 1997. *Towards an holistic approach to security management in Southern Africa and Africa.* Broederstroom: African Studies Association of South Africa.

Clapham, C. 1985. *Third World politics.* London: Croom Helm.

Coetzee, Z. Rian & Naude, W. A. 1995. Township economic infrastructure: quantifying the imbalances. *Development Southern Africa* **12**(6).

Cohen, J. & Arato, A. 1995. *Civil society and political theory.* Cambridge, Massachusetts: MIT Press.

Coleman, J. 1960. The political systems of the developing world. In *The Politics of the Developing Areas*, G. Almond & J. Coleman (eds). New Jersey: Princeton University Press.

COMSA (Commonwealth Observer Mission to South Africa) 1993. *Violence in South Africa.* The Report of the Commonwealth Secretariat, Pall Mall, London.

Constitution of the Republic of South Africa 1993.

Constitution of the Republic of South Africa 1996. Johannesburg: Government Publication.

Cuadra, X. Z. 1992. Fostering democratic culture in Central America. In *The Democratic Revolution*, L. Diamond (ed.). New York: Freedom House.

Daalder, H. & Mair, P. (eds) 1983. *Western European party systems.* London: Sage.

Dahl, R. 1989. *Democracy and its critics.* New Haven: Yale University Press.

Deegan, H. 1993. *The Middle East and problems of democracy.* Buckingham: Open University Press.

Deegan, H. 1996. *Third worlds.* London: Routledge.

*Democracy in Action* 15 December 1995. Cape Town: IDASA.

Democratic Trends. Cape Town: Urban Foundation.

Deutsch, K. 1967. Social mobilisation and political development. In *Political modernisation*, C. Welch (ed.). California: Wadsworth Publishing Co.

Diamond, L. (ed.) 1994. *Political Culture and Democracy in Developing Countries.* Boulder, Colorado: Lynne Rienner.

Diamond, L., Linz, J. & Lipset, S. M. 1988. *Democracy in developing countries.* Boulder, Colorado: Lynne Reinner.

Duvenage, P. 1995. In a field of tension: historical interpretation after and through Auschwitz and apartheid. Conference: Postmodernism in Africa. University of Port Elizabeth, South Africa.

Duverger, M. 1967. *The idea of politics*. London: Methuen.

Economic Intelligence Unit 1996. *Country Profile: South Africa*. London: Economic Intelligence Unit.

Ehteshami, A. 1995. *After Khomeini*. London: Routledge.

Epstein, L. D. 1967. *Political parties in Western democracies*. New York: Praeger.

Erasmus, G. 1994. *Politikon* **21**(1).

Everatt, D. 1995. *Finishing the job?* Focus Group Survey on Local Government Elections, Cape Town: Project Vote.

Faure, M. & Lane, J. E. 1996. *South Africa: designing new political institutions*. London: Sage.

Foltz, W. 1967. Building the newest nations: short-run strategies and long-run problems. In *Political modernisation*, C. Welch (ed.). California: Wadsworth Publishing.

Foucault, M. 1995. Truth & power. In *Critical Theory*, D. Tallak (ed.). Hertfordshire: Harvester Wheatsheaf.

Frey, F. W. 1963. Political development, power and communications in Turkey. In *Communications and political development*, L. Pye (ed.). Princeton: Princeton University Press.

Friedman, S. 1996. No easy stroll to dominance. *Towards Democracy* 4th quarter.

Fukuyama, F. 1992. *The end of history and the last man*. London: Penguin.

Geertz, C. 1967. The integrative revolution: primordial sentiments and civic justice. In *Political modernisation*, C. Welch (ed.). California: Wadworth Publishing.

Giliomee, H. 1994. The National Party's campaign for a liberation election. In *Election 94*, A. Reynolds (ed.). London: James Currey.

Giliomee, H., Schlemmer, L. & Hauptfleisch, S. 1994. The bold experiment: South Africa's new democracy. South Africa: Southern Book Publishers.

Gotz, G. 1995. Cracks in the edifice. *Indicator South Africa* **12**(3).

Gouws, A. 1996. *The role of women in the democratising process*, paper presented at University of Stellenbosch, 12 June.

*GTMC Perspective*, May 1996. Johannesburg: The Greater Johannesburg Transitional Metropolitan Council.

Gumede, W.-M. 1996. Civics at the crossroads. *Democracy in Action* **10**(5).

van Gunsteren, H. 1978. Notes on a theory of citizenship. In *Democracy, consensus and social contract*, P. Birnbaum, J. Lively & G. Parry (eds). London: Sage.

Habermas, J. 1979. *Communication and the evolution of society*. London: Macmillan.

Habermas, J. 1995. Questions and counter questions. In *Critical Theory*, D. Tallak (ed.). Hertfordshire: Harvester Wheatsheaf.

Hamilton, G. & Mare, G. 1994. The Inkatha Freedom Party. In *Election 94 South Africa*, A. Reynolds (ed.). London: James Currey.

Held, D. 1996. *Models of Democracy*. Cambridge: Polity Press.

Hirst, P. 1994. *Associative Democracy*. Cambridge: Polity Press.

van Hoek & Bussuyt, G. 1993. Democracy in Sub-Saharan Africa: the search for a new institutional set up. *Revue Africaine de Development*. African Development Bank.

Hooper-Box, C. 1996. New gen(d)eration. *Democracy in Action* **10**(3).

Horowitz, D. 1991 *A Democratic South Africa*. Berkeley: University of California Press.

*Human Rights Watch Africa* 1994. *The global report on women's rights* **6**(1) January.

*Human Rights Watch Africa* 1995 **7**(3), May.

Huntington, S. 1967. Political development and political decay. In *Political Modernisation*, C. Welch (ed.). California: Wadworth Publishing.

Hyden, G. 1996. Rethinking theories of the state. *Africa Insight* **26**(1).

Hyslop, J. 1996. *Tertiary educational reform in South Africa*. Discussion Paper: University of Witwatersrand.

IDASA 1995. What language would you like your children to be educated in?, *Opinion Poll* **1**(1), October.

IDASA 1996a. *Public Opinion Survey*, Report No. 3, February. Cape Town.

IDASA 1996b. *Public Opinion Survey*, Report No. 4, March. Cape Town.

IDASA 1996c. *Public Opinion Survey*, Report No. 6, *Voter Education and the 1995 Local Government Elections*, March. Cape Town.

IDASA 1996d. *Public Opinion Survey*, Report No. 8, May. Cape Town.

Independent Board of Enquiry 1994. *Fortresses of Fear*. Johannesburg: Broomfontein.

*Infospec* 1994. **3**(6), June–July.

*Infospec* 1995. April–May.

Inkatha Freedom Party 1987. *Inkatha and the struggle for liberation in South Africa*. Durban: Inkatha Freedom Party.

James, W. 1996. NP walk-out speeds up democratic evolution, *Democracy in Action* **10**(3).

James, W., Caliguire, D., Cullinan, K. 1996. *Now that we are free*. Boulder, Colorado: Lynne Rienner.

Johnson, R. W. 1996. *Focus Letter*. October, No. 4. Parklands: Helen Suzman Foundation.

Johnston, R. W. 1997. *Focus Letter*. May, No. 7. Parklands: Helen Suzman Foundation.

Johnston, R. W. & Schlemmer, L. (eds) 1996. *Launching democracy in South Africa*. New Haven: Yale University Press.

Johnston, A. 1996. *Peace and realignment*. KwaZulu Natal Briefing No. 3.

Johnston, A. & Spence, J. E. 1995. *South Africa's local government elections*. RIIA Briefing Paper No. 27.

Joseph, R. 1987. *Democracy and prebendal politics in Nigeria. The rise and fall of the Second Republic*. Cambridge: Cambridge University Press.

Kahn, B. 1996. *Exchange control liberalisation in South Africa*. Cape Town: IDASA.

Kariel H. (ed) 1970. *Frontiers of democratic theory*. New York: Syracuse University Press.

Kornhauser, W. 1957. *The politics of mass society*. New York: Free Press.

Kuper, R. 1995. Democracy as process and the green and socialist agendas. *Contemporary Politics* **1**(4).

Leftwich, A. (ed) 1996. *Democracy and development*. Cambridge: Polity Press.

Lerner, D. 1958. *The passing of traditional society*. Glencoe: Free Press.

Lewis, S. 1994. Economic realities and prospects for trade, investment and growth in Southern Africa. *Africa Insight* **24**(4).

Lijphart, A. 1977. *Democracy in plural societies: a comparative exploration*. New Haver: Yale University Press.

Lipset, S. 1960. *Political man*. London: Heinemann.

Lipton, M., Ellis, F. & Lipton, M. 1996. *Land, labour and livelihoods in rural South Africa*. Durban: Indicator Press.

Lodge, T. 1983. *Black politics in South Africa since 1945*. London: Longman.

Lodge, T. 1996. South Africa: democracy and development in a post-apartheid society. In *Democracy and development*, A. Leftwich. Cambridge: Polity Press.

Lodge, T. 1997 *Political corruption in South Africa*. Broederstroom: African Studies Association of South Africa.

Lodge, T. & Nasson, B. 1991. *South Africa: time running out*. United States: Ford Foundation.

Macpherson, C. B. 1973. *Democratic theory – essays in retrieval*. Oxford: Oxford University Press.

Mafenya, J. 1997. Speech cited in *Parliamentary Whip*, 5 November. Cape Town: IDASA.

Magliolo, J. 1998. Investment strategist. *Business Report*, 21 January.

Mandela, N. 1998. *The Star*, 1 January.

Marshall, T. 1950. *Citizenship and social class*. Cambridge: Cambridge University Press.

Mattes, R., Giliomee, H. & James, W. 1996. The election in the Western Cape. In *Launching democracy in South Africa*, R. W. Johnson & L. Schlemmer. New Haven: Yale University Press.

*Mayibuye* June 1996 Johannesburg: ANC Newspaper.

Mbembe, A. 1991. Power and obscenity in the post colonial period: the case of Cameroon. In *Rethinking third world politics*, J. Manor. Harlow: Longman.

Mehl, M. & Ashby, M. 1994. *From state provision to NGO initiative. A South African case study*. Cape Town: Independent Development Trust.

Meyer, R. P. 1995. Text of speech presented to the Institute for Strategic Studies, Pretoria.

Mill, J. S. undated. *Considerations of representative government*. London: H. Brown & Co.

Miller, D. 1995. Citizenship and pluralism. *Political Studies* **43**.

Mini, S. E. 1994. Gender relations of production in the Eastern Cape and the restructuring of rural apartheid. *Africa Insight* **24**(4).

Mokaba, P. 1997. Speech cited in *Parliamentary Whip*, 5 November. Cape Town: IDASA.

Moller, V. & Hanf, T. 1995. *Learning to vote*. Durban: Indicator Press.

Motsei, M. 1995. *RDP News*, June. South Africa.

Mouffe, C. 1995. *Citizenship and the political community*. Cambridge: Polity Press.

Mtintso, T. 1996. *The Star*, 25 September.

*Mzabalazo* 1994. Johannesburg: African National Congress Publication.

Nedcor Economic Unit 1996. *Guide to the economy* 2nd quarter. Johannesburg: Nedcor Economic Unit.

Neumann, R. G. 1960. *European and comparative government*. New York: McGraw-Hill.

Ngwema, S. 1996. No consultation no cash flow. *Democracy in Action* **10**(1).

Ngwema, S. 1997. Article cited in *Parliamentary Whip*, 5 November. Cape Town: IDASA.

Nyatsumba, K. 1996a. Challenges facing South Africa. *The Star*, 11 September.

Nyatsumba, K. 1996b. *Cape Argus*, 24 September.

O'Donnell, G. & Schmitter, P. C. 1986. *Transitions from authoritarian rule: Tentative conclusions about uncertain democracies*. Baltimore: John's Hopkins University Press.

Ottoway, M. 1991. Liberation movements and democracy, *Journal of Modern African Studies* **3**, 57–70.

Overseas Development Institute 1994a. *Political liberalisation and economic reform.* London: ODI.

Overseas Development Institute 1994b. *Economic policies in the new South Africa.* London: ODI.

Parry, G. 1978. Citizenship and knowledge. In *Democracy, consensus and social contract,* P. Birnbaum, J. Lively & G. Parry (eds). London: Sage.

Partridge, P. H. 1975. *Consent and consensus.* London: Macmillan.

Pateman, C. 1991. *The sexual contract.* Cambridge: Polity Press.

Poole, D. 1991. *Democratisation and its limits in the Middle East.* University of Lancaster: Political Studies Association Conference.

Pye, L. (ed.) 1963. *Communications and political development.* Princeton: Princeton University Press.

Race Relations Survey 1994/1995. Johannesburg: South African Institute of Race Relations.

Ramphele, M. 1995. *Affirmative action.* South Africa: IDASA.

Randall, V. (ed.) 1988. *Political parties in the third world.* London: Sage.

*RDP Vision* (1995) Gauteng Provincial Government, **1**, January.

Republic of South Africa 1994. *White paper on reconstruction and development: government's strategy for fundamental transformation.*

Reynolds, A. 1994. *Election 94 South Africa.* London: James Currey.

*RSA Review* (1995) **8**, September.

Sandifer, D. & Scheman, L. R. 1966 *The foundations of freedom.* New York: Praeger.

Sartori, G. 1976. *Parties and party systems.* Cambridge: Cambridge University Press.

Scott, T. 1995. An overview of South Africa's future international economic relations. In *South Africa in the global economy,* G. Mills, A. Begg & A. van Nieuwkerk (eds). South African Institute of International Affairs.

Seekings, J. 1995. *Media images of 'youth' during the South Africa transition 1989–1994.* Grahamstown: South Africa Sociological Association, Rhodes University.

Shear, K. 1996. Not welfare or uplife work: white women, masculinity and policing in South Africa. *Gender and History* **8**(3).

Shilowa, S. 1997. Speech cited in *Parliamentary Whip,* 5 November. Cape Town: IDASA.

Sibisi, J. 1996. *Democracy in Action* **10**(5), 1 September.

*South African Yearbook* 1995. Johannesburg: South African Communication Service.

South African Institute of Race Relations 1996. *Fast Facts,* September.

South African Police Service 1997. *Report on crime figures.* Crime Information Management Centre, South Africa.

South African Reserve Bank 1996. *Quarterly Bulletin.* Pretoria.

South African Reserve Bank 1997. *Quarterly Bulletin.* Pretoria.

Southall, R. 1997. Party dominance and development: South Africa's prospects in the light of Malaysia's experience. *Journal of Commonwealth and Comparative Politics* **35**(2).

Thabethe, F. 1997. Speech cited in *Parliamentary Whip,* 5 November. Cape Town: IDASA.

Turok, B. 1997. Development in South Africa. In *South Africa and Africa: within or apart,* A. Adedeji (ed.). London: Zed.

Tyson, H. 1996. *Sunday Independent,* 2 June. South Africa.

Unterhalter, E. 1989. Class, race, and gender. In *South Africa in question,* J. Lonsdale. Cambridge: University of Cambridge Press.

Uys, S. 1994. *South Africa's Elections.* London: RIIA Chatham House.

Wagner, R. 1991. Political institutions, discourse and imagination in China at Tiannanmen. In *Rethinking third world politics,* J. Manor (ed.). Harlow: Longman.

Ward, R. & Rustow, D. (eds) 1964. *Political modernisation in Japan and Turkey.* Princeton: Princeton University Press.

Webster, E. 1996. *Democratic consolidation in Southern Africa.* Witwatersrand: University of Witwatersrand.

Weiner, M. 1967. Political integration and political development. In *Political modernisation,* C. Welch. California: Wadsworth Publishing Co.

Welch, C. 1967. *Political modernisation.* California: Wadsworth Publishing Co.

Welsh, D. 1994. *The South African Elections.* London: RIIA.

White, C. 1995a. *Democratic societies? Voluntary association and democratic culture in a South African towhsip.* Johannesburg: Centre for Policy Studies.

White, C. 1995b. Gender on the agenda. Centre for Policy Studies, *Current Trends Series* **8**(7).

Williams, D. & Young, T. 1993. *Civil Society and Democratisation.* Warwick: British International Studies Association.

Worden, N. 1995. *The making of modern South Africa.* Oxford: Blackwell.

World Bank 1993. *Characteristics of the constraints facing black businesses in South Africa.* Washington: Thyra A. Riley.

World Bank 1995. *South Africa: reducing financial constraints to emerging enterprises.* Washington: World Bank.

Zuma, J. 1997. *KwaZulu Briefing,* No. 6.

# Index

Note: major treatments of topics (mainly chapters) are in **bold**